Green Accounting and Digitalization of E-Business for Sustainable Development

Shakhlo T. Ergasheva
Tashkent State University of Economics, Uzbekistan

IGI Global
Scientific Publishing
Publishing Tomorrow's Research Today

Vice President of Editorial Melissa Wagner
Director of Acquisitions Mikaela Felty
Director of Book Development Jocelynn Hessler
Production Manager Mike Brehm
Cover Design Jose Rosado

Published in the United States of America by
IGI Global Scientific Publishing
701 East Chocolate Avenue
Hershey, PA, 17033, USA
Tel: 717-533-8845
Fax: 717-533-7115
Website: https://www.igi-global.com E-mail: cust@igi-global.com

Library of Congress Cataloging-in-Publication Data

Names: Ergasheva, Shakhlo T. editor
Title: Green accounting and digitalization of e-business for sustainable development / [edited by] Shakhlo T. Ergasheva.
Description: Herhsey, PA : IGI Global Scientific Publishing, [2025] | Includes bibliographical references and index. | Summary: "This book aims to discuss the systematization and discussion of international experience of prospects for the sustainable development of e-business due to green accounting and digitalization"-- Provided by publisher.
Identifiers: LCCN 2025013669 (print) | LCCN 2025013670 (ebook) | ISBN 9798369383629 hardcover | ISBN 9798369383636 paperback | ISBN 9798369383643 ebook
Subjects: LCSH: Electronic commerce--Accounting | Environmental auditing | Sustainable development--Accounting
Classification: LCC HF5548.32 .G73 2025 (print) | LCC HF5548.32 (ebook) | DDC 658.8/72--dc23/eng/20250818
LC record available at https://lccn.loc.gov/2025013669
LC ebook record available at https://lccn.loc.gov/2025013670

British Cataloguing in Publication Data
A Cataloguing in Publication record for this book is available from the British Library.

Table of Contents

Detailed Table of Contents

The research aims to justify the preference for a systemic approach to organizing "green" accounting and digitalizing e-business for its sustainable development. Moreover, the research aims to develop recommendations for implementing this approach in Uzbekistan. To this end, the author conducted an empirical study on the experience of 15 countries with moderately sustainable e-business development in 2025, including Uzbekistan. Thus, the author developed a regression model to assess the impact of e-business adaptation tools to current global trends on its sustainability. According to the model, sustainable development in e-business is primarily ensured through the use of corporate accounting modernization tools (e.g., acquiring state-of-the-art software, making green investments, and engaging in green trade), while HRM tools play a secondary role. Furthermore, the systemic application of green accounting and digitalization significantly enhances its sustainability.

Modern economic conditions require from companies the effective management of green accounting. This is connected with an increasing role of environmental aspects in companies' activities. Environmental factors become very important for the competitiveness of companies since they influence their financial results, reputation, and image. Unlike traditional financial reporting, green accounting is an expanded concept, which includes non-financial indicators, such as environment, social impact, and sustainable development. E-business and e-commerce form a quickly growing industry, which offers many advantages for consumers. However, e-business has a large environmental impact, which is manifested in particular in

culture inside firms as well as the necessity of stakeholder participation. While the practical recommendations urge firms to establish quantifiable sustainability.

Preface

INTRODUCTION

In recent years, the rapid integration of digital technologies into all aspects of business has prompted a parallel and pressing need to align these advancements with global sustainability goals. *Green Accounting and Digitalization of E-Business for Sustainable Development* emerges at this critical intersection, where environmental stewardship, digital transformation, and economic resilience converge. This volume brings together diverse research efforts from across Eurasia and beyond, illuminating how e-business models are being recalibrated to embrace environmental considerations through green accounting systems and sustainability metrics. It reflects a shared commitment among scholars and practitioners to shape a more responsible and forward-thinking economic future.

This edited book provides a comprehensive framework for understanding how green accounting—once considered a supplementary component of corporate reporting—is evolving into a strategic pillar for sustainable development. As the chapters show, digital tools and platforms can significantly enhance the scope, accuracy, and influence of green accounting practices. The collected studies examine this phenomenon across a range of contexts, from energy efficiency and climate resilience in e-commerce to investment attractiveness, agricultural innovation, and industrial competitiveness. The book emphasizes that green digital transformation is not only a technical upgrade but a fundamental shift in business philosophy, rooted in environmental ethics, social responsibility, and long-term value creation.

As editor, I am especially proud to highlight the contributions from a wide array of regional researchers who offer both theoretical rigor and empirical insight. Their studies, many of which focus on the evolving economic landscape in Uzbekistan and neighboring countries, underscore the relevance of local perspectives in a global discourse. By examining sustainable practices through the lens of regional development, this volume bridges the gap between international frameworks and national priorities, offering actionable knowledge for academics, policymakers, and business leaders alike.

Chapter 1: A Systemic Approach to Organizing "Green" Accounting and Digitalizing E-business for Sustainable Development

This chapter presents a systemic approach to integrating green accounting with digitalized e-business practices to promote sustainable development, particularly in Uzbekistan. Drawing on a comparative analysis of 15 countries, the study uses a regression model to highlight the dominant role of corporate accounting modernization—such as green investments and digital tools—over HRM measures in driving sustainability. The author proposes actionable strategies for fostering sustainability in e-business through comprehensive digital transformation and environmental accounting.

Chapter 2: Digital "Green" Accounting of E-business to Raise its Energy Efficiency in Support of Sustainable Development

The authors explore how digital green accounting can improve energy efficiency in e-business and contribute to broader sustainability goals. This chapter argues that traditional financial reporting is insufficient, and emphasizes the importance of including environmental and social indicators. The adoption of renewable energy and eco-friendly materials is framed as both a competitive strategy and a necessity for reducing the environmental impact of e-commerce operations.

Chapter 3: Digital Model of Green Accounting of E-business in Agriculture for the Sustainable Development of the Agrarian Economy

Focusing on the agricultural sector, this chapter introduces a digital model of green accounting tailored to e-business in agriculture. Using case studies from India and Nigeria, the authors demonstrate how private sector-led digital platforms can enhance sustainability even in the absence of government support. The chapter concludes with a call for greater government involvement in agricultural digitalization to reinforce the sustainable development of the agrarian economy.

Chapter 4: Digitalization of Green Accounting of Climate-resilient E-business in Support of Decarbonization

This chapter investigates how digital green accounting can enhance the climate resilience and decarbonization of e-businesses. It analyzes the role of data centers and other energy-intensive components of digital infrastructure in environmental degradation and argues for integrating digital technologies into green accounting frameworks. By positioning green accounting as an analytical and management tool, the chapter outlines how companies can better align their operations with ecological and climate objectives.

Chapter 5: Contribution of Digital Green Accounting to the Investment Attractiveness of E-business for Its Sustainable Development

The chapter examines the impact of digital green accounting on the investment appeal of e-businesses. It identifies how environmental, social, and economic initiatives—such as reducing emissions, improving labor conditions, and ensuring financial viability—are captured through green accounting practices. The authors emphasize the strategic value of transparent sustainability reporting in attracting investment and aligning with Sustainable Development Goals.

Chapter 6: Digital Green Accounting in the Marketing Mix of E-business for Its Sustainable Development

This chapter explores how digital green accounting can be embedded in the marketing mix of e-businesses to support environmental sustainability and business competitiveness. It shows how digitalization transforms the traditional marketing mix into a more flexible and environmentally conscious structure. Green accounting is presented as a vital tool for ensuring the integrity and relevance of information used in marketing strategies that support sustainable development.

Chapter 7: Green Accounting and Digitalization of E-Business for Sustainable Development: A Methodological Toolkit for Forecasting Enterprise Competitiveness

This chapter introduces a methodological framework for forecasting the competitiveness of Uzbek enterprises by incorporating green accounting and digital tools. It includes an econometric model tied to marketing practices and offers a forecast extending to 2030. Through a comparative analysis with other competitive economies, the authors develop practical recommendations for enhancing the marketing and sustainability capabilities of local businesses.

Chapter 8: The Development and Enhancement of a Balanced Scorecard System in Management Accounting of an Enterprise

The authors propose an enhanced version of the Balanced Scorecard (BSC) that incorporates additional perspectives on quality and compliance, and cost management. This refined model aims to address evolving business challenges and regulatory demands. The chapter discusses how the extended BSC supports strategic alignment and decision-making across departments while promoting sustainable operational excellence.

Chapter 9: Econometric Analysis of Factors Affecting the Competitiveness of Industrial Enterprises

This chapter presents an econometric analysis of the macroeconomic factors that shape the global competitiveness of Uzbekistan's industrial sector. The authors develop a unique three-dimensional classification model that assesses these factors by management domain, statistical influence, and favorability. The research offers practical insights for optimizing industrial strategy in the context of the Fifth Industrial Revolution.

Chapter 10: Sustainable Finance and Impact Investing

This chapter outlines the principles and practices of sustainable finance, with a focus on aligning financial activities with ESG criteria. It highlights the potential for impact investing to generate both financial returns and measurable social or environmental benefits. Despite challenges in standardizing impact evaluation, the chapter emphasizes the growing role of ethical finance in supporting sustainable development.

Chapter 11: Contribution of Local E-Business to the Sustainable Development of Smart Territories: The Mediation of Green Accounting in Logistics Complexes of Ethiopia

The final chapter analyzes how green accounting mediates the relationship between local e-business practices and sustainable development in smart territories, using Ethiopia as a case study. Employing exploratory factor analysis, the authors identify key drivers of sustainability and advocate for the integration of environmentally conscious accounting practices. They stress the importance of stakeholder engagement and fostering a culture of sustainability within local enterprises.

A recurring theme throughout the book is the importance of integrating green principles into the operational and strategic dimensions of e-business. Whether through balanced scorecards, econometric modeling, or sustainability-focused marketing strategies, each chapter advances our understanding of how environmental accounting can shape corporate behavior, improve transparency, and build resilience. Importantly, this volume does not limit itself to theoretical models—it also provides robust methodological toolkits and policy recommendations, paving the way for future research and practical implementation.

Ultimately, this book offers a multidimensional view of sustainable digital transformation. It affirms that aligning business with environmental imperatives is not merely a moral obligation, but a strategic necessity for long-term success. I extend my sincere gratitude to all the contributing authors whose dedicated work has made this volume possible. It is my hope that this compilation serves as both a scholarly resource and a practical guide, empowering readers to harness green accounting and digital innovation for a more sustainable and inclusive economic future.

Shakhlo Ergasheva
Tashkent State University of Economics, Uzbekistan

Chapter 1
A Systemic Approach to Organizing "Green" Accounting and Digitalizing E-Business for Sustainable Development

Shakhlo T. Ergasheva
https://orcid.org/0000-0001-9896-3953
Tashkent State University of Economics, Uzbekistan

ABSTRACT

The research aims to justify the preference for a systemic approach to organizing "green" accounting and digitalizing e-business for its sustainable development. Moreover, the research aims to develop recommendations for implementing this approach in Uzbekistan. To this end, the author conducted an empirical study on the experience of 15 countries with moderately sustainable e-business development in 2025, including Uzbekistan. Thus, the author developed a regression model to assess the impact of e-business adaptation tools to current global trends on its sustainability. According to the model, sustainable development in e-business is primarily ensured through the use of corporate accounting modernization tools (e.g., acquiring state-of-the-art software, making green investments, and engaging in green trade), while HRM tools play a secondary role. Furthermore, the systemic application of green accounting and digitalization significantly enhances its sustainability.

DOI: 10.4018/979-8-3693-8362-9.ch001

INTRODUCTION

Based on numerous published sources, including the works of Abdurakhmanova et al. (2022), the author determines e-business as the collection of business entities engaged in electronic commerce. Emerging just a few decades ago with the widespread proliferation of the Internet, e-business has become a principal actor in the digital economy, with its significance and scale of operations continuously growing.

Initially, e-business appeared as a supplement to traditional offline commerce. However, as internet penetration became widespread among businesses and households, the popularity of e-business surged. It is now rapidly displacing traditional offline commerce in digital economy markets. Depending on the specific digital market, e-business takes on various forms.

In the B2C market, e-business is embodied in online marketplaces where retail transactions occur. In the B2B market, it appears as wholesale online trading, seamlessly integrated into the supply and distribution chains of the digital economy. In the B2G market, e-business is unique, taking the form of electronic auctions where digital economy business entities compete for exclusive rights to participate in public-private partnership projects and execute government contracts.

E-business offers a robust set of technological competitive advantages compared to traditional offline commerce. These advantages include reduced logistical costs through enhanced accessibility and the integration of "just-in-case" and "just-in-time" logistics, lower transaction costs owing to advanced search optimization and intelligent decision support for purchases, and an expanded geographical reach through online trading, which operates within the boundless Internet space.

This underscores the relevance of sustainable development in e-business because its uninterrupted functioning is crucial for the digital economy and its potential to enhance market efficiency and global competitiveness. Currently, e-business is strongly influenced by two major, though misaligned, global trends.

The first trend is the digital development of e-business. In response to this trend, e-business modernizes its processes and increases the level of high technology in online commerce (Tursunov et al., 2022). The second trend is the green development of e-business, which involves greening business activities to support the fight against climate change, specifically through decarbonizing the digital economy and more rational use of natural resources (Tolmachev et al., 2023).

The challenge is that contemporary e-businesses adapt to these trends separately, which hampers their sustainable development. One common feature of these trends is the modernization of corporate accounting, which potentially creates an opportunity to harmonize them. This research aims to substantiate the preference for a systemic approach to organizing green accounting and digitalizing e-business for its sustainable development. Moreover, the research aims to develop recommendations for implementing this approach in Uzbekistan.

BACKGROUND

The existing scholarly literature presents two alternative approaches for organizing the adaptation process of e-business to contemporary global trends. The first approach involves the exclusive digitalization of e-business activities using the following instruments:

- Involving leading specialists from among researchers and practitioners in the field of ICT (DA_1) (Mkrtchyan et al., 2024);
- Investing in telecommunications services to enhance the efficiency of e-business infrastructure (DA_2) (Przhedetskiy et al., 2019);
- Acquiring state-of-the-art software to improve the functionality of e-business services (DA_3) (Kirillova et al., 2023).

The second approach focuses solely on greening e-business activities through the following instruments:

- Ensuring green employment in e-business to bolster the human resource base for its greening processes (GA_1) (Bogoviz et al., 2023);
- Green investments to finance modernization projects in the greening of e-business activities (GA_2) (Rogachev et al., 2018);
- Green trade for the comprehensive ecological transformation of online trading processes (GA_3) (Bogoviz et al., 2017).

The modernization of corporate accounting is envisaged through instruments such as DA_2, DA_3, GA_1, and GA_2. Drawing on the work of Popkova & Ergasheva (2024), which highlights the critically important role of corporate accounting for the market adaptation of e-business, this research proposes hypothesis (H_1) that the sustainable development of e-business is primarily ensured by the application of corporate accounting modernization tools (namely, investments in telecommunications services, acquisition of state-of-the-art software, green investments, and green trade) while HRM tools (ICT specialists and green personnel) play a secondary role.

Furthermore, based on the publications by Kazambayeva et al. (2023), which present successful examples of combining green accounting and digitalization in the practical activities of e-business, this research posits hypothesis ($H_{2)}$ that the sustainability of e-business increases when green accounting and digitalization are implemented systematically.

MAIN FOCUS OF THE CHAPTER

To study Uzbekistan's experience and to obtain conclusions that are reliable for the Uzbek economy, the author formed a sample of 15 countries worldwide with moderately sustainable e-business development. The inclusion criterion was the share of e-business in the country's trade structure (SEb) as estimated by UNDP & MBRF (2023). This indicator equals 19.7% in Uzbekistan. For the countries in the sample, it must range between 10% and 20%.

To test the proposed hypotheses using regression analysis, the author determined the impact of the identified instruments (i.e., $DA_{1\text{-}3}$, determined based on UNDP & MBRF (2023) statistics, and $GA_{1\text{-}3}$, determined based on Global Green Growth Institute (GGGI, 2025) statistics) on SEb in the sample countries. The study period is 2025 (Table 1).

Table 1. Statistics on sustainable development of e-business in 2025

Country	Trade in digitally deliverable services (% total trade)	Tertiary graduates from ICT programs (%)	Investment in telecommunication services (% GDP)	Computer software spending (% GDP)	Green employment (score 0–100)	Green investment (score 0–100)	Green trade (score 0–100)
	SEb	DA_1	DA_2	DA_3	GA_1	GA_2	GA_3
Albania	12.1	36.3	29.9	11.6	38.48	24.10	65.55
Armenia	18.2	43.1	23.3	23.1	68.14	38.97	68.86
Bangladesh	16.7	10.9	12.0	17.5	35.32	53.29	63.77
Benin	15.7	29.6	24.7	4.3	0.00	37.49	66.58
Bhutan	17.7	0.0	34.4	0.0	0.00	42.94	55.93
Bolivia	17.6	0.0	61.7	26.0	49.48	44.98	50.74
Bosnia and Herzegovina	15.1	37.5	45.5	5.9	66.25	41.29	67.47
Burundi	12.6	37.6	12.0	5.5	22.60	15.90	52.23
Cabo Verde	11.7	10.5	93.6	25.7	52.06	56.00	0.00
Cambodia	14.5	58.1	39.2	2.3	29.95	53.83	59.70
Dominican Republic	12.5	30.7	24.6	1.4	39.64	34.67	68.32
Ecuador	18.7	9.4	27.2	19.9	49.69	22.70	65.88
Egypt	16.3	31.7	21.4	18.9	51.14	35.79	71.46

continued on following page

Table 1. Continued

Country	Trade in digitally deliverable services (% total trade)	Tertiary graduates from ICT programs (%)	Investment in telecommunication services (% GDP)	Computer software spending (% GDP)	Green employment (score 0–100)	Green investment (score 0–100)	Green trade (score 0–100)
	SEb	DA_1	DA_2	DA_3	GA_1	GA_2	GA_3
Georgia	14.8	18.0	25.8	6.1	61.23	30.20	73.12
Uzbekistan	19.7	28.8	15.9	15.3	41.96	43.66	51.02

Source: Developed by the authors based on the materials from Global Green Growth Institute (GGGI, 2023) and UNDP & MBRF (2023)

The regression analysis of the data from Table 1 provided the following model (1) for the impact of instruments adapting e-business to contemporary global trends on its sustainable development:

$$SEb=10.23-0.05DA_1-0.05DA_2+0.14DA_3-0.01GA_1+0.09GA_2+0.06GA_3 \quad (1)$$

According to model (1), for every 1% increase in the share of ICT specialists in e-business, its share in trade decreases by 0.05%. Similarly, a one-point increase in the level of green employment in e-business results in a 0.01% decrease in its trade share. This indicates the ineffectiveness of HRM instruments for the sustainable development of e-business in countries with moderately sustainable development (e.g., Uzbekistan).

Model (1) also shows that a 1% increase in investments in telecommunications services as a share of GDP leads to a 0.05% reduction in the trade share of e-business. However, other tools for modernizing corporate accounting have proven effective in countries with moderately sustainable e-businesses (e.g., Uzbekistan).

Thus, a 1% GDP increase in funding for acquiring state-of-the-art software by e-businesses boosts their trade share by 0.14%. A one-point increase in green investments raises the trade share by 0.09%. A one-point increase in the level of green trade results in a 0.06% growth in the trade share.

By supplementing the regression analysis with correlation analysis and forecasting based on model (1), the author identified a synergistic effect for sustainable development, which emerges from the systematic organization of green accounting and the digitalization of e-business (Figure 1).

Figure 1. A synergistic effect for sustainable development arising from the systemic application of green accounting and the digitalization of e-business

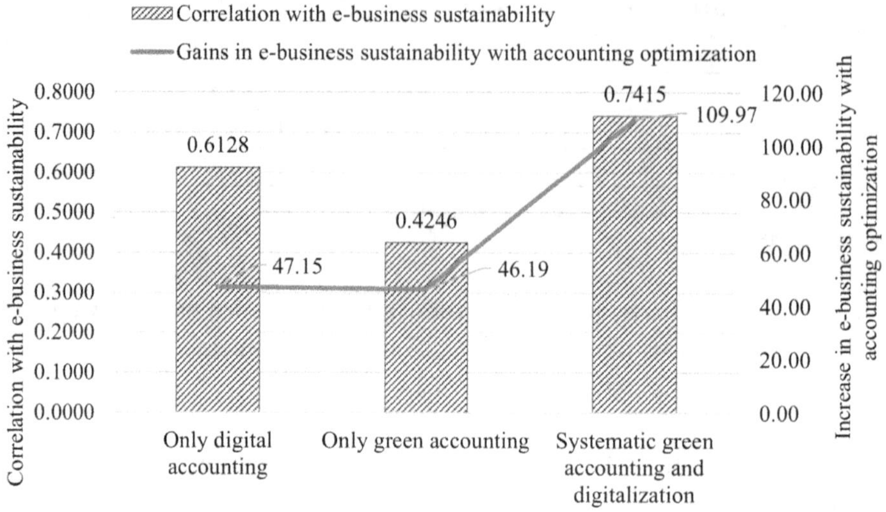

Source: Developed by the authors

Figure 1 shows that the instruments of exclusive digital accounting account for 61.28% of the sustainable development of e-business in countries such as Uzbekistan, while the instruments of exclusive green accounting account for 42.46%. The combined set of these instruments, when applied systemically through green accounting and digitalization, determines 74.15% sustainability of e-business in such countries.

Optimizing the use of the most promising selected instruments yields an increase in the sustainability of e-business in Uzbekistan up to 47.15% with exclusive digital accounting (increasing DA_3 to 100% of GDP) up to 46.19% with exclusive green accounting (increasing GA_2 and GA_3 to 100 points), and up to 109.97% with a systemic approach combining green accounting and digitalization.

SOLUTIONS AND RECOMMENDATIONS

To fully realize the potential of sustainable development of e-business in Uzbekistan during the Decade of Action (until 2030), the author developed a systemic approach to organizing green accounting and digitalization in the country. The author's recommendations for the practical application of this new approach in Uzbekistan, along with a forecast of its consequences for the sustainable development of Uzbek e-business, are presented in Figure 2. To formulate the forecast, the maximum (100) values of the selected effective instruments ensuring sustainable development of e-business (DA_3, GA_2, and GA_3) were substituted into the model (1) for Uzbekistan.

Figure 2. Recommendations for improving the organization of green accounting and digitalization of e-business for its sustainable development

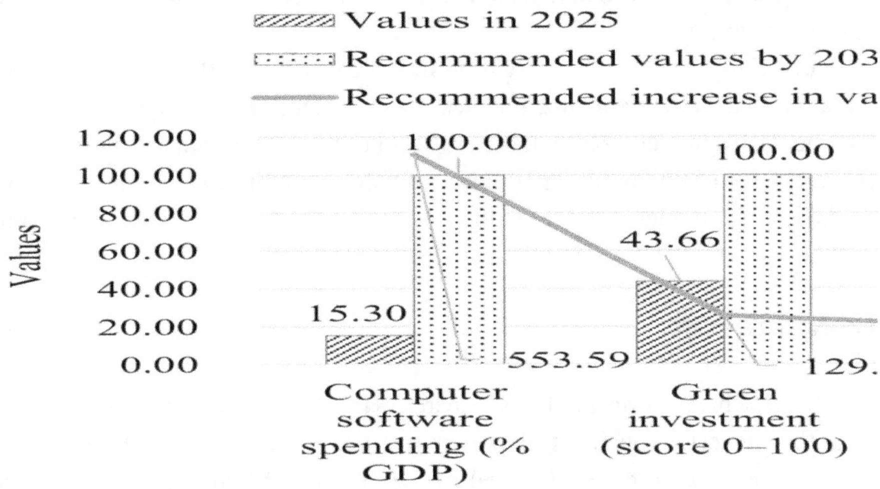

Source: Developed by the authors

Based on Figure 2, the author proposed the following recommendations to improve the organization of green accounting and digitalization of e-business in support of its sustainable development in Uzbekistan:

- Increase funding for the acquisition of state-of-the-art software by e-businesses by 553.59%;
- Boost green investments by 129.04%;
- Enhance the level of green trade by 96.00%.

By implementing these recommendations, it is forecasted that the share of e-business in trade in Uzbekistan will increase by 109.97% (from 19.70% in 2025 to 41.36% by 2030).

FUTURE RESEARCH DIRECTIONS

In future research, it is advisable to focus on the empirical experiences of countries with lower (trade share below 10%) and higher (trade share above 20%) sustainable development of e-business compared to Uzbekistan and examine the specifics of applying adaptation instruments to the global trends of digitalization and greening in these countries.

Particularly, a deeper investigation into the effects of HRM instruments on the sustainable development of e-business is warranted. It is essential to determine whether HRM modernization tools are secondary to corporate accounting modernization instruments for ensuring the sustainable development of e-business only in countries with moderate sustainability, such as Uzbekistan, or across all countries.

CONCLUSION

Thus, the primary result of this research is the development of a model that delineates the impact of e-business adaptation instruments on its sustainable development in response to contemporary global trends. The contribution of this model to the literature on e-business (Abdurakhmanova et al., 2022) lies in its elucidation of the consequences of digitalization and greening for the sustainability of e-business in Uzbekistan and other countries with moderately sustainable e-business (Table 2).

Table 2. Alternative approaches to organizing the process of e-business adaptation to contemporary global trends

Criteria for comparing alternative approaches		Approach to organizing the process of e-business adaptation to current global trends		
		Reflection in literature		Systems approach (regression)
		Exceptional digitalization	Exceptional greening	
Adaptation tools	HRM modernization	Involvement of ICT specialists (DA_1) (Mkrtchyan et al., 2024)	Green employment (GA_1) (Bogoviz et al., 2023)	negative impact (regression at DA_1=-0.05, at GA_1=-0.01)
	Modernization of corporate accounting	Investments in telecommunication services (DA_2) (Przhedetskiy et al., 2019)	Green investments t(GA_2) (Rogachev et al., 2018)	overall positive impact (regression at DA_2=-0.05, at GA_2=0.09, at DA_3=0.14, and at GA_3=0.06)
		Acquisition of the latest software (DA_3) (Kirillova et al., 2023)	Green trade (GA_3) (Bogoviz et al., 2017)	

continued on following page

Table 2. Continued

Criteria for comparing alternative approaches	Approach to organizing the process of e-business adaptation to current global trends		
	Reflection in literature		Systems approach (regression)
	Exceptional digitalization	Exceptional greening	
Effect of tools application (correlation with SEb)	0.6128	0.4246	synergistic effect: 0.7415
Perspective on sustainability accrual (growth of SEb)	+47.15%	+46.19%	+109.97%

Source: Developed by the authors

As shown in Table 2, unlike the findings of Bogoviz et al. (2023) and Mkrtchyan et al. (2024), an empirical study of countries with moderately sustainable e-businesses, such as Uzbekistan in 2025, revealed the ineffectiveness of HRM modernization tools for ensuring its sustainability. In contrast, in support of Bogoviz et al. (2017), Kirillova et al. (2023), and Rogachev et al. (2018), the author found that corporate accounting modernization tools in Uzbekistan (namely, acquiring state-of-the-art software, green investments, and green trade) are highly effective in enhancing the sustainability of e-business. This evidence supports hypothesis H_1.

Furthermore, in line with Kazambayeva et al. (2023), the author confirmed that the systemic implementation of green accounting and digitalization increases the sustainability of e-business. A synergistic effect was identified, manifesting, firstly, in a stronger correlation between adaptation tools for contemporary global trends and the sustainability of e-business when applied systemically (0.7415) compared to their individual application (0.6128 with exclusive digitalization or 0.4246 with exclusive greening).

Second, the prospect of significantly greater increases in the sustainability of e-business is evident with the systemic application of these tools (+109.97%) compared to their individual application (+47.15% with exclusive digitalization or +46.19% with exclusive greening). This confirms hypothesis H_2. Consequently, a systemic approach to organizing green accounting and digitalization of e-business is preferable for its sustainable development in Uzbekistan.

The author's recommendations for enhancing the organization of green accounting and digitalization of e-business in Uzbekistan during the Decade of Action are of practical significance because they will ensure better coordination of adaptation measures in e-business operations and fully unlock its sustainable development potential. In turn, this will contribute to a more stable functioning of the digital economy, increased market efficiency in Uzbekistan, and enhanced global competitiveness of Uzbek e-business.

REFERENCES

Abdurakhmanova, G. K., Astanakulov, O. T., Goyipnazarov, S. B., & Irmatova, A. B. (2022). Tourism 4.0: opportunities for applying industry 4.0 technologies in tourism. Proceedings of ICFNDS '22: *The 6th International Conference on Future Networks & Distributed Systems* (pp. 33-38). New York, NY: Association for Computing Machinery. DOI: 10.1145/3584202.3584208

Bogoviz, A. V., Lobova, S. V., Ragulina, Y. V., & Alekseev, A. N. (2017). A comprehensive analysis of energy security in the member states of the Eurasian economic union, 2000-2014. *International Journal of Energy Economics and Policy*, *7*(5), 93–101. Retrieved March 07, 2025, from https://econjournals.com/index.php/ijeep/article/view/5447/3311

Bogoviz, A. V., Tolmachev, A. V., Sozinova, A. A., & Gyiazov, A. T. (2023). The leading experience of ESG management of business in support of decarbonisation and development of the green economy in the Eurasian Economic Union (EAEU). In Popkova, E. G., & Sergi, B. S. (Eds.), *ESG Management of the Development of the Green Economy in Central Asia* (pp. 145–153). Springer., DOI: 10.1007/978-3-031-46525-3_16

Global Green Growth Institute (GGGI). (2023). Green growth index 2023: Measuring performance in achieving SDG targets. *GGGI Technical Report No. 32*. Seoul, Republic of Korea: GGGI. Retrieved March 07, 2025, from https://gggi.org/report/green-growth-index-2023/

Kazambayeva, A. M., Begeyeva, M. K., Nursapina, K. U., & Rakhmetova, R. (2023). Systematic approach to sustainable development in agricultural and food systems – Example of Republic of Sakha (Yakutia) and the Arctic Zone. [Problems of Sustainable Development]. *Problemy Ekorozwoju*, *18*(1), 226–234. DOI: 10.35784/pe.2023.1.24

Kirillova, E., Otcheskiy, I., Ivanova, S., Verkhovod, A., Stepanova, D., Karlibaeva, R., & Sekerin, V. (2023). Developing methods for assessing the introduction of smart technologies into the socio-economic sphere within the framework of open innovation. *International Journal of Sustainable Development and Planning*, *18*(3), 693–702. DOI: 10.18280/ijsdp.180305

Mkrtchyan, T. M., Karbekova, A. B., Zakharov, D. S., & Pakhomova, O. K. (2024). AI and machine learning in inclusive development to personalize user experience and increase digital literacy. In Popkova, E. G. (Ed.), *Digital inclusiveness: Bridging the divide in the digital economy* (pp. 25–35). World Scientific Publishing., DOI: 10.1142/9789811270826_0003

Popkova, E. G., & Ergasheva, S. T. (2024). Favorable business climate for transition to international financial reporting standards: criteria and pathways for achievement. In Eshov, M. P., Abdurakhmanova, G. K., Burkhanov, A. U., Abdusalomova, N. B., & Ergasheva, S. T. (Eds.), *Development of international entrepreneurship based on corporate accounting and reporting according to IFRS* (pp. 7–13). Emerald Publishing Limited., DOI: 10.1108/S1877-63612024000033A001

Przhedetskiy, Yu. V., Przhedetskaya, N. V., Borzenko, K. V., & Bondarenko, V. A. (2019). Blockchain technologies in healthcare institutions: Focus on security and effective cooperation with the government. *International Journal of Economics and Business Administration, 7*(Special Issue 2, SI2), 92–99. DOI: 10.35808/ijeba/373

Rogachev, A. F., Ostrovskaya, V. N., Natsubidze, A. S., Litvinova, T. N., & Yakovleva, E. A. (2018). Tools for sustainability management of socio-ecological systems in the globalizing world. In Popkova, E. (Ed.), *The impact of information on modern humans* (pp. 241–247). Springer., DOI: 10.1007/978-3-319-75383-6_31

Tolmachev, A. V., Lifanov, P. A., Ketko, N. V., & Smetanina, A. I. (2023). The model of organisation of green entrepreneurship and the climate-responsible management of production factors in the digital economy markets. In Popkova, E. G. (Ed.), *Smart green innovations in industry 4.0 for climate change risk management* (pp. 145–153). Springer., DOI: 10.1007/978-3-031-28457-1_15

Tursunov, B. O., Uktamov, K. F., & Tukhtamuratova, A. (2022). Ways to ensure food security in the development of a digital economy. Proceedings of ICFNDS '22: *The 6th International Conference on Future Networks & Distributed Systems* (pp. 548-555). New York, NY: Association for Computing Machinery. DOI: 10.1145/3584202.3584284

UNDP & MBRF. (2023). *Global Knowledge Index 2023*. Retrieved March 07, 2025, from https://knowledge4all.com/admin/2023/Methodology/GKI2023_Methodology_EN.pdf

ADDITIONAL READING

Alsulami, F. H. A. (2025). Digital innovation and sustainable accounting practices: A systematic literature review through the governance context. *Journal of Governance and Regulation, 14*(1), 38–48. DOI: 10.22495/jgrv14i1art4

Changalima, I. A., Ismail, I. J., & Amani, D. (2025). Driving SME performance through technological absorptive capacity and e-business innovation. *Sustainable Technology and Entrepreneurship*, *4*(1), 100089. DOI: 10.1016/j.stae.2024.100089

Huy, P. Q., & Phuc, V. K. (2025). Does effectiveness of digital accounting system intensify sustainable business model innovation with mediating role of digital business ecosystem? *Journal of Innovation and Entrepreneurship*, *14*(1), 3. DOI: 10.1186/s13731-024-00444-x

Lisnawati, L., Aryati, T., & Gunawan, J. (2024). Implementation of digital innovation on sustainability performance: The moderating role of green accounting in the industrial sector. *Eastern-European Journal of Enterprise Technologies*, *1*(13), 59–68. DOI: 10.15587/1729-4061.2024.298639

Martínez-Falcó, J., Sánchez-García, E., Marco-Lajara, B., & Zaragoza-Sáez, P. (2025). Green intellectual capital and sustainable competitive advantage: Unraveling role of environmental management accounting and green entrepreneurship orientation. *Journal of Intellectual Capital*, *26*(1), 104–129. DOI: 10.1108/JIC-07-2024-0204

Rasyid, S., Azis, N. A., & Rahmat, A. (2025). Green accounting for medium-sized enterprises: A review of participatory action research towards a sustainable future. *International Journal of Economics and Financial Issues*, *15*(1), 84–92. DOI: 10.32479/ijefi.17331

Routaib, H., Seddik, S., Elmounadi, A., & Haddadi, A. E. (2025). Enhancing E-business in Industry 4.0: Integrating fog/edge computing with Data LakeHouse for IIoT. *Future Generation Computer Systems*, *166*, 107653. DOI: 10.1016/j.future.2024.107653

Xu, Y., & Pan, H. (2025). The effects of enterprises' e-business adoptions on cross-border firm internationalization. *Systems*, *13*(2), 84. DOI: 10.3390/systems13020084

KEY TERMS AND DEFINITIONS

Digital development of e-business: the modernization of business processes and the enhancement of the technological sophistication of online trade.

E-business in the B2B market: wholesale online trade, seamlessly integrated into the supply and distribution chains of the digital economy.

E-business in the B2C market: online marketplaces where retail trade is conducted.

E-business in the B2G market: electronic auctions where digital economy business entities compete for the exclusive right to participate in public-private partnership projects and execute government contracts.

E-business: a collection of business entities engaged in electronic commerce.

Green development of e-business: the greening of e-business activities in support of combating climate change, particularly through the decarbonization of the digital economy and the rational use of natural resources.

Modernization of corporate accounting in e-business: investments in telecommunications services, the acquisition of state-of-the-art software, green investments, and green trade in e-business operations.

Modernization of HRM in e-business: attracting ICT specialists and green personnel to e-business.

Traditional trade: the offline sale of products.

Chapter 2
Digital "Green" Accounting of E-Business to Raise Its Energy Efficiency in Support of Sustainable Development

Arzybek O. Kozhoshev
https://orcid.org/0009-0003-3703-5856
Eurasian Economic Commission, Russia

Nargul A. Sydykova
https://orcid.org/0009-0002-8445-5717
Osh State University, Kyrgyzstan

Tatiana N. Litvinova
https://orcid.org/0000-0003-3101-2621
Volgograd State Agricultural University, Russia

Elena G. Popkova
https://orcid.org/0000-0003-2136-2767
Armenian State University of Economics, Armenia

ABSTRACT

Modern economic conditions require from companies the effective management of green accounting. This is connected with an increasing role of environmental aspects in companies' activities. Environmental factors become very important for the competitiveness of companies since they influence their financial results, reputation, and image. Unlike traditional financial reporting, green accounting is an

DOI: 10.4018/979-8-3693-8362-9.ch002

expanded concept, which includes non-financial indicators, such as environment, social impact, and sustainable development. E-business and e-commerce form a quickly growing industry, which offers many advantages for consumers. However, e-business has a large environmental impact, which is manifested in particular in energy consumption and emissions. E-business needs to implement renewable energy into the supply chain, to reduce their carbon footprint, save costs, and meet customer expectations. E-business and e-commerce use environmentally friendly materials in their activities, to preserve the environment and make it sustainable.

INTRODUCTION

E-business (electronic business) means the use of digital technologies for online business processes. E-business includes a variety of customer, internal, and management processes.

Electronic commerce, or e-commerce, means buying and selling goods on the Internet. At present, almost all existing products and services can be sold and purchased with the help of e-commerce.

Green accounting is a form of accounting according to which environmental costs are seen as a part of operations' financial results. Green accounting deals with the impact of human activities on environmental systems and resources, not just the financial effects of such activities.

According to Gogoleva and Bakhturina (2016), green accounting is the formation of documents systematized information about the environmental activities of the economic subject according to the requirements for the accounting information and its compilation based on environmental reporting.

Environmental problems, which are an inseparable component of the development of modern economic models, require the formation of environmentally conscious activities of companies. Ecosystems, which are the main elements of the environment, have complex sets of positive and negative reverse connections. The diversity of the ecosystems' services, namely support, provision, regulation, and culture, influence society to a large extent. Some of them are decisive for the safety of humans, quality of life, and health.

The environmental impact of e-business is a very important issue. Ensuring sustainable development is one of the main goals of the digitalization of green accounting. This includes improvement of energy efficiency, preservation of biodiversity, reduction of greenhouse emissions, and effective use of natural resources.

To decrease the environmental impact, all companies and organizations must implement measures for environmental protection. Thus, the issues of environmental cost accounting are very important (Yerdavletova et al., 2020).

Green accounting could be also defined as a form of financial accounting that includes environmental factors and ideas of sustainability in the traditional practice of financial accounting. Its goal is to ensure fuller and more precise view of the company's economic activities through considering the influence on the environment. By implementing the methods of green accounting, organizations can see their environmental indicators, determine spheres for improvement, and make more justified decisions, which take into account the long-term sustainability of their activities.

The notion of sustainable development is very important in the context of the digitalization of business processes. Sustainable development envisages the balance between economic, environmental, and social aspects of the activities, ensuring the satisfaction of current needs without damage to the future generation's opportunities (Kelchevskaya and Zhaparov, 2024).

The goal of this study was to study the role of digital green accounting of e-business and e-commerce in the improvement of energy efficiency and support of sustainable development.

BACKGROUND

E-business could be defined as using modern electronic technologies and networks for the organization and implementation of business processes in the conditions of active globalization of the world economy. As for green accounting, it could be treated as a very important framework that integrates environmental data and ideas into traditional accounting practices. Its main goal is to manage the effect of economic activities on the environment, providing a better understanding of economic development, which includes environmental sustainability.

The issues of green accounting, e-business, e-commerce, energy efficiency, and sustainable development have been studied by many scholars.

Wiredu et al. (2023) studied the influence of green accounting on environmental sustainability and considered environmental costs as a link between green accounting and sustainability, stating that stakeholders deal large pressure on businesses to manufacture products in a sustainable way, which has to be competitive and economical at the same time.

Gonzalez and Peña-Vinces (2022) state that environmental performance factors need to include green accounting in the accounting system and offer implications for economies and businesses.

Xie et al. (2022) provide proof concerning the connection between e-commerce and environmental sustainability. The scholars state that it is possible to reach human progress through the approaches of e-commerce and aim at filling the literature gap by revealing the influence of e-commerce on environmental sustainability.

Sundarasen et al. (2024) strive to fill the gaps between theory and practice, providing a comprehensive view of environmental accounting and sustainability. The researchers present information about the evolution of environmental accounting and its future directions, demonstrating the relevance of comprehensive reviews in the synthesis of the existing research, identification of trends, and filling the research gaps.

Fuadah et al. (2022) determine the influence of e-commerce and sustainability reporting on tax avoidance and corporate results, trying to find out whether organizational culture is a moderating variable in small and medium enterprises, by the example of Indonesia.

Imran et al. (2023) dwelt on the optical effects of e-commerce, demand for renewable energy, and services trade on carbon emissions. Based on the analysis of carbon emissions in five of Asia's most advanced ICT markets over 1990-2020, the scholars state that innovative packaging methods allow reducing the carbon impact.

Popkova (2024) conducted comprehensive research on e-business 5.0, discussing the international experience and perspectives and providing recommendations to improve the management of smart technologies and innovations in e-business 5.0. The research includes such topics as entrepreneurial development and dynamics, Big Data, and mobile payment systems.

Popkova et al. (2024) revealed and assessed the directions for achieving environmental friendliness of products as a measure of product quality in the context of management from the position of sustainable development. The scholars elaborate on the main directions for the achievement of the environmental friendliness of products, which include responsible production and consumption, as well as the use of climate measures for the reduction of emissions in the environment.

Mkrtchyan et al. (2023) dwelt on the state of tourism in Armenia, an innovative economy, and opportunities for the development of tourism in this economy. The authors offered a new tool for the assessment of the achievement of sustainable tourism development goals.

Based on the overview of the literature on the selected topic, Antonini (2024) found that the most dominant idea is connected with the ability of environmental accounting to improve decisions and support the protection of the environment. The study's results emphasize the importance of research on the interconnection between accounting, digitalization, information systems, and environmental protection.

Kwilinski et al. (2023) studied the character of digital businesses' influence on energy efficiency to determine the tools for the development of the potential of European countries in sustainable development. The scholars also showed the large effect of digital business on energy intensity, $CO2$ emissions, and renewable energy share.

Further in this study, the concepts of e-commerce, green accounting, improvement of energy efficiency, and sustainable development are considered.

MAIN FOCUS OF THE CHAPTER

E-business is growing very quickly, compared to other forms of business. In particular, this is due to an increase in the number of Internet users, growth of trust in electronic payment systems, and convenience and speed of purchases in online stores.

Information technologies and their development led to a change in the means of doing business. Organization of electronic information exchange between companies allows for a significant increase in effective activities, which leads to a reduction of communication costs, a decrease in personnel involved with document turnover, a reduction of time required for the organization of different operations, and a growth of speed and precision of receiving information and conducting financial transactions. E-commerce equals chances in the competitive struggle. This allows large and small enterprises to compete in equal conditions in the context of an assortment of products, quality, and price. E-business and e-commerce provide companies access to the world market. Online stores provide managers with diverse aspects of doing business.

Integration of green accounting into corporate governance frameworks, in particular, in emerging markets, can improve companies' transparency and accountability. Clear reporting of environmental effects builds trust among stakeholders, including investors, consumers, and regulators (Sundarasen et al, 2024).

E-commerce provides sustainability advantages, compared to traditional retail methods. These include decreased environmental footprint, energy-efficient transportation and packaging, less food waste, transparency, and awareness.

E-business, as one of the forms of economic activities, has certain features: 1) it is directly connected with the use of information and communication technologies and the Internet, which are its technological basis; 2) it is oriented towards the achievement of a certain goal of the economic subject (making of profit, optimization of economic activities, management of information, transformation and optimization of business processes, change in the marketing practice, optimization of interrelations with consumers, improvement of the company's image, expansion of the market, development of new spheres of activities, etc.) with the help of information technologies; 3) it is a system, i.e., a combination of certain components: a system of information exchange, a system of online marketing, a system of online payments, a system of global information search, a system of online consulting, mobile office system, online banking, etc.

E-business has positive and negative effects on sustainability. An increase in online commerce led to the growth of the number of shipments and transportation. This is not always negative. Thanks to home deliveries, online shipping decreased the number of individual consumer trips and, therefore, emissions, which is a positive feature.

E-business eliminated geographical barriers, which allows companies to expand market coverage beyond local borders. Small companies receive access to global customer databases and can compete with larger enterprises. This led to an increase in competition and opportunities for growth. E-business optimizes business operations, reducing expenditures connected with physical stores, stock management, and operational costs. Online platforms allow for the automatization of processes, raising the effectiveness of work. E-business generates a lot of data about consumer behavior, preferences, and models of purchases. Companies can use this data to receive information, optimize marketing strategies, personalize their interaction with customers, and make justified decisions for an increase in customer satisfaction levels. E-business platforms ensure direct and interactive communication between companies and customers. Using personalized recommendations, targeted marketing campaigns, and feedback mechanisms, companies can strengthen relations, raise customer loyalty, and ensure better customer support.

Green accounting is a means of planning, management, and control over the influence of companies, organizations, and other economic subjects on the environment. It is an effective tool for reflecting expenditures and results on the natural resources used and environmental protection, as well as an element of the activities of companies, organizations, or other economic subjects.

Green accounting is a complex process, which includes numerous challenges for accountants. The main ones include the absence of common international standards for green accounting; difficulty of precise assessment of expenditures for environmental measures, given the fact that certain expenditures and indirect and hidden; insufficient level of accountants' qualification, which requires training and certification; demands regarding transparency and reliability of information from investors, regulators, the public, etc.

There are three key elements of green accounting: 1) collection and preparation of environmental data with the help of differentiation and expansion of the traditional accounting system (e.g., structuring of accounting of different types of expenditures and places of their emergence, expanded accounting of investments, analysis of financial results, calculation of external expenditures that are specific for the given company); 2) System of environmental control with constant planning, management, and control; 3) environmental audit as internal and external processes for the control over functional capabilities and effectiveness of the system of environmental management.

Green accounting covers the economic, environmental, and social aspects of organizations' activities. It helps ensure sustainable development, raise the effectiveness of resource use, and strengthen the company's reputation. Thus, the implementation of green accounting is an important step for any organization that wants to be responsible and successful in the modern world.

Green accounting should perform the following functions:

- Optimistic, which lies in the creation of the basis for the best selection of optimal variants of environmentally-oriented activities;
- Motivational, which is manifested in the provision of information to stimulate solutions to environmental problems;
- Regulatory, which consists in controlling measures on expenditures for the environment.

In the context of green accounting, digitalization is manifested in the application of digital technologies for the collection, analysis, and monitoring of environmental data for the effective management of companies' impact on the environment. Implementation of digital technologies in green accounting allows for the automatization of the process of collection and analysis of data on emissions, simplifies the procedures of reporting, and raises the precision and objectivity of results received. For example, the use of sensors and AI systems allows for constant monitoring of emissions and tracking of dynamics of changes in environmental indicators in real-time.

Tables 1 and 2 show the largest internet and e-commerce companies by market capitalization.

Table 1. Largest internet companies, by market capitalization (as of October 2024)

No.	Company	Market capitalization, $ billion
1.	Alphabet (USA)	2,028
2.	Amazon (USA)	1,966
3.	Meta (USA)	1,448
4.	Tencent (China)	499.53
5.	Netflix (USA)	326.26
6.	Alibaba (China)	244.29
7.	ServiceNow (USA)	186.99
8.	Pinduoduo (China)	174.83
9.	Uber (USA)	168.99
10.	Booking Holdings (USA)	145.24

Source: Compiled by the authors based on Statista (2024b).

Table 2. Largest e-commerce companies, by market capitalization (as of December 2024)

No.	Company	Market capitalization, $ billion
1.	Amazon (USA)	2,215
2.	Alibaba (China)	206.09
3.	Shopify (Canada)	146.29
4.	Pinduoduo (China)	137.46
5.	Meituan (China)	128.53
6.	MercadoLibre (Argentina)	98.98
7.	Sea (Singapore)	65.03
8.	Jingdong Mall (China)	60.98
9.	Copart (USA)	59.75
10.	Coupang (South Korea)	44.7

Source: Compiled by the authors based on Statista (2024a)

Sustainable development is a process of managing economic, social, and environmental aspects of business in a well-balanced and responsible way. This means creating value for stakeholders, employees, and society, minimizing the negative influence on natural resources and climate.

To develop in the modern dynamic and competitive market, companies should implement goals and values of sustainable development. This is a moral obligation and, at the same time, a strategic advantage, which ensures leadership. The use of sustainable practices allows businesses to raise effectiveness, innovativeness, reputation, and resilience, gaining a competitive advantage in the market.

Support of the Sustainable Development Goals is an important component in the context of environmental protection and sustainable use of resources. Implementation of digitalization in green accounting can help achieve the targeted indicators of sustainable development, in particular, reduction of the pollution level, preservation of biodiversity, and ensuring sustainable use of natural resources. Digitalization can help improve the monitoring of environmental indicators and develop more effective strategies for environmental management, which will facilitate the reduction of the negative influence of economic activities on the environment and more effective use of natural resources for sustainable development.

Digital green accounting of e-business in the context of ensuring its energy efficiency is connected with the implementation of measures at the level of the main management spheres which contribute to the reduction of energy consumption. Companies that provide digital services and products have a smaller effect on the environment compared to companies in the production sectors. Thus, it is necessary to consider the specifics of digital green accounting of e-business of manufacturing companies. In the context of the focus on the digitalization of the main processes, these companies implement energy-efficient technologies and equipment in the production and management of the energy sector, and apply information management systems and digital applications to control energy usage and product movement in logistics and delivery.

Let us consider the specifics of green accounting of e-business by the example of the leading manufacturing companies of the EU.

ThyssenKrupp AG (Germany) is among the leaders in industrial production in the EU (Adams, 2023). The company works in the sector of metallurgy and machine-building. Analysis of materials of green accounting of e-business allowed revealing the measures of energy efficiency and sustainable development of the company (Table 3).

Table 3. The influence of digital green accounting of e-business on energy efficiency and sustainable development of ThyssenKrupp AG

	Indicator	Description
1	Organization of communication with customers, sales, control of product supply chain, production, and logistics	Digital form. The company's website and electronic marketplaces are used for sales and communication. Digital interaction allows avoiding spending energy on office premises for contact with visitors (consumers, suppliers, etc.). Expenditures for companies' personnel in 48 countries (98,000 people) are lower compared to potential expenditures in the case of traditional office work. The companies practise remote work for certain categories of personnel, which also contributes to energy efficiency. Smart control systems are used for control of energy consumption in offices and production premises and storage.
2	Quantitative assessment of energy efficiency measures of the company (according to the data of green accounting from the sustainable development report)	Indicator of the growth of energy efficiency: - Factual values for the period of 01.01.2022-30.09.2023 – 340 GW, with the planned indicator of 250 GW for 2022-2023; - Factual values for the period of 01.01.2024-30.09.2024 – 360 GW, with the planned indicator of 125 GW for 2022-2023.
3	Influence of green accounting of e-business and energy efficiency on sustainable development	Reduction of CO2 emissions (t CO2 per million € sales): - for 2023-2024, the planned indicator was 34.5 t CO2 per million € sales, with the factual indicator of 31.1 t CO2 per million € sales (as of 30.09.2024). The factual indicator is below the planned one, which is a sign of the positive influence of energy efficiency measures.

Source: Compiled by the author based on (ThyssenKrupp AG, 2025)

As shown in Table 3, green accounting of e-business positively influences energy efficiency and sustainable development of the company. According to corporate reports of the company (ThyssenKrupp AG, 2025), it is planning on continuing the above trends. The key feature of green accounting of the company's e-business in the sphere of energy efficiency is the resource and technological approach. The company uses measures to save energy resources and applies modern intellectual digital technologies, which allow for their effective distribution.

Another example of the influence of digital green accounting of e-business on energy efficiency and sustainable development is Schneider Electric SE (France) (Adams, 2023). The company manufactures electrical equipment, including electrical wiring, switchboards, chargers for cars, information systems for energy efficiency management, etc.

Measures ensuring the company's energy efficiency are as follows (Schneider Electric SE, 2025):

- Integration of information systems (developed by the company for the internal and foreign markets), which ensure processing of the data about consumed energy at the level of corporate networks and equipment. These systems include smart control of energy consumption, the system of cooling of buildings, and systems of management of switching, low voltage, and medium voltage devices;
- Modernization of buildings used for offices, production, and logistics to raise energy efficiency.

These measures allowed the optimization of energy consumption, which led to the reduction of CO_2 emissions. In 2023, the reduction equaled 553 MT CO_2 emissions. This indicator improved by 112 MT compared to 2022 (Schneider Electric SE, 2025). This shows the results of the measures of energy efficiency of the company and allows stating that the company, similar to ThyssenKrupp AG, uses the resource and technological approach in this sphere.

SOLUTIONS AND RECOMMENDATIONS

In the modern conditions of digitalization, the development of information technologies, and the popularization of online services, e-business is a very promising form of economic activity.

E-business is a promising direction of entrepreneurial activities that can raise the level of competitiveness of individual companies and sectors and entire countries. E-business is a means of doing business with the use of the capabilities of the Internet. This is a rather wide notion, which includes a lot of aspects, including e-commerce. The main feature of e-business is the total digitalization of all processes, not only trade, which leads to the growth of effectiveness, profit, and capabilities of business.

Businesses use a large range of sustainability practices to reach their goals connected with environmental protection. Businesses undertake a lot of changes in their activities and infrastructures to perform sustainable operations. The most popular e-commerce sustainability practices, which become very popular among online sellers and consumers, include packaging, labeling, sourcing, dispatching & shipping, and carbon footprint.

FUTURE RESEARCH DIRECTIONS

The future of sustainable e-business lies in sustainable packaging, sustainable shipping, supply chain integration, and decreased energy waste.

Green accounting is a process of collection, analysis, and presentation of data on environmental aspects of a company's activities. Its goal is to help in decision-making aimed at minimization of environmental influence and support of the balance of economic and environmental goals.

Green accounting can also be seen as a system of collection, processing, storing, and analysis of data about the companies' or country's influence on the environment. The main goal of green accounting is an assessment of environmental costs and profits, which allows making justified decisions on environmental protection. Green accounting is aimed at the assessment of environmental factors and preparation of financial environmental accounting of the adopted form and contents, which is aimed mainly at external and internal users.

CONCLUSION

E-business is a business in which all internal and external relationships and processes are supported and ensured by information computer technologies. E-business is a system of conducting economic activities based on the use of the latest technologies in the organization of business and financial interrelations between counterparties. It is based on the transformation of the main business processes through using automatized information systems, the Internet, and web technologies, as a means of communication with potential and real customers, with a well-developed information infrastructure and new information culture.

With the growing presence and reach of the internet, e-business has become a very important component of modern business operations. E-business allows companies to attract more customers and provide personalized experiences that satisfy customer needs.

Green accounting is one of the most important tools that influence the national economy. Green accounting implements the concept of sustainability into economic development and to help reach a better future for the planet.

There are a lot of challenges on the path of e-business to sustainability. These challenges can be overcome with the help of transparency, innovations, consumer education, and strategic partnerships.

Green accounting, as a tool aimed at the preservation of the favorable state of the environment, is very important, for it allows the management and external users to receive environmental information about the activities of the company, organization, or another economic subject, which is necessary for the effective management of the environment. Achievement of sustainability helps protect the environment and natural resources and facilitates the growth of business.

E-business, as a model of sustainable development, has substantial potential for the transformation of the world economy. Due to integration of economic, social, and environmental aspects, helps create stable economic systems, which ensure harmonious and stable growth. In the modern globalized world, where digital technologies play a key role, models of sustainable development, in particular, e-business, become a central element of the strategies of development of national and international levels, facilitating the achievement of the Sustainable Development Goals and ensuring a better future for everyone.

REFERENCES

Adams, H. S. (2023). Top 10 European manufacturing companies. URL: https://manufacturingdigital.com/ai-and-automation/top-10-european-manufacturing-companies (data accessed: 19.02.2025)

Antonini, C. (2024). Accounting digitalization in the quest for environmental sustainability. *Current Opinion in Environmental Sustainability*, *66*, 101399. DOI: 10.1016/j.cosust.2023.101399

Fuadah, L. L., Dewi, K., Mukhtaruddin, M., Kalsum, U., & Arisman, A. (2022). The Relationship between Sustainability Reporting, E-Commerce, Firm Performance and Tax Avoidance with Organizational Culture as Moderating Variable in Small and Medium Enterprises in Palembang. *Sustainability (Basel)*, *14*(7), 3738. DOI: 10.3390/su14073738

Gogoleva, T. N., & Bakhturina, Yu. I. Environmental accounting in the system of accounting types // International accounting. 2016. No. 12 (402). URL: https://cyberleninka.ru/article/n/ekologicheskiy-uchet-v-sisteme-vidov-ucheta-1 (Accessed: 06.02.2025).

Gonzalez, C. C., & Peña-Vinces, J. (2023). A framework for a green accounting system-exploratory study in a developing country context, Colombia. *Environment, Development and Sustainability*, *25*(9), 9517–9541. DOI: 10.1007/s10668-022-02445-w

Imran, M., Khan, I., Nassani, A. A., Binsaeed, R. H., Khan, H. R., Abro, M. M. Q., Zaman, K., & Haffar, M. (2023). A green perspective: Investigating the optical effects of e-commerce, renewable energy demand, and services trade on carbon emissions. *Optik (Stuttgart)*, *283*, 170918. Advance online publication. DOI: 10.1016/j.ijleo.2023.170918

Kelchevskaya, N. R., & Zhaparov, R. N. (2024) Integration of digital technologies into the strategy of company's sustainable development // Bulletin of South Ural State University, Series "Economics and management", 2024, No. 3. URL: https://cyberleninka.ru/article/n/integratsiya-tsifrovyh-tehnologiy-v-strategiyu-ustoychivogo-razvitiya-promyshlennogo-predpriyatiya (Accessed: 06.02.2025).

Kwilinski, A., Lyulyov, O., & Pimonenko, T. (2023). The Impact of Digital Business on Energy Efficiency in EU Countries. *Information (Basel)*, *14*(9), 480. DOI: 10.3390/info14090480

Mkrtchyan, T. M., Tovmasyan, G. R., & Dallakyan, S. A. (2023). Sustainable Development of the Tourism Sector of the Republic of Armenia in the Context of an Innovative Economy. In Popkova, E. G. (Ed.), *Smart Green Innovations in Industry 4.0. Springer Climate*. Springer., DOI: 10.1007/978-3-031-45830-9_43

Popkova, E. G. (Ed.). (2024). *Smart Technologies and Innovations in E-Business*. IGI Global., DOI: 10.4018/978-1-6684-7840-0

Popkova, E. G., Ustenko, V. S., Petrenko, Y. S., & Bratukhina, E. A. (2024). ENVIRONMENTAL FRIENDLINESS OF PRODUCTS AS A MEASURE OF QUALITY: MANAGEMENT FROM THE POSITION OF SUSTAINABLE DEVELOPMENT. *International Journal of Qualitative Research*, *18*(4), 1159–1170. DOI: 10.24874/IJQR18.04-15

Schneider Electric, S. E. (2025). Financial and Sustainable Development Report 2023 Universal Registration Document. URL: chrome- https://www.se.com/ww/en/assets/564/document/462018/2023-universal-registration-document.pdf (data accessed: 19.02.2025)

Statista (2024a) Leading e-commerce companies worldwide as of December 2024, by market cap. URL: https://www.statista.com/statistics/245340/leading-large-cap-e-commerce-companies-market-cap/ Accessed: 06.02.2025

Statista (2024b). Market capitalization of the largest internet companies worldwide as of October 2024. URL: https://www.statista.com/statistics/277483/market-value-of-the-largest-internet-companies-worldwide/ Accessed: 06.02.2025

Sundarasen, S., Rajagopalan, U., & Alsmady, A. A. (2024). Environmental Accounting and Sustainability: A Meta-Synthesis. *Sustainability (Basel)*, *16*(21), 9341. DOI: 10.3390/su16219341

ThyssenKrupp AG. (2025). Environment, Social, Governance (ESG). URL: https://www.thyssenkrupp.com/en/investors/esg-information-for-capital-markets (data accessed: 19.02.2025)

Wiredu, I., Osei Agyemang, A., & Agbadzidah, S. Y. (2023). Does green accounting influences ecological sustainability? Evidence from a developing economy. *Cogent Business & Management*, *10*(2), 2240559. Advance online publication. DOI: 10.1080/23311975.2023.2240559

Xie, H., Chang, S., Wang, Y., & Afzal, A. (2022). The impact of e-commerce on environmental sustainability targets in selected European countries. *Ekonomska Istrazivanja*, *36*(1), 230–242. DOI: 10.1080/1331677X.2022.2117718

. Yerdavletova, Farida & Zhumabayeva, Myrzabike & Nurkasheva, Nursulu. (2020). State and problems of development of environmental accounting: experience of Kazakhstan. The economy: strategy and practice. 15. 139-150. .DOI: 10.51176/JESP/issue_2_T12

ADDITIONAL READING

Čečević, N. (2023). *Bojana & Đorđević, Milica & Stanojević, Marina*. The Role and Significance of Environmental Accounting for Sustainable Business Development., DOI: 10.4018/978-1-6684-7730-4.ch011

Endiana, D., Dicriyani, N. L. G. M., Adiyadnya, M. S. P., & Putra, I. P. M. J. S. (2020). The Effect of Green Accounting on Corporate Sustainability and Financial Performance. *The Journal of Asian Finance, Economics and Business*, *7*(12), 731–738. DOI: 10.13106/jafeb.2020.vol7.no12.731

Oláh, J., Kitukutha, N., Haddad, H., Pakurár, M., Máté, D., & Popp, J. (2019). Achieving Sustainable E-Commerce in Environmental, Social and Economic Dimensions by Taking Possible Trade-Offs. *Sustainability (Basel)*, *11*(1), 89. DOI: 10.3390/su11010089

Rasyid, S., Azis, N., & Rahmat, A. (2024). Green Accounting for Medium-Sized Enterprises: A Review of Participatory Action Research Towards A Sustainable Future. *International Journal of Economics and Financial Issues.*, *15*(1), 84–92. DOI: 10.32479/ijefi.17331

Revinova, S. (2021). E-commerce effects for the sustainable development goals. SHS Web of Conferences. 114. 01013. DOI: 10.1051/shsconf/202111401013

Shakour, Amer, & Alaodat, Hamza & Alghazawi, Ali & al-Qaisi, Emad. (2018). The Role of Environmental Accounting in Sustainable Development Empirical Study. *Journal of Applied Econometrics*, *8*, 71–87.

Wati, Y., Chandra, T., Irman, M., & Rahman, S. (2024). Green Accounting, Corporate Governance, Sustainable Development: The Moderating Effect of Corporate Social Responsibility. *The Indonesian Journal of Accounting Research.*, *27*(2). Advance online publication. DOI: 10.33312/ijar.786

KEY TERMS AND DEFINITIONS

E-business: Way of doing business with the help of the capabilities of the Internet; transforming the main business processes with the help of Internet technologies; a type of business activity in which the commercial interaction of subjects in buying and selling products and services is performed with the help of information networks.

E-commerce: Sphere of economy in which all transactions take place on the Internet; the sphere of the economy that includes all trade and financial operations performed with computer networks and all business processes related to these transactions. It consists of all actions connected with online transactions, including marketing, selling, processing of orders, delivery, and customer services.

Green accounting: A type of accounting that considers environmental costs in the company's financial activities. A system of identifying, measuring, registering, generalizing, and storing information about the company's activities in the sphere of nature for its transfer to customers for the most optimal managerial decisions.

Information systems: Totality of organizational and technical means for storing and processing information to ensure customers' information needs.

Sustainable development: The practice of development that satisfies current needs without depleting natural resources and without damage to the health and well-being of future generations.

Sustainable Development Goals: Key directions of development of countries adopted by the UN; a general call for actions aimed at overcoming poverty, protecting the planet, and ensuring peace and prosperity of all people.

Chapter 3

Digital Model of Green Accounting of E-Business in Agriculture for the Sustainable Development of the Agrarian Economy

Elena G. Popkova
https://orcid.org/0000-0003-2136-2767
Armenian State University of Economics, Armenia

Begaim T. Toichieva
https://orcid.org/0009-0004-3004-8870
Osh State University, Kyrgyzstan

Kholisa K. Kuldasheva
https://orcid.org/0009-0007-1746-4740
Tashkent State University of Economics, Uzbekistan

Alexey V. Tolmachev
https://orcid.org/0000-0001-9991-685X
Kuban State Agrarian University Named After I.T. Trubilin, Russia

ABSTRACT

Green accounting of e-business in agriculture contributes to achieving the key goals of sustainable development in the agrarian sector of the economy. We compile a digital model of green accounting of e-business in agriculture for sustainable development of the agrarian economy, the frameworks of which allow assessing indicators and characteristics of this process at the level of companies and the country. This model

DOI: 10.4018/979-8-3693-8362-9.ch003

allows evaluating green accounting of e-business in this sector by the example of India and Nigeria. The presented results show that at the current stage, these developing countries use the financing of digital communication and trade platforms without the participation of the government. Despite the absence of government support, this approach contributes to an increase in the level of sustainable development of the agrarian sector. However, our recommendations include the need to attract the government to the digitalization of agriculture.

INTRODUCTION

Organization of accounting and reporting of companies is equally important for management as production, supply chain management, financial management, etc. Modern trends of ensuring sustainable development led to the integration of a range of tasks, which stimulate the growth of the ecologization of companies' activities, into this sphere. Activities of agricultural companies are connected with sufficiently serious environmental effects on the environment. The quality of agricultural products, which is influenced by transportation and correct storage, influences the environment as well. All types of the agrarian sector's products have certain requirements for storing, transporting, and packaging. Their violation raises the level of waste. Accordingly, waste management costs must be taken into account, which is a task of green accounting.

E-business contributes to the reduction of such waste management costs for companies in the agrarian sector. Its organization, which ensures the minimum movement of agricultural products and is connected with the direct interaction of consumer and manufacturer, is less costly compared to expenditures required for waste management. Agricultural producers, which selected the method of product promotion through electronic platforms, have a higher organizational and technological potential compared to small farms. However, in certain countries that have digital platforms for the electronic trade of agricultural products, deals are concluded at the level of small companies (farmers) and consumers.

Agricultural producers, which are aimed at openness and transparency in informing about the results of economic activities with the help of e-business, conduct green accounting of costs and indicators. This allows positioning themselves as market players aimed at long-term activities and sustainable development of the agrarian economy. Commitment to the use of a digital model of green accounting of e-business in agriculture for sustainable development of the agrarian economy is the advantage of these companies. This advantage is important for consumers (the possibility to purchase agricultural products from the field, which influences product quality), investors (expenditures for ecologization are the basis for the agrarian sector's subject's observing the standards of ecologization and demonstrate a focus on support of external image), and government (agricultural company ensures environmental production due to responsible business).

Given the importance of studying the influence of digitalization of green accounting of e-business on the level of sustainable development of the agrarian economy, the considered topic is very relevant.

The goal of this research is to establish the effectiveness of the influence of green accounting of e-business in agriculture on the level of sustainability of the agrarian sector of countries. To reach this goal, we use the comparative method, the factor method, and the framework method.

The novelty of this research consists in determining the specifics of the formation of green accounting of e-business in agriculture of developing countries and revealing the influence of this process on the sustainable development of the agrarian sector.

BACKGROUND

To study the connection between the implementation of the digital model of green accounting of e-business and the indicator of sustainability of the agrarian sector's development, it is necessary to determine the categorical apparatus in this sphere.

Analysis of scientific materials allows stating that such notion as a digital model of any process could be viewed as a typical example of its implementation in the electronic form. According to van der Valk et al. (2024), the digital model of any process is connected with the establishment of framework parameters, conditions, and functional load. Zarubin and Deev (2017) state that the digital model of the process (in this case – production) includes a list of functions, stages, and attributes of its implementation, modeled in the electronic form.

We need to determine the essence of the notion of green accounting at the general level and the essence of the notion of green accounting of e-business in agriculture.

According to Maama and Appiah (2019), green accounting is a process of financial and economic assessment with a focus on the environmental and socio-economic responsibility of companies in various sectors of the economy.

Khan and Gupta (2024) state that this process is based on the systemic inclusion of ecologization costs of the activities in the total costs of the corresponding category (production costs, administrative costs, sales costs, etc.).

Burkhanov et al. (2024) dwelt on the important issues of individual health, environmental health, and public health and identified the potential for deep learning in organic agriculture to improve food security and promote individual, public, and environmental health.

Rounaghi (2019) also believes that this process envisages systemic calculation of environmental costs connected with company management.

Green accounting should be considered in the context of the calculation of expenditures for sustainable development in the complex of financial and economic accounting. Expenditures for the sustainable development of the company include expenditures for the balance of ecologization, social sector, and economic environment.

The second considered notion is green accounting of e-business in agriculture. E-business in this sector involves a focus on trading on digital platforms. We believe that green accounting is based on the accounting of the costs of this trade. Accordingly, green accounting of e-business in agriculture is a process of calculation of costs of ensuring sustainable development through selling products in the electronic form. These costs are connected with the promotion, payment, and digital control of delivery with a minimal negative effect on ecology and ensuring the social and economic development of the company.

Given the above theoretical basis, we developed a digital model of green accounting of e-business in the studied sector of the economy (Table 1).

Table 1. Digital model of green accounting of e-business in agriculture for the sustainable development of the agrarian economy

<table>
<tr><td colspan="4">1st stage – creation of a digital platform for promoting and selling products of agricultural producers directly to consumers</td></tr>
<tr><td colspan="4">↓</td></tr>
<tr><td colspan="4">Determining the subjects of financing of this information and communication system at the level of the territory of functioning (region, macroregion, country, etc.)</td></tr>
<tr><td colspan="4">↓</td></tr>
<tr><td colspan="4">For the type of digital platforms</td></tr>
<tr><td colspan="3">1. Agricultural producers - consumers</td><td>2. Sellers - buyers</td></tr>
<tr><td>1.1. Government, regional authorities, municipal authorities</td><td>1.2. Public-private partnership</td><td>1.3. Private business structure, private business structures in partnership with institutional funds (including international)</td><td>2.1. Agricultural producers independently promote and sell products on standard digital platforms</td></tr>
<tr><td colspan="4">↓</td></tr>
<tr><td colspan="4">2nd stage – Organisation of green accounting of e-business of agricultural producers with the use of digital platforms</td></tr>
<tr><td colspan="4">↓</td></tr>
<tr><td>1.1.</td><td>1.2</td><td>1.3</td><td>2.1</td></tr>
</table>

continued on following page

Table 1. Continued

Direction 1. Accounting of costs of participation in electronic promotion and sales of products. Direction 2. Accounting of the growth capital and stock price due to participation in sustainable development through the provision of information about the use of green accounting. The openness of information about image advantages of implementation of the Sustainable Development Goals, reduction of waste, reduction of the negative influence on ecology, growth of product quality due to direct sales, an increase in the social well-being of personnel, and growth of the volumes of product sales. Direction 3. Moving the costs of sustainable development to the financial reporting of the company. Presence of information system of accounting. Compilation of reporting.	Directions 1, 2, and 3 – similar to the categories of subjects within three digital models. Direction 4. Accounting of costs of the complex organization of the search for consumers, management of electronic payments, and organization of delivery.
↓	
3rd stage – Determining the influence of green accounting of e-business of agricultural producers on sustainable development with the use of all digital platforms	
↓	
1. Effects in the sphere of ecologization for territories and product safety and quality. 2. Effects in the social sphere. 3. Effects in the economic sphere.	

Source: Compiled by the authors

The presented model is a methodological basis for analysis of the level of implementing green accounting.

In this research, we use a comparative method to compare the selected indicators in dynamics (GDP of agriculture, prices for stock of agrarian companies, etc.). The factor method is used to reveal the factors of formation of the level of green accounting of e-business in the given sector. The framework method is used to determine the characteristics of green accounting of e-business in agriculture.

MAIN FOCUS OF THE CHAPTER

Implementation of e-business in agriculture contributes to the ecologization and competitiveness of agrarian companies, as well as the economic development of the country. One of the countries whose experience deserves attention is India. Analysis of statistical data (Government of India, 2024) shows that over the last five years, the country has been demonstrating a stable growth of GDP from selling agricultural products with stable prices. The indicator of the annual average growth rate of GDP from selling these products was 4.18% over 2018-2022. Stable prices for agricultural products of the country show that farms and large agrarian companies reached a high quality of crops. GDP from selling the products of fisheries, forestry, and agricultural sector equaled $ 273.2 billion in 2009, $ 338.8 billion in 2013, $ 387 billion in 2017, $ 456.9 billion in 2021, and $ 485.3 billion in 2023 (World Bank

Group, 2025a). The growth of the dynamics of the indicator was achieved due to an increase in yield, obtained thanks to the use of digital intellectual technologies and implementation of the tool of e-business – electronic trade on specialized trade platforms. It should be noted that the growth of grain yield in India (Figure 1) also became a factor in implementing the Sustainable Development Goals.

Figure 1. Dynamics of the grain yield growth in India

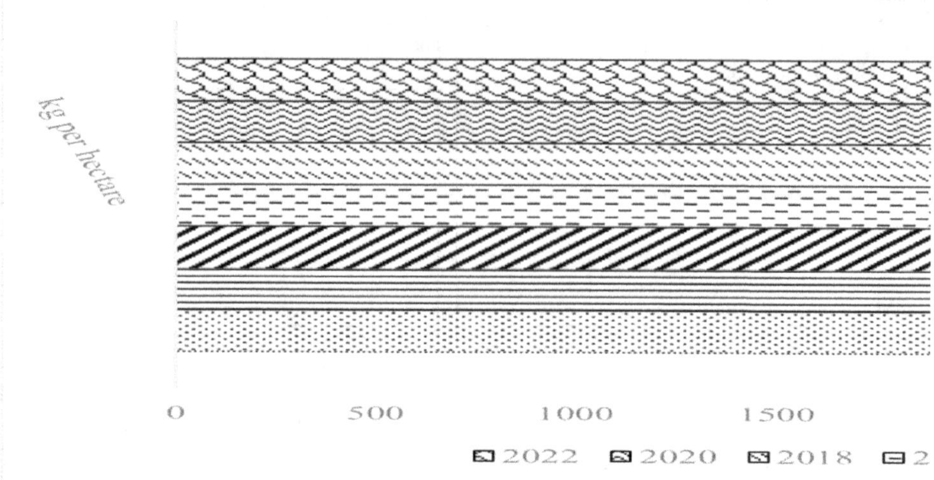

Source: Compiled by the authors based on the World Bank Group (2025b)

According to the statistical materials (Onwude, 2023), the leading digital trading platform in India, which ensures direct communication and transaction between agricultural producers and consumers, is AgroStar. Analysis of the main features of this digital trading platform (AgroStar, 2025) enabled us to formulate the key directions of its functioning, which include the following:

1) Support of individual farmers, farms, and agrarian companies in the process of transition to digital (including green) technologies. Consulting agricultural producers by the platform's operators with the use of a multichannel form of interaction, and support in installing and working with the digital app of this resource or software. AgroStar consultants help subjects of the agrarian sector in the setup of digital technologies of communications and sales to consumers in offices and stores. AgroStar has retail stores in 11 Indian states (more than 9,500 retail outlets);
2) Supporting agricultural producers in smart management of processes. The function of support of smart agriculture ensures an increase in the value-added of products in this sector. Also, in cooperation with various scientific and technical

organizations, AgroStar created and patented more than 200 agrarian resources (seed material, certified means of plant care), which are offered in the company's stress. These agrarian resources allow raising yield, avoiding the negative influence on product safety and environmental indicators. AgroStar becomes not only an electronic resource for communication and sales but also forms a strong intellectual capital and raises sustainable development of the country's agriculture. All consultations, provided to farmers and agrarian companies in India and other Asian countries, are free. However, they raise the level of intellectualization of agricultural companies. If the agricultural company wants to receive professional support in smart production management, it can order this service from AgroStar;

3) Help in the organization of product sales directly to consumers in India and other countries. As of early 2025, this digital marketplace helps agricultural producers export products to more than 25 countries. If the agricultural company wants to receive individual support in this sphere on a constant or temporary basis, its cost will depend on the selected options, and expenditures for those services will require the corresponding reflection in green accounting and reporting on the sustainable development of the agricultural company;
4) Financing of AgroStar is conducted by private organizations and institutional international partners (International Finance Corporation, Rabo Frontier Ventures, Evolvence India, Hero Enterprise, British International Investment, Bertelsmann Investments, Chiratae Ventures, Accel, Schroders Capital, and Aavishkaar Group). Activities of the studied digital marketplace in the sphere of sustainable management of India's agriculture are not financed by the government. However, it is supported by large investors and international financial organizations, which cover expenditures for the activities in 11 states of India;
5) Digital marketplace AgroStar contributed to the following (since 2013):
    - Fighting hunger in the world, through the improvement of farms' yield in India by 27% (with observation of environmental norms). An increase in yield was ensured due to the application of the agrarian resources AgroStar and the consultations on smart agriculture;
    - Support of gender equality (one of the SDGs declared by the UN and member-states). Over 2013-2025, AgroStar increased the number of female employees;
    - Protection of biosystems due to reduction of agricultural waste from products of manufacturers which are participants of the digital marketplace AgroStar and receive recommendations on the management in this sphere. Over the entire period of the platform's activities, farmers reduced harvesting waste by 1%. This has a direct environmental effect and influence on support of humanitarian food security;

- Preservation of water resources of territories due to farms' using new technological solutions and approaches to smart agriculture. Over the entire period of the activities of the digital marketplace AgroStar, farms were able to save around 423 billion liters of water;
- Improvement of soils of India's territories in which farmers working with AgroStar are located. This effect was achieved due to consultations provided to farmers within smart agriculture;
- Influence on the creation of conditions for the improvement of the social well-being of people residing in India's rural territories. More than 9,500 innovative information solutions were developed and integrated for agriculture at the microbusiness level.

Expenditures seen in articles of green accounting and sustainable development reports of companies working with AgroStar include the following:

- Materials costs of purchasing agrarian resources which ensure environmental effects and perspectives for farms, territories, national ecology, and product effects for food security;
- Costs of the platform's services, required by agricultural companies in the management of electronic interaction and trade. This category of costs could be assigned to distribution costs. Their application ensures the achievement of economic goals of sustainable development, stimulating the reduction of unproductive costs, and decrease in the level of ineffective management of logistics, calculations, and product sales.

Special attention should be paid to reflection in green accounting of all positive transformations ensured by e-business in agriculture. Even if the agricultural company does not spend funds for transformations, it is important to determine such reforms. This ensures competitive positions (including in the world markets), and growth of the market cost of stock (in the agrarian company is public). In the case of India, these are small, medium, and large cooperatives of farmers. Improvement of skills, quality of seed materials, and materials of crop care could be assessed at the level of such cooperatives. Corporate reporting on the sustainable development of such organizations reflects the directions of green accounting, including in the context of using e-business in agriculture.

One example is the experience of green accounting of e-business by Godrej Agrovet Limited – a subsidiary of Godrej Group (India). The main office is located in Mumbai, Maharashtra. The sustainable development report of Godrej Agrovet Limited states that 101,000 farmers, who are part of the company by cooperative terms, undertook training and received consultations on labor efficiency and growth of yield (smart agriculture) (Godrej Agrovet Limited, 2025b). The report also contains information on the improvement of the level of knowledge and skills of farmers in this sphere. The cooperative association of Godrej Agrovet Limited distributes products on the AgroStar digital marketplace, which helps reduce the supply chain and contributes to the direct interaction between producers and customers.

Farmers consultations by Godrej Agrovet Limited ensured the achievement of 0% of product waste from the stage after harvesting to distribution and delivery to consumers. The sustainable development report of Godrej Agrovet Limited states 0% of waste for the types of economic activities in the sphere of agricultural production and product processing (Godrej Agrovet Limited, 2025b). Costs of waste management during processing (another direction of the activities of Godrej Agrovet Limited) are reflected in the sustainable development report as ecologization costs. Measures of environmentally oriented management of waste and measures of raising farmers' readiness in smart agriculture belong to the indicators of the improvement of market cost of Godrej Agrovet Limited and lead to an increase in stock price. According to Trading View, Inc. (2025), stock prices changed in the following way: over the entire period of trading, the indicator grew by 23.58%, which is a sign of the effectiveness of management, including the efficiency of implementing measures on the organization of green accounting of e-business in agrarian production.

Implementation of green accounting of e-business in the production, promotion, and distribution of agricultural products contributed to financial and economic growth. An increase in product quality led to the growth of the indicator Total Revenue From Operations: 11.3% in 2023 compared to 2022 (Godrej Agrovet Limited, 2025a).

There are also other digital marketplaces whose activities are similar to the functioning of AgroStar. However, AgroStart is known due to its high level of organization, digital support, focus on modern biotechnologies, and investing.

The second considered country is Nigeria. Its GDP started growing quickly since 2002. According to the World Bank Group (2025a), this indicator equaled $ 49.9 billion in 2022, $ 60.7 billion in 2005, $ 74.3 billion in 2008, $ 85.6 billion in 2011, $ 98.1 billion in 2014, $ 109.6 billion in 2017, $ 117 billion in 2020, and $123.1 in 2023. Similar to India, this growth was connected with the implementation of smart agriculture technologies, including e-business, which contributes to an increase in value-added and a reduction of producers' losses from the functioning of additional intermediary supply chains.

Due to geographical and climate specifics, farmers of Nigeria have not been able to reach a high level of grain yield – despite the use of smart agriculture practices. Over 2002-2022, this indicator grew - 1,255 kg per hectare in 2022 and 1,656 kg per hectare in 2022 (World Bank Group, 2025b). The measures on implementing smart agriculture practices, as well as the organization of green accounting of e-business, are achieved due to external support of the national digital resource FC Foods by the global agrotech company Farmcrowdy.

FC Foods is a digital technological platform, which ensures the creation of conditions for the interaction between agricultural producers and consumers. The final consumers here are companies in the food industry, retailers, public catering companies, and foreign customers (Farmcrowdy, 2025).

Analysis of the materials by Atuahene-Gima and Amuzu (2019) and Farmcrowdy (2025) allowed determining the key features of the platform FC Foods (Table 2).

Table 2. Characteristics of digital communication and trade platform FC Foods

	Indicator	Characteristics
1	Subjects of financing of FC Foods platform	Foreign private business structures, which function in capital markets: venture company Social Capital (USA), venture company Cox Ventures (India), and venture company Techstars (USA)
2	Territories covered by the activities of the FC Foods platform	All regions and territories of Nigeria that have agricultural production. All regions and territories of Nigeria in which the agrarian sector's products are processed. Farmcrowdy's website states that the platform FC Foods has products from three African countries, though only Nigerian farmers promote their products on this platform.
3	Directions of services provided to subjects of agriculture	1. Satellite probing of territories for monitoring of crop quality. Paid service. 2. Informing farmers about the time of harvesting on their territories. Free service. 3. Other consultations in the sphere of smart agriculture. Free and paid services. 4. Attraction of investors (mostly foreign), which finance innovations in the context of smart agriculture. This "sponsor package" service is paid, and the price depends on the investment return. 5. Organization of communication and trade between agricultural producers and consumers. Free service. 6. Support of farmers in the use of the platform's digital technologies. There is free support for the installation of the app, and there are paid services for order processing and communications. 7. Equipment and technologies lease. Paid service; the price depends on different options.
4	Indicators of effectiveness	Number of customers over the entire period of the activities – 427,000. Reduction of informal trade of agricultural products and food products in Nigeria. Support of the implementation of smart agriculture practices, which helps reach environmental, social, and economic effects. Increase in digital skills of Nigerian farmers.

Source: Compiled by the authors based on Farmcrowdy (2025) and Atuahene-Gima and Amuzu (2019)

As shown in Table 2, the digital platform of Farmcrowdy ensures the achievement of the following aspects of the Sustainable Development Goals:

- Overcoming hunger and reduction of poverty due to employment at farms, which expand due to attracted investments and the growth of yield. In this case, this is the achievement of social goals at the level of agricultural territories of the country. It is possible to suggest that for Farmcrowdy, the achievement of these goals is secondary compared to its financial and economic objectives, but its innovative approach to the activities raises the parameters of the formation of the social sphere at the national level;
- Fighting poverty among farmers and farm employees due to the growth of labor efficiency and effectiveness of smart agriculture. These goals are also connected with an increase in social well-being, though they are concerned with the financial and economic sphere of functioning as well;
- Reduction of negative environmental influence of the activities of farmers and farms, achieved thanks to smart agriculture measures. Implementation of smart agriculture is supported by Farmcrowdy (consultations of specialists), and its directions are selected during the interaction of agricultural producers and scholars. Farmcrowdy is oriented towards responsible production in its activities and the activities of the subjects of agrarian business in Nigeria.

The following services provided by Farmcrowdy could be seen as part of the green accounting of Nigerian agrarian companies:

- All paid services, provided by the company and required by farms. These services are not sufficiently affordable to individual farmers due to the high price, but they are used by farmers' cooperatives. In Nigeria, farmers' cooperatives have a higher financial and economic potential (Usman et al., 2022). Free support of these cooperatives by Farmcrowdy and local services concerned with smart agriculture is of higher priority compared to individual farmers. This is because training and consultations are conducted during group meetings (including in the remote form), which is more convenient than individual consultations for each farmer. These paid services belong to the costs of the corresponding categories. In sustainable development reports, costs of e-business are assigned to costs of sustainable development;
- All free services regarding e-business in agriculture are denoted as measures aimed at the achievement of the corresponding Sustainable Development Goals.

At the current stage, it is possible to see the development of information and technological infrastructure in Nigeria due to the large prospects of the development of farms and farmers entering regional and international markets. 2024 saw the start of the functioning of a new information and technological platform Farmstarck, which is Farmcrowdy's rival. It provides similar services to farms and farmers (Farmstarck, 2025). However, Farmstarck uses a simpler and more affordable system of farmers' training and pays attention to possible support in the purchase of communication means and doing e-business.

SOLUTIONS AND RECOMMENDATIONS

In this research, we considered two forms of financing of digital technological communication & trade platforms in the interaction at the level of agricultural producers and consumers. The Indian digital platform AgroStar is financed by an institutional organization and private financial partners (national and international capital). The second considered resource is the Nigerian digital technological platform FC Foods, which is oriented towards support of communication and deals with direct sales of agricultural products at the level of farms and consumers. A larger number of the subjects of financing and targeted priorities of investors are more acceptable for the quality and level of information and technological support of similar resources. In this case, the Indian digital platform has higher loyalty towards farmers and farm cooperatives that seek its services.

The considered digital platforms are tools of e-business in agriculture. Their financing is one of the factors of effectiveness of achievement of the Sustainable Development Goals in the sector. An important factor of a higher level of sustainable development during the use of e-business is the level of education and digital readiness of farmers and farm employees. In India, this indicator is higher, compared to Nigeria. According to the World Bank Group (2025c), school education in India covers 79% of the population in India, while in Nigeria – 47% (2021). Knowledge at the level of secondary school education allows farmers and consultants to better learn the information environment and ensure interaction in the business environment with the use of information and communication technologies.

The quick growth of smart agriculture in India and Nigeria is a sign of the socio-economic perspectives of these countries. An important role in this belongs to green accounting of expenditures for e-business and assessment of advantages gained due to its organization. These accounting data are reflected in sustainable development reports. Promotion of information about the focus on green accounting of e-business is performed at the level of farms and farmers cooperatives, which helps attract investors.

FUTURE RESEARCH DIRECTIONS

Effective adaptation of green accounting of e-business at the level of small and medium agricultural companies, which strive toward sustainable development, is connected with the growth of scientific and practical research and forecasting of projects of digital communication and trade platforms. Creation of the scientific basis of the activities of these platforms will allow creating them in various regions and territories of developing agrarian countries.

CONCLUSION

Green accounting of e-business in agriculture allows subjects of this sector and interested parties to reach sustainable development of territories, regions, and countries. According to the existing approach to corporate and financial accounting, open reporting of the results of market subjects' activities is a privilege for companies. Individual entrepreneurs (farmers) should use the opportunities for economic integration with other market participants to promote their businesses. This could be cooperatives or network organization structures, integrated within a level entity. This allows them to be more independent in capital, technology, and HR markets.

Uniting with interested parties who function in the adjacent segments (growing other crops) requires serious legal support. In case of the emergence of conflict issues regarding the rights and interests of each participant, there is a need to protect them in the court of law. In developed countries, this aspect is ensured by the legislative and executive systems, while in developing countries this direction is more difficult to implement. That is why farmers in such countries as Nigeria have problems with the achievement of results in the organization of e-business both individually and within integrated business structures. An important place in the protection of such interests belongs to the acceptance of offers by companies that manage digital services platforms on the provision of various services (communication, trade, processing of orders, lease, search for investors, etc.).

Recommendations for agricultural producers regarding green accounting in e-business to achieve the sustainable development of the agrarian economy include as follows:

- Lobbying their rights and interests with the national government and local authorities. Public authorities should participate in guaranteeing the protection of the agricultural sector and supporting the well-being of labor resources involved in the sector. According to Kantor et al. (2023), the government can help stimulate investors and participants in the infrastructure for the functioning of the agrarian sector;

- Improvement of the level of special knowledge in the organization of smart agriculture (including the use of green accounting of e-business). This direction can be implemented at the cooperative level: cooperatives of farmers can delegate and finance training in the digital sphere for young specialists;
- Use of the offers of alternative digital platforms or change of digital platforms will allow further development of the market, improvement of the quality of services, and liberalization of prices.

REFERENCES

AgroStar. (2025). *Who are we.*https://www.corporate.agrostar.in/

Atuahene-Gima, K., & Amuzu, J. (2019). Farmcrowdy: Digital business model innovation for farming in Nigeria. *Emerald Emerging Markets Case Studies, 9*(2), 1–22. Advance online publication. DOI: 10.1108/EEMCS-03-2019-0065

Burkhanov, A., Popkova, E., Galoyan, D., Mkrtchyan, T., & Sergi, B. (2024). Deep learning, irrigation enhancement, and agricultural economics for ensuring food security in emerging economies. *Global Transitions, 6*, 164–172. DOI: 10.1016/j.glt.2024.06.002

Farmcrowdy. (2025). *FC Foods.* https://farmcrowdyweb.netlify.app/fcfood

Farmstarck (2025). *Join Us in Achieving Agricultural Excellence.* https://www.farmstarck.com/

Godrej Agrovet Limited. (2025a). *Annual Reports.*https://www.godrejagrovet.com/investors/annual-reports

Godrej Agrovet Limited. (2025b). *Sustainability.*https://www.godrejagrovet.com/sustainability

Government of India. (2024). Agriculture *Sector has registered an average annual Growth Rate of 4.18 per cent over the last five years: Economic survey.*https://pib.gov.in/PressReleasePage.aspx?PRID=2034943

. Kantor, O.G., Rudneva, Y.R., Dunov, D.Y., Ergasheva, S.T., & Leybert, B.M. (2023). *Green Finance: Analysis of Prospects of the Russian Market. Food Security in the Economy of the Future: Transition from Digital Agriculture to Agriculture 4.0 Based on Deep Learning,* 45-56. DOI: DOI: 10.1007/978-3-031-23511-5_6

Khan, S., & Gupta, S. (2024). The interplay of sustainability, corporate green accounting and firm financial performance: A meta-analytical investigation. Sustainability Accounting. *Management and Policy Journal, 15*(5), 1038–1066. DOI: 10.1108/SAMPJ-01-2022-0016

Maama, H., & Appiah, K. O. (2019). Green accounting practices: Lesson from an emerging economy. *Qualitative Research in Financial Markets, 11*(4), 456–478. DOI: 10.1108/QRFM-02-2017-0013

Onwude, D. (2023). *What is the role of digitalisation for a sustainable agri-food system?*https://energy-base.org/news/what-is-the-role-of-digitalisation-for-a-sustainable-agri-food-system/

Rounaghi, M. M. (2019). Economic analysis of using green accounting and environmental accounting to identify environmental costs and sustainability indicators. *International Journal of Ethics and Systems*, *35*(4), 504–512. DOI: 10.1108/IJOES-03-2019-0056

Trading View, Inc. (2025). Overview Godrej Agrovet LTD.https://www.tradingview.com/symbols/NSE-GODREJAGRO/

Usman, A. B., Babaji, A. U., & Muhammad, R. (2022). Performance of Cooperatives among Farmers in Gombe State, Nigeria. *Nigerian Journal of Agriculture and Agricultural Technology*, *2*, 2. DOI: 10.59331/njaat.v2i2.351

van der Valk, H., Schmelzer, R., Rose, D., & Dinter, B. (2024). Towards a Process Model for Digital Twin Implementation: The Implementation Canvas. *Procedia CIRP*, *122*, 903–908. DOI: 10.1016/j.procir.2024.01.123

World Bank Group. (2025a). Agriculture, forestry, and fishing, value added (constant 2015 US$) – India, Nigeria. https://data.worldbank.org/indicator/NV.AGR.TOTL.KD?locations=IN-NG&view=chart

World Bank Group. (2025b). *Cereal yield (kg per hectare) – India, Nigeria.*https://data.worldbank.org/indicator/AG.YLD.CREL.KG?locations=IN-NG&view=chart

World Bank Group. (2025c). *School enrollment, secondary (% gross). – India, Nigeria.*https://data.worldbank.org/indicator/SE.SEC.ENRR?locations=IN-NG&view=chart

Zarubin, S. G., & Deev, K. A. (2017). Process model of digital manufacturing. *Russian Engineering Research*, *37*(8), 714–719. DOI: 10.3103/S1068798X17080214

ADDITIONAL READING

Arellano, J. (2022). Green accounting in cotton white and its effect on agriculture. A documentary review. *Económicas CUC*, *43*(2), 139–156. DOI: 10.17981/econcuc.43.2.2022.Econ.3

He, L., Zhou, L., Qi, J., Song, Y., & Jiang, M. (2024). The Role of Digital Finance Embedded in Green Agricultural Development: Evidence from Agribusiness Enterprises in China. *Land (Basel)*, *13*(10), 1649. DOI: 10.3390/land13101649

Laurett, R., Paço, A., & Wagner Mainardes, E. (2021). Sustainable Development in Agriculture and its Antecedents, Barriers and Consequences – An Exploratory Study. *Sustainable Production and Consumption*, *27*, 298–311. DOI: 10.1016/j.spc.2020.10.032

Qin, Z., Pei, X., Andrianarimanana, M. H., & Wen, S. (2023). Digital inclusive finance and the development of rural logistics in China. *Heliyon*, *9*(6), e17329. DOI: 10.1016/j.heliyon.2023.e17329 PMID: 37383193

Rudnicki, R., Biczkowski, M., Wiśniewski, Ł., Wiśniewski, P., Bielski, S., & Marks-Bielska, R. (2023). Towards Green Agriculture and Sustainable Development: Pro-Environmental Activity of Farms under the Common Agricultural Policy. *Energies*, *16*(4), 1770. DOI: 10.3390/en16041770

Yu, G., & Xiang, H. (2021). Rural E-commerce development and farmers' digital credit behavior: Evidence from China family panel studies. *PLoS One*, *16*(10), e0258162. DOI: 10.1371/journal.pone.0258162 PMID: 34653212

Yuan, B., & Cao, X. (2022). Do corporate social responsibility practices contribute to green innovation? The mediating role of green dynamic capability. *Technology in Society*, *68*, 101868. DOI: 10.1016/j.techsoc.2022.101868

Zhang, Y., Long, H., Ma, L., Tu, S., Li, Y., & Ge, D. (2018). Analysis of rural economic restructuring driven by e-commerce based on the space of flows: The case of Xiaying village in central China. *Journal of Rural Studies*, *93*, 196–209. DOI: 10.1016/j.jrurstud.2018.12.001

KEY TERMS AND DEFINITIONS

Digital communication and trade platforms: Communication and information systems that are used by e-business.

E-business: All business processes that are organized in electronic form.

Ecologization: Policy of agrarian companies that involves socially responsible production aimed at protecting the environment from the negative consequences of economic activities.

Smart agriculture: Approach to the organization of agricultural processes that is based on digital intellectual technologies that ensure effectiveness.

Sustainable development of the agrarian economy: Functioning of the agrarian economy given the balanced formation of social and economic sectors and environment.

Sustainable development report: Company's corporate report containing information on green accounting.

Yield: Indicator of the effectiveness of the activities of farms that use the practices of smart agriculture.

Chapter 4
Digitalization of Green Accounting of Climate-Resilient E-Business in Support of Decarbonization

Ilham M. Saipidinov
https://orcid.org/0000-0001-9378-7313
Osh State University, Kyrgyzstan

Elena G. Popkova
https://orcid.org/0000-0003-2136-2767
Armenian State University of Economics, Armenia

Yulduz P. Khalikulova
https://orcid.org/0009-0002-5542-5367
Tashkent State University of Economics, Uzbekistan

Inna P. Bandurina
https://orcid.org/0000-0003-3251-325X
Kuban State Agrarian University Named After I.T. Trubilin, Russia

ABSTRACT

This work elaborates on the problem of using green accounting in e-business, as one of the tools of support of decarbonization and facilitation of climate resilience of companies, and digitalization of accounting and analytical processes. Theoretical and methodological principles of decarbonization are considered in the context of climate change and anthropogenic influence on ecology, specifics of e-business and

DOI: 10.4018/979-8-3693-8362-9.ch004

its interconnection with the processes of environmental and climate resilience are described, the problem of energy consumption of data processing centers as objects of e-business infrastructure is emphasized, importance of green accounting as a tool of information and analytical support of the management of sustainable development at companies is analyzed, and priority of using digital technologies in the system of environmental accounting to raise its potential and achieve significant effects in the sphere of ecological and climate resilience of e-business companies is determined.

INTRODUCTION

Determinants of world development define cause-and-effect relationships between the current state and past events. According to this, most of the current problems stem from the past, and ways to solve them should also be found in the past. In this context, global warming, which is seen as one of the biggest challenges of the 21st century, is closely connected with CO2 emissions and other greenhouse gas emissions.

Since the beginning of the industrial age in 1850, the average temperature on our planet grew by more than 1.5 C^0, of which an increase of 1.2 C^0 took place in the last 45 years (Ritchie et al., 2025). According to reports by climate change experts, the main reason for these changes is anthropogenic influence (Hausfather, 2017). According to the analysis by Carbon Brief, almost 100% of global warming since 1950 has been caused by human activities (Stocker et al., 2013). The main factor of anthropogenic influence on climate is economic activities, especially industrial production and energy consumption. Historically, the main drivers of an increase in greenhouse gas emissions were the growth of the population and its energy needs. However, since the 1990s, due to the realization of threats of global warming, reverse processes were started, connected with the reduction of industrial emissions, development of alternative energy sources, implementation of sustainable development culture, and decarbonization.

In the context of the Fourth Industrial Revolution, traditional models of production, distribution, consumption, and disposal of products were transformed significantly. Information computer technologies, including the Internet of Things, blockchain, artificial intelligence, and cloud computing, ensured new opportunities for the optimization of economic processes. They include reduction of physical movement for transfer of information, automatization of production and managerial systems, forecasting based on big data, and creation of new sectors of the economy (e-commerce, digital marketing, e-government, etc.).

Due to large-scale and quick changes, sectors of e-business were deeply integrated into economic and social structures, demonstrating a large potential in the sphere of decarbonization. From the position of using resources, energy consumption, and logistics processes, they demonstrated a much higher level of effectiveness and neutrality towards the environment and climate processes. Moreover, accounting and analytical tools of e-business demonstrated high potential for the optimization of logistics processes, growth of the effectiveness of resources management, and reduction of greenhouse gas emissions and economic decarbonization.

Given this, the issue of digitalization of green accounting and climate-resilient e-business in the conditions of decarbonization form the current agenda in the scientific sphere, with goals and tasks for further development of human civilization. In this context, studying the potential of the digital tools of green accounting as to their influence on decarbonization requires more in-depth research to reveal their potential and possibility to ensure targeted effect on the sphere of digital commerce from the position of raising climate and environmental resilience.

The methodological framework of the research is formed by the complex approach, which covers the spheres of economic cybernetics, ecology, management, entrepreneurship, and trade, which are set onto the processes of sustainable development, decarbonization, and digitalization. To reach this work's tasks, a selected methodology is used, which includes the methods of observation, generalization, comparison, analysis, synthesis, and other methods.

The main value of the work is the assessment and characteristics of the key digital technologies in the context of their usage in the system of green accounting. This work presents the specifics and advantages of each digital tool, characterizes their influence on the accounting and analytical system of e-business companies, and distinguishes the advantages of their application from the position of environmental sustainability and decarbonization.

BACKGROUND

The issues of environmental accounting, digitalization, and the development of e-business form an important interdisciplinary direction for the research, which conforms to the relevant global challenges. In this context, studying the problems of digitalization of environmental accounting of climate-responsible companies of the e-business sphere with a special focus on decarbonization requires the use of literature sources belonging to different spheres of scientific and practical activities. The basis for understanding the processes of climate change and global initiatives is formed by scientific works focused on human activities from the position of influence on processes of climate change (Hausfather, 2017; Stocker et al., 2013). Global initiatives on the mitigation of implications or solving climate problems (United Nations, 2015a, United Nations, 2015b), realized in international documents, determine the key institutional conditions of the activities of companies and governments to solve them. However, the factual state of execution of the outlined plan demonstrates significant problems in executing the adopted commitments (International Energy Agency, 2025; Ritchie et al., 2025).

In the context of an increase in the relevance of initiatives aimed at the achievement of the Sustainable Development Goals and decarbonization, green accounting is viewed as an important tool of information and analytical support of managerial influence (Van, 2012), which is implemented in different forms and has a special role in the system of non-financial accounting (Lestari et al., 2023). In the conditions of active digitalization, its potential is expanded through digital transformation, which causes a change in approaches to financial accounting and reporting (Petcu et al., 2024). Directions of digitalization's influence on environmental accounting are determined depending on the spheres of the use of certain digital technologies, among which artificial intelligence facilitates an increase in precision and speed of accounting and reporting (Antwi et al., 2024), and other digital tools ensure better transparency and precision of data and a higher level of objectivity of information and effectiveness of environmental solutions (Alshdaifat et al., 2024; Soraya et al., 2024).

Against this background, an increase in the role of ICT in economic systems determines new directions for the research, aimed at identifying their impact on ecology. These actions are connected with the growth of the need for energy resources and digital technologies' potential in the sphere of improvement of energy- and resource efficiency and decarbonization (Data Center Knowledge, 2024; Rozite, 2023), which is especially relevant for the sphere of digital business (Zhu et al., 2024). Financial aspects of digital transformation will determine the perspectives of the development of the green financing market (Kantor et al., 2023), which is set onto effective practices of using modern methodologies of green accounting and reporting (Zrnić et al., 2020).

Practical measures and recommendations, aimed at decarbonization and fighting climate change (Basil-Jones, 2023), are combined with general economic processes (D'Arcangelo et al., 2022) and study in detail the connection between the reduction of greenhouse gas emissions and implementation of digital technologies (Kare et al., 2024). Attention is paid to all digital tools in their totality (Sheth, 2024), or individual tools (Garrigós-Simón et al., 2021), as well as a strategy for business entities adaptation in the conditions of digital transformation of the economy (Galoyan et al., 2023). In this context, relevant issues on mitigation of the consequences of climate change through rational management of knowledge (Dzhumakova et al., 2024) or wider application of intellectual technologies and innovations in the system of sustainable development (Popkova, 2024) are raised.

The literature review demonstrates a domination of a stable belief regarding the positive influence of digital tools on the problems of sustainable development and climate resilience. Among the current problems, the focus is on large energy needs for support of the ICT infrastructure of e-business, as well as the necessity for improvement of the system of green accounting to avoid the problems of bias or limitations of the information basis for reporting, analytics, or substantiation of managerial solutions. Thus, the purpose of the research is the comprehensive assessment of the problem of green accounting of climate-resilient e-business, as well as substantiation of the potential of its digitalization to raise the level of effectiveness of environmental solutions and stimulate the reduction of greenhouse gas emissions.

This research topic includes several interconnected directions, which are concerned with the issues of climate change and decarbonization, digitalization, and development of e-business, support of its climate resilience, and development of new information & accounting and analytical technologies. Integration of these directions within one research requires a comprehensive methodology, which would include theories and approaches of cybernetics, economics, management, accounting, ecology, and a range of other scientific spheres.

The theoretical and methodological foundations of this research are based on the concept of sustainable development, which is implemented within the triad "economy-society-ecology" and aimed at the search for balance between economic interests, preservation of the environment, and ensuring social justice. Combining these directions requires the use of the system approach, which allows viewing decarbonization as a certain unity, in which parameters are determined not only by volumes of greenhouse gas emissions but also by other connected processes, which cover the sphere of production, social behavior, environmental protection, etc. These aspects are executed in the best way in the circular economy, which offers methodological tools for the comprehensive reduction of anthropogenic influence on environmental processes.

The methodological apparatus of this research includes general scientific and special scientific methods, inherent to cybernetic, accounting & analytical, trade, environmental, economic, and other systems. General scientific methods include observation, generalization, comparison, and grouping, as well as methods of analysis, synthesis, empirical methods, etc. An important task within this research is the development and application of a rational system of metrics for measuring processes connected with environmental pollution, CO2 emissions, energy consumption, etc. According to this, accounting tools in the context of decarbonization and climate-resilient e-business form a separate methodological block, which involves the use of quantitative and qualitative methods, including Life Cycle Assessment (LCA), carbon audit, and metrics and indices of sustainable development (e.g., Power Usage Effectiveness, PUE).

MAIN FOCUS OF THE CHAPTER

CO2 emissions are growing. After a temporary decrease in this indicator in 2020, its growth continued. As of year-end 2020, total CO2 emissions reached the level of 34,116.8 Mt CO_2, which is 1.7 times more than in 1990. Since 2007, growth rates of emissions reduced, equaling 1.17 times vs. 1.4 times from 1990 to 2007. Moreover, from 2007 to 2022, the reduction of emissions took place three times. In 2009, the reason was the global financial crisis, in 2005 – the slowdown of the Chinese economy and growth of energy efficiency, and in 2020 – COVID-19 restrictions. The global indicator of CO_2 emissions per capita in this period was at the level of 4.2–4.5 t per capita. However, it does not reflect the regional differences. Thus, the indicator is 15 t per capita in the USA, 6-8 t per capita in the EU, and less than 2 t per capita in India. Most emissions are produced by the energy sector (around 40%), industry (25%), and transport (20%) (International Energy Agency, 2025).

The recent period was marked by trends connected with the development of renewable energy, an increase in energy efficiency in industry, and the electrification of transport. These and other trends led to a certain demarcation between the processes of economic growth and CO2 emissions, which confirmed the possibility of achievement of the economy's sustainable development with a simultaneous decrease in the carbon footprint products. Important factors of these processes were the implementation of the tools of carbon pricing and the realization of the goals of the Paris Agreement and national strategies for the formation of a low-carbon economy. The main goals declared in this context for the short-term include keeping global warming within 1.5 ^{0}, which requires a reduction of CO_2 by two times and the achievement of zero emissions by 2050. These goals require large-scale transformation and modernization of all spheres of the economy, as well as substantial investments in the sphere of clean technologies and energy efficiency, which are combined with decarbonization.

Decarbonization is viewed as a process of reducing the volumes of greenhouse gas emissions through transforming industrial energy and transport systems through the use of renewable energy sources, the use of energy-efficient technologies, and the implementation of low-carbon solutions. According to the OECD report "A framework to decarbonize the economy" (2022), the directions for decarbonization are expanded by supplementing them with green investments, implementing the corresponding political decisions, and supporting international cooperation for a fair green transition (D'Arcangelo et al., 2022).

The global nature of the policy of decarbonization is based on the combination of institutionalism and regulatory and comparative approaches. Its institutional aspects are disclosed through the interaction between global and government bodies, civil society, and representatives of business and are implemented through the development and implementation of sustainable development tools. The regulatory provisions are based on the UN Sustainable Development Goals (United Nations, 2015a), the Paris Agreement (United Nations, 2015b), and other legal and regulatory documents. The comparative approach is based on a comparison of different approaches and practices of low-carbon development to reveal the most effective measures that can ensure the achievement of results with minimal resources spent.

Challenges of climate changes and processes caused by them predetermined and started large-scale transformations, which were reflected in the economy and public, political, and economic relationships. One of the top-priority directions of mankind's development in these conditions is digitalization. Integration of digital technologies into the organization of business processes and growth of the role of ICT ensured the active development of e-business, which acquired the status of one of the drivers of economic transformations. Its components and tools, such as e-commerce, financial technologies, blockchain, and artificial intelligence, were successfully integrated into business models and allowed companies to become more flexible and adaptable. They also created new opportunities for the development of small and medium businesses through the reduction of barriers to entering foreign markets and forming online marketplaces and specialized platforms.

The development of e-business is directly connected with the Fourth Industrial Revolution and digitalization. It involves the active use of information and communication technologies in different spheres of activities and is based on the application of online technologies to support managerial and socio-economic processes. The main component of e-business is e-commerce. The volume of the world market of e-commerce reached $26.8 trillion in 2024. According to the forecast of IMARC Group, the market volume will reach $214.5 trillion by 2033, with a growth rate (CAGR) of 25.83%. Thus, e-commerce is one of the largest sectors of e-business. It covers more than 18% of all retail sales in the world (Basil-Jones, 2023). The structure of e-business defines the necessity for evaluating the interaction between its subjects and environmental factors from three different positions: production and product shipping, support, and maintenance of digital infrastructure.

Among other elements, the digital structure of e-business includes data processing centers and data transfer networks. They perform an important role in the communication of business with consumers and are an important resource for deep analytics of market participants' behavior. From the position of climate-responsible processes, centers of processing and networks of data transfer are factors in an increase in volumes of energy consumption. Each of them consumes around 1-1.5% of the world's electric energy, and, in total, they produce 1% of greenhouse gas emissions connected with energy (Rozite, 2023).

As of year-end 2023, there were more than 10,900 data processing centers, of which half were located in the USA. All data processing centers consumed 7.4 GW of electric energy in 2023, compared to 4.9 GW in 2022. In 2022, the average index of Power Usage Effectiveness (PUE) was 1.55, compared to 2.5 in 2007. There is significant progress. However, only a small part of technology giants, like Google or Facebook, can demonstrate the desired effectiveness of energy consumption (Data Center Knowledge, 2024).

Traditional business and e-business seek common goals and have many similarities. At the same time, they have significant differences. These differences concern mainly the spatial and time restrictions of traditional business from the position of transporting and delivery of resources and workforce in one direction, and final products and production waste – in another direction. On the contrary, digital business, using the capabilities of the Internet and digital technologies, allows reducing transaction costs, reducing the volumes of energy consumption, and ensuring high effectiveness due to the digital character of the large volume of digital products. This approach conforms to the policy of sustainable development and demonstrates environmentally stable characteristics of e-business and the potential for the reduction of CO2 emissions.

Thus, information and communication technologies are viewed as factors in the reduction of energy consumption volumes, which is achieved due to an increase in energy efficiency and a decrease in CO2 emissions. Apart from this, digitalization at different stages of the supply chain, which covers production, transportation, processing, consumption, and disposal, allows forming additional environmental effects. They are manifested through optimization of transport routes, reduction of the volumes of stock and waste, search for opportunities for reuse of resources, reduction of the need for manual labor, etc. However, the application of information technologies is closely connected with energy consumption. Therefore, active digitalization and automatization of production and logistics processes require additional energy support, which can lead to a rebound effect and an increase in CO2 emissions (Zhu et al., 2024). Climate-responsible e-business functions in the conditions of active development of offer and demand for environmentally-oriented solutions. According to this, many buyers are ready to choose safer – from the environmental position – products and options of delivery – even with larger time of transportation. The same is true for the offer when production companies adapt their products and processes to the demands of sustainable development according to GRI (Global Reporting Initiative) or ISO 14001.

Apart from direct actions aimed at the reduction of the negative anthropogenic influence on the environment, e-business offers additional tools for sustainable development. They directly influence the parameters of ecologization and can be presented in three forms:

- Digitalized business processes, which can ensure the reduction of the volume of material resources, necessary for doing business. An example of this could be electronic document turnover, which replaces printed documents and materials, and physical transactions. These measures contribute to the reduction of transportation costs and reduce the need for paper production, saving trees;
- Automatized operations, which allow for optimization of logistics flows, reducing the cases of excessive transportation and stimulating the effectiveness of delivery routes. In aggregate, this leads to the reduction of the volumes of consumption of car fuel and the reduction of CO_2 emissions;
- Development of the market of digital products which do not require space for storing or transporting requires small physical resources and is simple for disposal.

Despite the large potential of the position of decarbonization, digital business has certain environmental effects. It is mainly connected with the functioning of data centers and cloud services, which require large energy resources. Reduction of the carbon footprint from the functioning of these objects of digital infrastructure is achieved due to the development and active use of alternative energy sources, as well as edge computing technologies.

In the conditions of climate challenges and threats, economic activities are subject to additional pressure from global institutions, which seek the goal of reducing the harmful anthropogenic influence on ecology. Thus, demands for compliance with the provisions of environmentally- and climate-responsible activities gradually become mandatory. They are integrated into companies' strategies, included in the system of their values, and formalized through changes in organizational structures and administration. Inseparable elements of such activities are the systems of environmental accounting and reporting.

Green accounting (environmental accounting or accounting of environmental responsibility) is closely connected with the dissemination of the tools, of social, non-financial, or sustainable reporting (Zrnić et al., 2020). It is used as an auxiliary element of the traditional system of financial accounting. Its main goal is the collection and provision of information about the measures of environmental character, which take place within the organization and are its reaction to actions taking place in the surrounding environment. The basis of this information is the data about the company's influence on the part of the ecosystem the company interacts with (Van, 2012).

Unlike traditional accounting, the goal of environmental accounting is not to record the short-term profitability of the company but to assess the level of its strategic resilience. Provisions of such accounting are not mandatory, and demands for forms, periodicity, and content are not sufficiently unified at the global level. Nevertheless, it reflects stable economic processes, which influence goes beyond the contacts between the company and stakeholders. It integrates environmental and social factors into financial and economic context, forming a basis for the comprehensive analysis of companies' activities, influences the investment attractiveness of the business, its image in the market, and strategic stability, and facilitates higher transparency through disclosure of internal processes of the company from the position of the influence on environmental sustainability and social equality. The main principles of green accounting are shown in Figure 1.

Figure 1. The main principles of green accounting

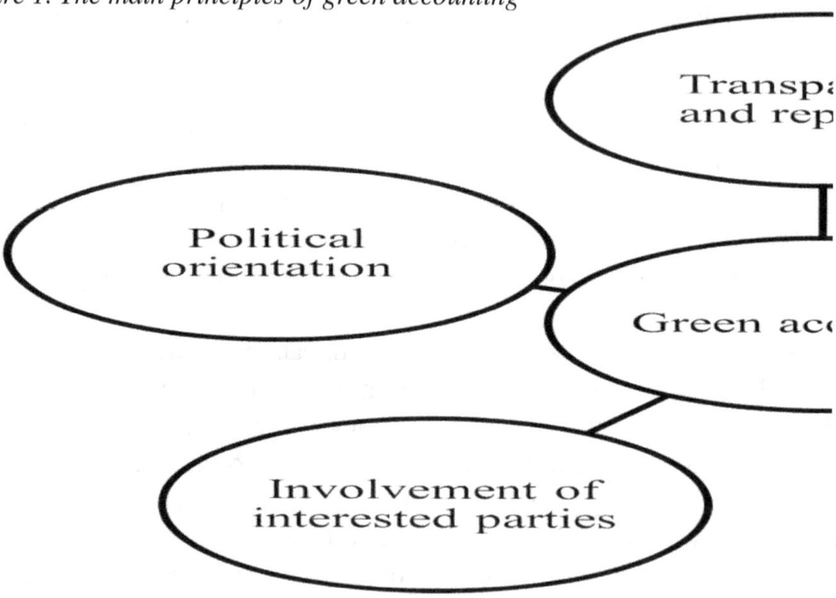

Source: Compiled by the authors based on Wall Street Mojo (2024)

The political orientation of accounting determines its relevance for governments and government bodies from the position of development of political and regulatory decisions. The results of environmental reporting could be used by government bodies to assess and plan government policy and to evaluate the efficiency of the applied methods of environmental resilience management. The principle of transparency and reporting characterizes the main values of green accounting regarding the absence of misuses and hidden processes. It allows presenting accounted processes as they are. The principle of compliance with international standards determines the basis for the unification of rules, approaches, and procedures for accounting of environmental and social processes that are based on the GRI (Global Reporting Initiative) and SASB (Sustainability Accounting Standards Board).

Measuring the effectiveness determines the methodological basis of accounting, aimed not only at the fixation of processes but also at their assessment and improvement. To determine the effectiveness of environmental and social indicators, the indicators of CO2 emissions, energy efficiency, waste production and recycling, social influence, and the use of water and other natural resources are used. Another important principle is the involvement of interested parties, which includes the integration of green accounting into a socioeconomic global context, according to which the environmental influence of the company does not have political or local boundaries and can affect a wide range of economic and social agents, including investors, employees, consumers, government, territorial communities, etc.

Despite the voluntary character, green accounting offers a range of advantages for business, which is manifested in the following:

- Growth of the level of justification of the solution, through accounting of environmental costs in financial accounting;
- Better balance of economic and environmental interests of the company in its interests and stakeholders' interests;
- Higher level of transparency of financial and accounting processes and reporting for stakeholders, demonstration of corporate responsibility, and increase in the company's image in the market;
- Better possibility of compliance with global regulatory demands through systemic tracking of environmental costs and influence;
- Improvement of competitive advantages in the conditions of popularity of the concept of responsible behavior in society, higher level of investment attractiveness, and additional economic opportunities for development (Soraya et al., 2024).

Despite significant advantages, the implementation of environmental accountancy is also connected with certain problems. The primary problem is the collection of precise environmental data. This type of information activity is not typical for the accounting services of the company. The absence of unified standards of environmental accounting can predetermine the inconsistency of information support of the corresponding processes and the complexity of comparison of results of companies' environmental activities. Since environmental aspects of management are difficult to assess and require subjective judgments, the additional problem of green accounting is a financial assessment of the company's influence on the natural environment.

To raise the value of the systems of green accounting as the basis for assessing the level of sustainable development, many countries implemented the system of Sustainability Accounting and Reporting (SAR). It is based on the model of Triple Bottom Line (TBL), which takes into account economic, environmental, and social aspects and involves reporting the results of the company's activities according to the interests and demands of stakeholders. Standards of this accounting are presented by the global initiative of Global Reporting Initiative (GRI) and involve the use of unified approaches to management in all three spheres: economic, environmental, and social. Responsible reporting reflects the information about these indicators, the level of their achievement, and their influence on the creation of the company's strategic value.

The application of digital technologies in the system of environmental accounting and reporting ensured a large impulse for the sector's development. Thus, the integration of such digital tools as cloud computing, AI, big data analytics, blockchain, and the Internet of Things into the accounting systems of companies raises the effectiveness, precision, and transparency of accounting processes. These advantages were manifested in the conditions of the COVID-19 pandemic when most information was collected and processed remotely. The level of integration of accounting processes was raised, the level of their automatization was improved, the number of errors was reduced, the level of access to data grew, and better precision and flexibility of accounting and reporting processes in the sphere of environmentally responsible activities of the company were achieved (Petcu et al., 2024).

Each of the digital tools, based on its potential, positively influences the processes of support of environmental accounting and the company itself. For example, big data analytics allows distinguishing hidden data on ESG reporting from the totality of information connected with the company; AI algorithms allow the processing of non-structured and non-formalized data, supplementing the information basis of green accounting; together with cloud computing, these algorithms ensure a high level of integration and accessibility of data; together with blockchain technologies, AI raises transparency and reliability of data and ensures their consistency. In general, the influence of digital technologies on environmental accounting and activities of e-business in the sphere of decarbonization are given in Table 1.

Table 1. The influence of digital tools on green accounting in e-business

Digital technologies	Influence on green accounting	Influence on the company and stakeholders	Usage in e-business
AI and machine learning	Supports automatization of the calculation of the carbon footprint based on transactions, offers environmental forecasts	Optimization of the use of resources and energy, improvement of the precision and systemic character of green accounting	Possibility to track the carbon footprint along the entire value chain
Blockchain	Ensures transparency of data, protects their invariability, and stimulates the tracking of the environmental footprint	Reduction of costs of fixation and checking of environmental indicators, improvement of trust in environmental reporting, prevention of misuse	Tracking the value chain for the carbon footprint and, the possibility of certification of CO_2 emissions in the logistics sphere
Big data	Expands the information basis for analysis, allows revealing trends in greenhouse gas emissions and analyzing the products' life cycle	Improvement of the level of information about environmental processes and their influence on the company, optimization of chains' logistics, better compliance with environmental norms	Analysis of environmental footprint at all stages of the product's life cycle, including delivery of e-commerce orders
Internet of Things (IoT)	Accumulates data about CO_2 emissions and energy consumption from sensors, including information from personal and household devices	Interactive monitoring of the processes of energy consumption and tracking of the carbon footprint in real-time, formation of opportunities for quick rational decisions	Possibility for control of the volumes and dynamics of energy consumption of any objects of e-business in the sphere of production, transporting, storing, or consumption
Cloud technologies	Ensures integration of information processes into one place, accessible for storing and processing, supports automatized formation of environmental reporting	Quick access to the database and calculation capacities without connection to the workplace, reduction of the cost of IT infrastructure maintenance, quick analytics	Possibility for joint formation and use of the unified information basis to track the carbon footprint and for monitoring and control of processes in e-business
Digital Twins	Creation of virtual models for forecasting the company's influence on the ecosystem	The basis for testing different scenarios and alternatives, the reduction of the risk of environmental sanctions	Using digital twins to substantiate managerial decisions and simulate the processes of energy consumption in e-business

continued on following page

Table 1. Continued

Digital technologies	Influence on green accounting	Influence on the company and stakeholders	Usage in e-business
Energy efficiency indices (PUE, CUE)	Implementation of the unified methodology of calculating environmental indicators	Ensuring compliance with ecological norms, reduction of energy and resource consumption, and reduction of the carbon footprint	Creation of the system of environmental monitoring of e-commerce based on the applied metrics
Automatized analytical platforms (ESG, CRM, etc.)	Automatized accounting and formation of non-financial reporting based on processing data from databases and platforms	Ensuring compliance with international standards, improvement of the company's image, and better interaction with stakeholders	Possibility for automatic environmental ranking of e-business, search for reserves for raising the indices of environmentally responsible activities.

Source: Compiled by the authors based on Antwi et al. (2024), Alshdaifat et al. (2024), Garrigós-Simón et al. (2021), Parthasarathy & Kumar (2012), Petcu et al. (2024), Ragin-Skorecka et al. (2024), and Treiblmaier & Sillaber (2021)

The table characterizes the influence of the eight main digital technologies and the connected platforms on green accounting and the activities of companies and stakeholders and determines the possibility of using them in e-business. The main advantages, provided by these tools from the position of environmental accounting, include improvement of transparency and reliability of environmental data, growth of analytical and forecasting ability of companies' accounting system, the possibility of tracking energy consumption and greenhouse gas emissions in real-time, and support of compliance with international standards and achievement of a high level of environmental effectiveness in the sphere of e-business.

Achievement of the above advantages takes place due to the specifics of digital technologies, which lie in the following:

- Reduction of the influence of human factors on data collection;
- Reduction of the level of the subjectivity of human assessment during the analysis of information;
- Ensuring complete tracking of information, its openness, and transparency;
- Possibility to ensure continuous fixation of data and their processing;
- Improvement of the level of forecasting of processes and search for reserves for their improvement;
- Possibility to make and implement decisions on the influence of e-business systems on the environment online.

Due to the digitalization of green accounting, these effects form significant advantages that could be used by different groups of stakeholders. Companies of e-business can achieve serious reduction of costs of environmental audit, raise the level of the effectiveness of sustainable development, and improve the state of resources and waste management. Government bodies can improve the state of monitoring of the companies' functioning and raise the level of effectiveness of regulation of environmental standards. Investors and financial establishments can receive reliable data to substantiate their decisions in the sphere of promotion of green financial products, such as Green Bonds, ESG investments, etc. Society can count on a significant reduction of the negative influence of the subjects of digital business on the environment and an improvement in the level of decarbonization. Implementation of digital tools in the system of green accounting is a valuable resource for raising the level of effectiveness of accounting and information processes in the sphere of environmental activities and substantial improvement of conditions from the position of the achievement of the UN Sustainable Development Goals.

SOLUTIONS AND RECOMMENDATIONS

The obtained results contain valuable conclusions regarding the possibility of using digital tools for green accounting in e-business. Characteristics of this influence on the process of green accounting, stakeholders, and e-business determine their pros and cons. Understanding the real potential of digital tools in connection with the above processes, it is necessary to focus on their drawbacks and issues that require more in-depth discussion.

The study of problems and perspectives of using green accounting and its digitalization in climate-resilient e-business from the position of its influence on decarbonization contains many debatable provisions, connected with different aspects of the problems posed. The basis of this discussion is determined by the specifics of drawbacks of green accounting as an additional tool of the financial and accounting services of e-business companies. This is primarily connected with the large resource intensity of the process of implementing the elements of non-financial reporting at companies, which requires the adoption of accounting policy, introducing changes in the organizational structure of companies, development, and implementation of the corresponding rules and procedures of collection and accounting of information, and preparation and filing of reporting. With the ambiguity in the establishment of the economic effectiveness of green accounting, the high level of costs during its implementation is a significant restraining factor. In this context, research aimed at the identification and economic assessment of the effectiveness of measures connected with the use of environmental accounting deserves special attention and has a high scientific and applied value.

Another aspect of the discussion around green accounting is the problem of greenwashing. It is connected with unfair practices of certain companies, which, striving toward the improvement of their image in an environmentally responsible community, resort to fraud, idealizing their indicators in non-financial reporting. This problem stems from the principles of voluntary environmental accounting and the absence of effective tools for audit and checking of reliability of this reporting. Another component of this problem is the policy of companies with high environmental risks (mining, chemical, and metallurgical industries), which account for the largest share of CO_2 emissions, but compensate for this influence with insignificant projects, which are not directly connected with decarbonization. Thus, the search for ways to ensure high standards of accounting and reporting in the studied system is a relevant task.

FUTURE RESEARCH DIRECTIONS

Problems of global warming, connected with the greenhouse effect and CO_2 emissions are among the largest challenges for humanity in the 21st century. A slight decrease in greenhouse gas emissions after 2007 is an important signal of the recovery of environmental balance. Still, its rates are too low. The main sources of CO2 that go into the atmosphere are the energy sphere, industry, and transport. However, their influence on the above processes is gradually reduced through the growth of the level of energy efficiency, the application of alternative energy sources, and the dissemination of electric cars. Despite this, the global strategy of decarbonization requires more large-scale and deep transformations of economic processes to achieve the declared goals.

The complexity and subjectivity of green accounting create additional obstacles to its wide usage. This problem could be solved through the use of digital tools that can ensure a clearer fixation of environmental processes and their objective accounting and analysis based on AI algorithms. Development of the corresponding parameters and offered on the implementation of such information systems of green accounting in e-commerce companies will allow for a significant increase in the level of objectivity of accounting systems and growth of the level of trust to reporting that is formed on its basis.

CONCLUSION

The Fourth Industrial Revolution and digitalization were important factors in the environmental transformation of the economy. The tools offered by them allowed companies to substantially raise the effectiveness of environmental actions and reduce the negative impact on the environment. One of the economic spheres in the conditions of digitalization that contributed to the reduction of greenhouse gas emissions and growth of the level of energy efficiency is digital business. It ensured the reduction of transport and logistics operations, stimulated the optimization of business models, and decreased the volumes of CO2 emissions at all stages of the formation of product value. At the same time, an increase in the need for maintenance of IT infrastructure led to the growth of energy spending for data processing centers.

An important tool for achieving environmental goals is green accounting. Unlike traditional accounting, it is focused not on the economic results of business but on its influence on the environment. Thus, it integrates environmental and social metrics and procedures into business processes, ensuring transparency of information activities and improving companies' image in the market. The use of international standards GRI and SASB stimulates an increase in the precision of environmental data, allows unifying accounting and analytical procedures, and stimulates the formation of a comprehensive system of accounting support of environmental solutions in e-business companies. A large share of problems connected with the human factor, misuse of environmental reporting, difficulties in receipt of environmental data, and subjectivity of their assessment could be solved through the use of the corresponding digital technologies, such as blockchain, artificial intelligence, cloud computing, big data analytics, etc. Their application contributes to an increase in the precision and reliability of data and protection from manipulations, improves the level of its analytical acceptability, and allows for optimization of resources management of the company, reduction of the anthropogenic pressure on the environment, and optimization of business processes in the sphere of e-business according to the Sustainable Development Goals.

REFERENCES

Alshdaifat, S. M., Aziz, N. H. A., Alhasnawi, M. Y., Alharasis, E. E., Al Qadi, F., & Al Amosh, H. (2024). The Role of Digital Technologies in Corporate Sustainability: A Bibliometric Review and Future Research Agenda. *Journal of Risk and Financial Management*, *17*(11), 509. DOI: 10.3390/jrfm17110509

Antwi, B. O., Adelakun, B., & Eziefule, A. (2024). Transforming financial reporting with AI: Enhancing accuracy and timeliness. *International Journal of Advanced Economics*, *6*(6), 205–223. DOI: 10.51594/ijae.v6i6.1229

Basil-Jones, W. (2023). How to decarbonise your e-commerce business? URL: https://plana.earth/academy/how-to-decarbonise-e-commerce-business (Accessed: 10.02.2025)

D'Arcangelo, F. M., Levin, I., Pagani, A., Pisu, M., & Johansson, Å. (2022). A framework to decarbonise the economy: Designing and monitoring strategies to achieve climate change targets while boosting growth and social cohesion (OECD Economic Policy Paper No. 31). *Organisation for Economic Co-operation and Development.* URL: https://www.oecd.org/content/dam/oecd/en/publications/reports/2022/02/a-framework-to-decarbonise-the-economy_642a6827/4e4d973d-en.pdf. (Accessed: 08.02.2025)

Data Center Knowledge. (2024). Data center power: Fueling the digital revolution. Data Center Knowledge. URL: https://www.datacenterknowledge.com/energy-power-supply/data-center-power-fueling-the-digital-revolution. (Accessed: 11.02.2025)

Dzhumakova, A., Nosirov, I., Rakhmatova, O., & Popkova, E. (2024). Fight against climate change in the digital economy based on green management of knowledge and information systems. *Proceedings on Engineering Sciences.*, *6*(3), 1239–1246. DOI: 10.24874/PES06.03A.018

Galoyan, D., Mkrtchyan, T., Hrosul, V., Buhrimenko, R., Smirnova, P., & Balamut, H. (2023).. . *Formation of Adaptation Strategy for Business Entities in the Context of Digital Transformation of the Economy.*, *21*, 2023. refpress.org/ref-vol21-a64/

Garrigós-Simón, F., Sanz-Blas, S., Narangajavana, Y., & Buzova, D. (2021). The Nexus between Big Data and Sustainability: An Analysis of Current Trends and Developments. *Sustainability (Basel)*, *13*(12), 6632. DOI: 10.3390/su13126632

Hausfather, Z. (2017). Analysis: Why scientists think 100% of global warming is due to humans. Carbon Brief. URL: https://www.carbonbrief.org/analysis-why-scientists-think-100-of-global-warming-is-due-to-humans/ (Accessed: 10.02.2025)

International Energy Agency. (2025). Climate pledges explorer: Data and statistics. International Energy Agency. URL: https://www.iea.org/data-and-statistics. (Accessed: 08.02.2025)

Kantor, O. G., Rudneva, Y. R., Dunov, D. Y., Ergasheva, S. T., & Leybert, B. M. (2023). Green Finance: Analysis of Prospects of the Russian Market. Food Security in the Economy of the Future: Transition from Digital Agriculture to Agriculture 4.0 Based on Deep Learning, pp. 45-56. DOI: DOI: 10.1007/978-3-031-23511-5_6

Kare, M. Š., Gavurová, B., & Porada Rochoń, M. (2024). Digitalization and carbon footprint: Building a path to sustainable economic growth. *Technological Forecasting and Social Change*, *199*(1), 123045. Advance online publication. DOI: 10.1016/j.techfore.2023.123045

Lestari, D. I., Adi, P. P., Kustinah, S., Jayanti, D., Mulyandini, V. C., Purwanti, M., & Kurniawan, A. (2023). Green accounting, environmental accounting, and carbon accounting: Is it the same? *Kurdish Studies*, *11*(2), 2359–2366. kurdishstudies.net/menu-script/index.php/KS/article/view/801

Parthasarathy, V., & Kumar, V. (2012). Cloud computing for business sustainability. *Asia-Pacific Journal of Management Research and Innovation*, *8*(4), 461–474. DOI: 10.1177/2319510X13481905

Petcu, M. A., Sobolevschi-David, M.-I., & Curea, S. C. (2024). Integrating Digital Technologies in Sustainability Accounting and Reporting: Perceptions of Professional Cloud Computing Users. *Electronics (Basel)*, *13*(14), 2684. DOI: 10.3390/electronics13142684

Popkova, E. G. (Ed.). (2024). *Smart Technologies and Innovations in E-Business*. IGI Global., DOI: 10.4018/978-1-6684-7840-0

Ragin-Skorecka, K., Grobelna, K., & Nowak, F. (2024). Identifying e-commerce processes is key to sustainable automation using AI. *European Research Studies*, *27*(Special Issue A, S2), 621–633. DOI: 10.35808/ersj/3740

Ritchie, H., Rosado, P., & Roser, M. (2025). CO_2 and greenhouse gas emissions. Our World in Data. URL: https://ourworldindata.org/co2-and-greenhouse-gas-emissions. (Accessed: 09.02.2025)

Rozite, V. (2023). Data centres and data transmission networks. International Energy Agency. URL: https://www.iea.org/energy-system/buildings/data-centres-and-data-transmission-networks. (Accessed: 10.02.2025)

Sheth, J. (2024). AI-powered sustainability in e-commerce: How smart technologies are reducing carbon footprints. *LinkedIn*. URL: https://www.linkedin.com/pulse/ai-powered-sustainability-e-commerce-how-smart-carbon-nyeff/. (Accessed: 12.02.2025)

Soraya, B., Nurrochmah, A., & Hwihanus. (2024). Business transformation towards sustainability: The role of green accounting in sustainability management. *Journal of Environmental Economics and Sustainability*, 1(3). URL: https://www.researchgate.net/publication/381573968_Business_Transformation_Towards_Sustainability_The_Role_of_Green_Accounting_in_Sustainability_Management. (Accessed: 08.02.2025)

Stocker, T. F., Qin, D., Plattner, G.-K., Alexander, L. V., Allen, S. K., Bindoff, N. L., Bréon, F.-M., Church, J. A., Cubasch, U., ... (2013). Technical Summary. In: Climate Change 2013: The Physical Science Basis. Contribution of Working Group I to the Fifth Assessment Report of the Intergovernmental Panel on Climate Change [Stocker, T.F., D. Qin, G.-K. Plattner, M. Tignor, S.K. Allen, J. Boschung, A. Nauels, Y. Xia, V. Bex and P.M. Midgley (eds.)]. Cambridge University Press, Cambridge, United Kingdom and New York, NY, USA. URL: URL: https://www.climatechange2013.org/images/report/WG1AR5_TS_FINAL.pdf. (Accessed: 09.02.2025)

Treiblmaier, H., & Sillaber, C. (2021). The impact of blockchain on e-commerce: A framework for salient research topics. *Electronic Commerce Research and Applications*, *48*, 101054. DOI: 10.1016/j.elerap.2021.101054

United Nations. (2015a). The Paris Agreement. United Nations Framework Convention on Climate Change. URL: https://unfccc.int/sites/default/files/english_paris_agreement.pdf. (Accessed: 10.02.2025)

United Nations. (2015b). Transforming our world: The 2030 agenda for sustainable development. United Nations. URL: https://sdgs.un.org/2030agenda. (Accessed: 11.02.2025)

Van, H. T. T. (2012). Environmental accounting – A new challenge for the accounting system. *Public Finance Quarterly*, *57*, 437–452. https://api.semanticscholar.org/CorpusID:15291846

Wall Street Mojo. (2024). What is green accounting? Wall Street Mojo. URL: https://www.wallstreetmojo.com/green-accounting/. (Accessed: 10.02.2025)

Zhu, H., Bao, W., & Qin, M. (2024). Impact analysis of digital trade on carbon emissions from the perspectives of supply and demand. *Scientific Reports*, *14*(1), 14540. DOI: 10.1038/s41598-024-65658-1 PMID: 38914673

Zrnić, A., Pekanov Starčević, D., & Mijoč, I. (2020). Evaluating environmental accounting and reporting: The case of Croatian listed manufacturing companies. *Pravni Vjesnik*, 36(1), 47-63. URL: https://www.academia.edu/52291685/Evaluating_Environmental_Accounting_and_Reporting_The_Case_of_Croatian_Listed_Manufacturing_Companies. (Accessed: 11.02.2025)

ADDITIONAL READING

Broccardo, L., Zicari, A., Jabeen, F., & Bhatti, Z. (2023). How digitalization supports a sustainable business model: A literature review. *Technological Forecasting and Social Change*, *187*, 122146. DOI: 10.1016/j.techfore.2022.122146

Garg, V., Aggarwal, S., Tiwari, P., & Chatterjee, P. (Eds.). (2021). *Applications of artificial intelligence in business and finance: Modern trends* (1st ed.). Apple Academic Press., DOI: 10.1201/9781003129639

Iqbal, S., Tian, H., Akhtar, S., & Javed, H. (2025). Effects of green entrepreneurship and digital transformation on eco-efficient e-commerce. *The International Entrepreneurship and Management Journal*, *21*(1), 8. DOI: 10.1007/s11365-024-01024-x

Khan, S. A. R., Godil, D. I., Jabbour, C. J. C., Shujaat, S., Razzaq, A., & Yu, Z. (2021). Green data analytics, blockchain technology for sustainable development, and sustainable supply chain practices: Evidence from small and medium enterprises. *Annals of Operations Research*. Advance online publication. DOI: 10.1007/s10479-021-04275-x

Özyürek, H. (2024). A bibliometric analysis of green accounting, environmental accounting, and green business publications in a global perspective. In Proceedings of the 21st International Conference on Smart Business Technologies (ICSBT 2024) (pp. 115–122). *SCITEPRESS – Science and Technology Publications*. https://www.scitepress.org/Papers/2024/128450/128450.pdf

Renaldo, N. (2024). Digital and Sustainable Accounting for Corporate Value Creation. *Nexus Synergy: A Business Perspective,* 2(1), 46–55. https://doi.org/DOI: 10.61230/nexus.v2i1.97

Shaheen, F., Khan, M. R., & Middlebrough, F. (2024). Green accounting practices: A pathway to sustainable business growth. *Environmental Earth Sciences, 2024*(02), 1–14. https://www.researchgate.net/profile/Rashed-Khan-7/publication/388146821_Green_Accounting_Practices_A_Pathway_to_Sustainable_Business_Growth/links/678bc6d61ec9f9589f4dd14b/Green-Accounting-Practices-A-Pathway-to-Sustainable-Business-Growth.pdf

Stasiskiene, Z. (2020). Environmental accounting: Concept, methodology, and application. In W. Leal Filho, A. M. Azul, L. Brandli, P. G. Özuyar, & T. Wall (Eds.), Responsible consumption and production (pp. 1–12). *Encyclopedia of the UN Sustainable Development Goals.* Springer. https://doi.org/DOI: 10.1007/978-3-319-95726-5_27

Suhardjo, S., Junaedi, A. T., Andi, A., Putri, N. Y., Renaldo, N., Musa, S., & Cecilia, C. (2024). Social Accounting in Sustainability Reporting for Digital Banking. *Nexus Synergy: A Business Perspective,* 2(1), 36–45. https://doi.org/DOI: 10.61230/nexus.v2i1.96

Unter, K., Park, S., & Rivera, J. (2024). Business response strategies to climate change: An integrative and research frontiers outlook. *Organization & Environment, 37*(2), 325–357. DOI: 10.1177/10860266231202819

Witt, J., & Schoop, M. (2023). Blockchain technology in e-business value chains. *Electronic Markets, 33*(1), 15. DOI: 10.1007/s12525-023-00636-5

KEY TERMS AND DEFINITIONS

Decarbonization: Process of reduction or full termination of CO_2 emissions into the atmosphere. It involves a range of measures, including the refusal of fossil fuels, the development of alternative energy, and the development of technologies that absorb CO2.

E-commerce: Component of e-business, which is connected with commercial transactions performed on the Internet. It includes online trade, digital marketing, electronic payments, etc.

E-business: A business model that is based on the use of information and communication technologies for optimization of business processes. It involves the automatization of production, commercial, and managerial processes and the integration of all elements of business into one ecosystem.

Green accounting: System of accounting that operates non-financial indicators of the company and reflects their influence on environment and consumption of resources.

Climate resilience: Ability of economic, social, and environmental systems to oppose climate change, adapt to it, or recover as a result of climate change.

Digital economy: Economic system that functions based on digital technologies. It includes the spheres of e-commerce, digital services, and business platforms.

Digital technologies: Systems and devices that operate information in the digital form. They include hardware and software, as well as network systems, blockchain, cloud technologies, big data, artificial intelligence, the Internet of Things, etc.

Digitalization: The process of implementing digital technologies in the economy and other spheres of life. It involves partial or full transition of production and economic processes to the digital form for the optimization of activities.

Chapter 5
Contribution of Digital Green Accounting to the Investment Attractiveness of E-Business for Its Sustainable Development

Maksatbek O. Orozov
https://orcid.org/0009-0002-8800-098X
Osh State University, Kyrgyzstan

Tolgonay S. Zhusueva
https://orcid.org/0009-0008-7770-3480
Osh State University, Kyrgyzstan

Tatiana N. Litvinova
https://orcid.org/0000-0003-3101-2621
Volgograd State Agricultural University, Russia

Vadim H. Grigoryan
https://orcid.org/0000-0002-8420-9682
Armenian State University of Economics, Armenia

ABSTRACT

Green accounting of e-business has specifics connected with the reflection of costs and/or measures on implementing the Sustainable Development Goals by companies. These costs are concerned with the main goals in environmental (reduction of CO2 emissions from all processes, transition to sustainable packaging, the use of materials and resources that are circular), social (creation of decent labor conditions,

DOI: 10.4018/979-8-3693-8362-9.ch005

support of the well-being of labor resources, an improvement of digital readiness of personnel given the challenges of the digital economy), and economic spheres (ensuring the level of financial and economic results of the company). The goal of this research was to reveal the features of the influence of green accounting on the state of investment attractiveness of e-business for its sustainable development. The novel aspect of this research consists in revealing the specifics of green accounting and reporting of e-business to attract investors in the context of well-balanced achievement of the Sustainable Development Goals.

INTRODUCTION

Green accounting is a new direction for company management in documenting expenditures for sustainable development. The focus on green accounting allows attracting more interested parties (consumers and investors). Consumers and investors are keen on the improvement and protection of the environment and achievement of the Sustainable Development Goals in the social and economic spheres. Through social corporate responsibility and under the influence of public trends, companies declare and implement policies aimed at the achievement of the Sustainable Development Goals. Declaring costs concerning green accounting in corporate reports and sustainable development reports allows ensuring the information basis for the growth of companies' market costs.

Scholars (Nico, 2023; Gantino et al., 2023) confirm the positive influence of green accounting on the capitalization of companies and stock prices. Reporting the information on a company's participation in the achievement of global, international, regional, and territorial aspects of the Sustainable Development Goals causes interest with investors who want to invest in companies that are aimed at receiving profit and creating a sustainable environment.

E-business supplements the investment attractiveness of companies conducting green accounting due to lower negative influence on the environment, compared to traditional business.

Thus, green accounting and e-business could be used for the growth of investment attractiveness and expansion of activities in new market segments.

In this paper, we develop a proprietary approach to assessing the influence of approaches to green accounting of e-business on the level of investment attractiveness of companies in the context of the focus on sustainable development. Based on the proprietary approach, we assessed this influence and proved the positive influence between the considered variables. We noted the revealed relevance of reflection of e-business costs in green accounting and reporting as a factor of ensuring investment attractiveness in the context of the achievement of the Sustainable Development Goals

The purpose of this research was to determine the specifics of the effect of green accounting on the state of investment attractiveness of e-business for its sustainable development. In the context of this purpose, we established the features of the connection between digital green accounting of e-business and sustainable development and systematized the subjects of green accounting of e-business, which ensures investment attractiveness.

BACKGROUND

The connection between green accounting and the investment attractiveness of e-business for sustainable development has its specific features. Revealing them allows establishing the scales of the interaction between the two parameters and determining their influence on sustainable development. For this, we need to formulate the methodological basis, which would allow establishing the connection.

Table 1. Order of the assessment of the influence of green accounting of e-business on companies' investment attractiveness to achieve the Sustainable Development Goals

Determining companies' expenditures on the organization of e-business (or measures for its organization), which ensures the achievement of the Sustainable Development Goals			
↓			
1st source: data of internal accounting	2nd source: open data of corporate accounting	3rd source: open data of the company's sustainable development report	4th source: open data published in mass media, obtained from official sources
↓			
Determining the type of e-business which organization requires costs or measures that influence sustainable development			
↓			
Based on the information sources, in the context of the focus on green accounting of e-business for its sustainable development			
↓			
Establishment of green accounting of the costs and their reflection in corporate reporting			
↓			
1st source: the fact of reflection of costs	2nd source: the fact of reflection of costs	3rd source: the fact of reflection of costs	4th source: need to check the implementation of green accounting and reflection of costs of measures in the sphere of sustainable development
↓			

continued on following page

Table 1. Continued

Determining companies' expenditures on the organization of e-business (or measures for its organization), which ensures the achievement of the Sustainable Development Goals			
Specifics of promotion of green accounting of e-business as a factor of the company's investment attractiveness			
↓			
1st source: informing at the level of the company; no access to data for investors	2nd source: open informing; access to data for investors	3rd source: open informing; access to data for investors	4th source: additional open informing; additional access to data for investors
↓			
Assessment of the influence of green accounting of e-business on companies' investment attractiveness			
↓			
1st source: assessment of the connection between the dynamics of costs, reflected in internal documents, and the dynamics of the company's investments.	2nd source: assessment of the connection between the dynamics of costs, reflected in this category of reporting, and the dynamics of the company's investments.	3rd source: assessment of the connection between the dynamics of costs, reflected in this category of reporting, and the dynamics of the company's investments.	4th source: assessment of the connection between the dynamics of costs, reflected in mass media and obtained from official sources, and the dynamics of the company's investments.

Source: Developed by the authors

The method of categorization was used to reveal the source of informing about costs of the organization of e-business. We also used factor analysis, based on the establishment of the influence of informing about costs on the dynamics of investment attraction. The comparative method allows revealing differences in the influence of the specifics of informing about the established costs on the growth of investments and implementation of the Sustainable Development Goals.

For the purpose of this research, we also analyzed the approaches of different scholars in the sphere of green accounting, e-business, and investment attractiveness of companies that implement the policy of sustainable development.

Jula et al. (2024) provided an assessment of the formation of e-commerce in the EU and revealed the factors of its dissemination (including implementation of innovations, improvement of the quality of the Internet, etc.). Oláh, et al. (2023) dwelt on the influence of e-commerce on sustainable development. The authors showed the measures of the EU countries in implementing the rules of managing this type of e-business in the conditions of reduction of the negative environmental influence and noted the positive role of investments in environmental ways of managing deliveries, logistics, etc.

Fatimah et al. (2023) considered the importance of using the capabilities of e-business in the formation of such components of sustainable development as circular economy. The authors presented an approach to the creation of a portfolio of circular production with the use of e-business means, which could be realized within digital applications.

Lin and Qamruzzaman (2023) elaborated on the assessment of using the tools of e-business, based on the infrastructure of information technologies and green accounting and reporting on the level of financial and economic indicators of economies.

Jabłoński (2018) determined a range of values of the activities of companies in various sectors of the economy, which conform to the Sustainable Development Goals within the focus on functioning on electronic markets. The scholars note the ambiguity of dependence between the activities on electronic markets and achievement of the Sustainable Development Goals and point to the need for the development of optimal variants of integration of these values in ecoogization and social and economic sectors.

Popkova and Ergasheva (2024) established the criteria and pathways to reach a favorable business climate for the transition to IFRS and reassessed the criteria for a favorable business climate for transitioning to IFRS in the context of new multipolar globalization.

JinRu et al. (2022) proved the connection between the growth of investments in companies of various sectors of the economy and the improvement of the level of sustainable development. The scholars confirmed the necessity for establishing the possibilities for the improvement of companies' investment attractiveness in the context of improvement of green accounting of e-business to achieve the Sustainable Development Goals.

MAIN FOCUS OF THE CHAPTER

Complex research on the influence of various components of the digital economy on sustainable development allows determining new opportunities for the effective management of the balance of environmental, social, and economic spheres of companies' activities. This balance could be achieved through the use of e-business, which ensures the resolution of environmental and social problems inherent to the modern economy. E-business can be done in any sphere of the economy. It envisages a focus on modern digital (including intellectual) technologies of process management. Let us evaluate the specifics of connection at the level of green accounting of e-business, investment attractiveness, and sustainable development according to the provisions of the presented methodological basis (Table 1).

We analyzed companies that are involved with e-business in world markets. The selected companies operated in the EU member states. This choice was due to the EU's being the leader in the sphere of implementation of green accounting.

The first considered company is Otto GmbH & Co KG (or The Otto Group), which functions in the world market of retail and e-commerce. The assortment of products (services), provided by the company, includes offers from around 30 participating companies, including clothing, footwear, household goods, financial services, etc. (The Otto Group, 2025a).

We analyzed the data of the company's sustainable development report, which can be found in open access (The Otto Group, 2025c). Let us determine the specifics of green accounting and reporting of the company. The company performs green accounting of e-business, distinguishing measures in the sphere of sustainable development. However, the company does not perform green accounting of direct costs in this sphere. Thus, it is impossible to establish the direct influence of each cost item of this category on the financial results of the activities of Otto GmbH & Co KG. It is possible to reveal the general influence of the main measures in the sphere of sustainable development, declared at the level of green accounting and reporting. We also assessed the connection between green accounting and reporting of the company's e-business and the level of its investment attractiveness.

Table 2. Assessment of the connection between green accounting of e-business and investment attractiveness of Otto GmbH & Co KG

	Indicator	Description of the indicator
1	Directions for green accounting of e-business	
1.1	Operational direction	Declaration and registration of measures on implementing innovations in the management of processes, materials, and measures which ensure the achievement of the Sustainable Development Goals
1.1.1	Responsible chain of supply of raw materials, resources, and products	Interaction with partners from 70 countries: - Requirements for transparency in wages (cooperation only with companies that practice official employment). This measure ensures social protection; - Requirements for certification of raw materials and resources purchased from suppliers by participation companies (compliance with international environmental standards); - Focus on purchasing raw materials and resources containing environmentally-clean components (so-called "preferred fibers").
1.1.2	Certification of furniture manufactured by the group's companies	Certification of correspondence of the quality and environmental safety of raw materials and resources. The level of certification of the company's furniture equaled 83% in 2023-2024.
1.1.3	Sustainability of packaging for products purchased online	The company is focused on the environmental friendliness of packaging. Packaging material is improved to minimize the negative influence on the environment. In 2022-2023, sustainability of packaging equaled 78%, and in 2023-2024 – 94%.

continued on following page

Table 2. Continued

	Indicator	Description of the indicator
1.1.4	Sustainability of paper used for post catalogs of the company	The sustainability of paper includes its environmental safety, confirmed by documents, and the social responsibility of paper manufacturers. The level of paper's sustainability equaled 90% in 2022-2023, and 94% in 2023-2024.
1.1.5	Reduction of CO2 emissions compared to 2018	Over 2022-2023, this indicator decreased by 21%, and over 2023-2024 – by 30%. The company's transition to the reduction of CO2 emissions includes the following aspects: - Reduction of the share of air transportation of materials and products. Over 2012-2024, the indicator of CO2 emissions from the group's companies' activities reduced by 68%. The priority is given to railroad and sea transport; - Transition to green energy. Complete refusal from non-renewable energy sources has been declared. Among renewable energy sources, the key role belongs to solar energy (all offices and production and logistics centers are equipped with solar stations); - Gradual refusal from personnel business trips in favor of remote meetings. This measure is directly connected with the opportunities for the development of e-business, which ensures environmental (reduction of the influence on the environment from the use of transport), social (exchange of knowledge and experience during remote meetings and conferences), and economic (saving expenses for organization of business trips) advantages.
1.2	Charity initiatives	Project on the protection of water biodiversity (project "toMOORow").
2	Object of green accounting of e-business	Measures in the sphere of sustainable development in the operational management. Expenditures for measures on charity initiatives.
3	Dynamics of the results of the influence of green accounting and reporting of e-business on sustainable development	Positive by the main indicators (environmental, social, and economic)
4	Financial and economic results of the company's activities	1) Revenue: 2022-2023: EUR 16.2 billion 2023-2024: EUR 15 billion Revenue in the e-commerce segment: 2022-2023: EUR 12 billion 2023-2024: EUR 10.8 billion 2) EBITDA 2022-2023: EUR 589 million 2023-2024: EUR 744. 3) Profit / Loss (financial result after taxes, amortization, and interest payments). 2022-2023: loss equaling EUR 413 million 2023-2024: loss equaling EUR 426 million.
5	Level of investment attractiveness (dynamics of investments)	The volume of investments: 2022-2023: EUR 593 2023-2024: EUR 418. The most important items of investments: - Investments in digital intellectual services on electronic marketplaces: 2022-2023 – EUR 332 million, 2023-2024 – EUR 283 million; - Investments in the company's brand and other corporate assets: 2022-2023 – EUR 215 million, 2023-2024 – EUR 176 million; - Investments in brands of partner companies: 2022-2023 - EUR 81 million, 2023-2024 – EUR 83 million; - Investments in the company's marketplace: 2022-2023 – EUR 76 million, 2023-2024 – EUR 79 million.

Source: Compiled by the authors based on (The Otto Group, 2025a; The Otto Group, 2025b; The Otto Group, 2025c)

Analysis of the results in Table 2 allows stating that despite the obvious reduction of sales revenue at the level of e-business and growth of losses, Otto GmbH & Co KG was able to increase the indicator EBITDA. This is a sign of an improvement in operational effectiveness. This was accompanied by the development of measures in the sphere of sustainable development, declared at the level of green accounting and the sustainable development report. The growth of the company's attention to implementing measures in this sphere is directly connected with an increase in targeted investing. It is possible to state a direct positive connection between the green accounting of e-business and the investment attractiveness of the company. This connection could grow under the influence of projects ensuring the balance of environmental, social, and economic components.

The second considered company is an EU-based company from Poland – Allegro Group. Allegro Group owns the online stores Allegro.pl and Allegrolokalnie.pl. Allegro.pl marketplace sells products around the country, while Allegrolokalnie.pl offers products only within certain regions. Online shopping at Allegrolokalnie.pl allows saving on shipping and thus achieves the reduction of CO2 emissions from transport. According to the materials of corporate reporting and sustainable development reporting, Allegrolokalnie.pl and Allegro.pl account for approximately equal shares of Allegro Group's sales revenue. The aspects of e-business in the context of the provision of services by Allegro Group are as follows (Allegrolokalnie.pl, 2025; Allegro.pl, 2025b):

- Seller and buyer must register on the website of one of the online marketplaces;
- Buyer uses the function of digital search to look for the required product;
- Seller provides all characteristics of the offered product;
- During the purchase, Allegro Group received a certain percent of the product cost, and the seller received payment for the product minus the commission for the digital platform's services;
- Allegro Group provides information and technological support for the processes of communication and payments;
- Each of the two online marketplaces has a function of free shipping (Allegro Group parcel lockers), but only for products of certain size and weight;
- There is an option for paid additional advertising at the online marketplace.

Allegro Group declares data on the measures in the sphere of sustainable development in internal green accounting and the sustainable development report (Allegro.pl, 2025a). Similar to Otto GmbH & Co KG, Allegro Group does not specify the volumes of expenditures for measures in the sphere of sustainable development, though describes the measures and their positive consequences. The main measures and their consequences are as follows (Allegro.pl, 2025a):

1) Annual reduction of the gap in male and female employees' wages. In 2022 and 2023, this gap was reduced by 5%. This measure concerns the entire personnel: employees and managers involved in e-business, and is aimed at the implementation of sustainable development in the social sector – gender equality and decent work;
2) Measures on an increase in the level of sustainability of packaging of products that are sold through electronic marketplaces. In this case, there are requirements for sellers that sell products on these electronic marketplaces. Allegro Group uses sustainable packaging in independent shipping. The company has packaging materials that are produced from raw materials with circular properties. By the year end 2023, the company achieved 49% sustainability of product packaging, sold at the electronic marketplaces. The aim is to ensure 100% sustainability of packaging by 2028. This will be the requirements for sellers whose products are presented on the two electronic marketplaces. This measure is aimed at achieving the goals of sustainable development in the sphere of responsible production;
3) Implementation of measures for the reduction of CO2 emissions. By 2030, the company aims to reduce CO2 emissions by 38%, compared to 2015. This goal is a part of the commitment to the achievement of the SDGs in the environmental sphere;
4) Growth of the level of digital readiness of the company's personnel to improve its resilience to new challenges of the digital economy. During the entire period of the activities of Allegro Group, there were no cyberattacks, which is a sign of technological growth as an element of economic development. By year-end 2025, the company plans to increase its digital readiness for cyber threats. The year 2023 was marked by measures in training 68% of personnel in observation of rights and interests of consumers and the company; 71% of personnel – in the improvement of the level of data protection on the Internet; 58% of personnel – in prevention and detection of cyber threats. We support the statement by Vanchukhina et al. (2022) regarding the necessity to use the systemic approach to training labor resources for changes introduced by the digital economy.

All of the above measures conform to the Sustainable Development Goals, and their implementation is described within open green reporting.

Based on the analysis of corporate reporting (Allegro.pl, 2025a), we established the dynamics of the key financial and economic indicators of the activities of Allegro Group:

1) Sales revenue and other operating revenue equaled PLN 3.977 billion; in 2020, this indicator grew by 125.2%, equaling PLN 9.0049; in 2023, the indicator grew by 13.8%, equaling PLN 10.2506 billion. This positive dynamics shows that

despite the crisis phenomena in the economy, Allegro Group works in the niche of online commerce which does not lose demand among consumers (consumer goods and brand consumer goods). Within green accounting and reporting, the company's focus on the achievement of Sustainable Development Goals is promoted. This facilitates the attraction of consumers that support the policy of sustainable development;

2) The indicator Profit / Loss changed over 2020-2023. In 2021, profit equaled PLN 616.7 million; in 2022, loss equaled PLN 1,639.5 billion; in 2023, optimization of costs (including saving on business trips and improvement of resources use) led to a profit of PLN 500.2 million. Thus, the company adequately reacts to external challenges, improving the management of internal potential;
3) The indicator of EBITDA on sales in the Polish market had a positive value. In 2020, it equaled PLN 1.5868 billion, in 2022 – PLN 2.2 billion, and in 2023 – PLN 2.86 billion. EBITDA on sales in the international market had a negative value. The company should reconsider sales costs on electronic marketplaces to foreign consumers and develop a profitable national direction, the results of which are rather attractive to investors.

It is also necessary to determine the effectiveness of the influence of green accounting and reporting of e-business on the company's investment attractiveness to achieve the Sustainable Development Goals. According to the balance data (Allegro.pl, 2025a), as of year-end 2022, the volume of investments in the company's activities equaled PLN 692 million, and as of year-end 2023 – PLN 695 million. We may note the direct dependence between green accounting and reporting of e-business and the growth of the company's investment attractiveness (in particular, regarding the activities at the national market of e-commerce of consumer goods).

SOLUTIONS AND RECOMMENDATIONS

This research enabled us to determine the specifics of the influence of green accounting of e-business on investing in the context of sustainable development. These specific features are formed under the influence of different factors.

The factor of the policy of the country, regions, and macro-regions, in which e-business subjects work, have a large impact on the specifics of its organizations, which include also the attraction of investors. In the case of companies, registered in the territory of the EU member states, there are requirements for trade (including online commerce). These requirements include environmental safety of raw materials and resources used in production; environmental safety of products; achievement of sustainability in the context of social management of producers; requirements for manufacturing products that have recycling properties (to reduce the level of waste and the level of CO2 emissions); requirement for the creation of digital passport of products; requirements for providing the right for product maintenances, etc. (Rödl & Partner, 2024). All the above requirements, which are mandatory for compliance, involve the organization of processes (including in the context of green accounting of e-business) and management of costs, which could be covered through price and profit.

The factor of external financial and economic instability, observed in recent years, became a serious challenge for the subjects of e-business, including the ones operating in the EU. The financial and economic crisis led to the reduction of the potential abilities of consumers to purchase products (services) that are not among consumer goods. Thus, European online stores (including those selling their products or products of partner companies, as is the case of Otto GmbH & Co KG) need to reconsider the assortment, prices, and order of organization of e-business. It is possible to perform rebranding given the focus on sustainable development and the creation of conditions for the effectiveness of e-business to attract more investors.

The specifics of the organization of green accounting of measures on the organization of e-business, based on the declaration of measures and results, does not involve the determination of costs in value terms. This does not allow revealing the economic effectiveness of costs, which could be a barrier to the attraction of new investors or growth of investments from the existing investors. This feature of green accounting and reporting was peculiar to the policy of the two European companies functioning in the e-commerce market (Otto GmbH & Co KG (Germany) and Allegro Group (Poland)). These companies have various forms of segments of online commerce. The former sells its products, manufactured by participating companies; the latter provides services for e-commerce on its digital platforms. The two companies use a universal approach to green accounting and reporting, connected with the insufficient transparency of costs in the sphere of achievement of the Sustainable Development Goals. This might be due to the fact that, as of now, the international standards of financial accounting and standards of reporting do not contain requirements for the disclosure of information about precise amounts of costs in this sphere. The introduction of such reporting data would raise the transparency of green accounting of e-business and would become a source of information for investors.

FUTURE RESEARCH DIRECTIONS

Prospects for scientific research on the considered topic may be seen in the search for new forms of digital green accounting and reporting of the indicators of e-business of companies which activities influence the indicators of sustainable development of territories and countries. Since their functioning is important for cities, regions, territories, and countries, it might be relevant to work on legislative regulation of the mandatory character of green accounting and reporting of all processes (including in the context of the activities of e-business companies).

CONCLUSION

This research demonstrated that European companies show commitment to the policy of sustainable development, which is adapted at the supra-national level of the EU in the provisions of various regulatory standards. Compliance with these standards is the priority for all subjects of the economy in various sectors. This is true for product manufacturers in various sectors of industry and for companies that sell consumer goods on online marketplaces. We revealed a positive dependence between green accounting and reporting of e-business and the growth of investments in companies. This connection is seen in local projects, which are characterized by balance, which includes the application of environmentally oriented measures and social measures, which positively influence the level of financial and economic indicators.

This shows that all measures of the environmental character, implemented by companies in the context of the policies of countries and supra-national structures (EU) must mutually supplement the level of formation of the social and financial & economic sectors.

Summing up the above, it is possible to offer a range of recommendations that would ensure an increase in the connection between green accounting of e-business and the growth of companies' investment attractiveness for sustainable development. These recommendations are as follows:

- Initiative on the development of new standards for adapting green projects in the context of achievement of social and economic goals. This initiative could be developed at the level of countries and supra-national unions. Its implementation will allow accelerating the participation of the business environment in the implementation of the Sustainable Development Goals, and investors will be able to assess the expedience of investing in companies contributing to sustainable development;
- Initiative on introducing changes to the provisions of international financial reporting standards to create costs items in the sphere of sustainable development of e-business;
- Revealing new directions of green accounting of e-business, which would, without changes in the standards of accounting and reporting, inform inter-

ested parties (including investors and consumers) about the effectiveness of measures on the company's sustainable development.

REFERENCES

Allegrolokalnie.pl. (2025). *Sprzedawaj, jak chcesz*. Retrieved February 12, 2025, from https://allegrolokalnie.pl/o/poznaj (data accessed: 12.02.2025).

Allegro.pl. (2025a). *Dla inwestorów*. Retrieved February 12, 2025, from https://about.allegro.eu/pl/esg (data accessed: 12.02.2025).

Allegro.pl. (2025b). *Kategorie*. Retrieved February 12, 2025, from https://allegro.pl/ (data accessed: 12.02.2025).

Fatimah, Y. A., Kannan, D., Govindan, K., & Hasibuan, Z. A. (2023). Circular economy e-business model portfolio development for e-business applications: Impacts on ESG and sustainability performance. *Journal of Cleaner Production*, *415*, 137528. Advance online publication. DOI: 10.1016/j.jclepro.2023.137528

Gantino, R., Ruswanti, E., & Widodo, A. M. (2023). Green accounting and intellectual capital effect on firm value moderated by business strategy. *Jurnal Akuntansi*, *27*(1), 38–61. DOI: 10.24912/ja.v27i1.1118

Jabłoński, M. (2018). Value migration to the sustainable business models of digital economy companies on the capital market. *Sustainability (Basel)*, *10*(9), 3113. DOI: 10.3390/su10093113

JinRu, L., Qamruzzaman, M., Hangyu, W., & Kler, R.JinRu. (2022). Do environmental quality, financial inclusion, and good governance ensure the FDI sustainably in Belt and Road countries? Evidence from an application of CS-ARDL and NARDL. *Frontiers in Environmental Science*, *10*, 936216. DOI: 10.3389/fenvs.2022.936216

Jula, N. M., Staicu, G. I., Moraru, L. C., & Bodislav, D. A. (2024). Toward a sustainable development of e-commerce in EU: The role of education, internet infrastructure, income, and economic freedom on e-commerce growth. *Sustainability (Basel)*, *16*(9), 3809. DOI: 10.3390/su16093809

Lin, J., & Qamruzzaman, M. (2023). The impact of environmental disclosure and the quality of financial disclosure and IT adoption on firm performance: Does corporate governance ensure sustainability? *Frontiers in Environmental Science*, *11*, 1002357. DOI: 10.3389/fenvs.2023.1002357

Nico, A. (2023). Green accounting and firm value. *Accounting and Finance Review*, 7(4), 12–18. DOI: 10.35609/afr.2023.7.4(2)

Oláh, J., Popp, J., Khan, M. A., & Kitukutha, N. (2023). Sustainable e-commerce and environmental impact on sustainability. *Economics & Sociology (Ternopil), 16*(1), 85–105. DOI: 10.14254/2071-789X.2023/16-1/6

Popkova, E. G., & Ergasheva, S. T. (2024). Favorable business climate for transition to international financial reporting standards: Criteria and pathways for achievement. In M. P. Eshov, G. K. Abdurakhmanova, A. U. Burkhanov, N. B. Abdusalomova, & S. T. Ergasheva (Eds.), *Development of international entrepreneurship based on corporate accounting and reporting according to IFRS* (*Advanced Series in Management,* Vol. 33A, pp. 7–13). Emerald Publishing. DOI: 10.1108/S1877-63612024000033A001

Rödl & Partner. (2024). *Current ESG and product compliance – New regulatory requirements due to the EU Green Deal.* Retrieved February 12, 2025, from https://www.roedl.com/insights/esg-news/2024-3/esg-product-compliance-new-regulatory-requirements-due-to-eu-green-deal- (data accessed: 12.02.2025).

Statista. (2025). *Income statement of Allegro in Poland from 2020 to 2023 (in million zloty).* Retrieved February 12, 2025, from https://www.statista.com/statistics/1219445/poland-income-statement-of-allegro/ (data accessed: 12.02.2025).

The Otto Group. (2025a). *About us.* Retrieved February 12, 2025, from https://www.ottogroup.com/en/nachhaltigkeit/ (data accessed: 12.02.2025).

The Otto Group. (2025b). *Annual reports.* Retrieved February 12, 2025, from https://www.ottogroup.com/en/medien/downloads/?categoryDocs=geschaeftsberichte (data accessed: 12.02.2025).

The Otto Group. (2025c). *Sustainability.* Retrieved February 12, 2025, from https://www.ottogroup.com/en/nachhaltigkeit/ (data accessed: 12.02.2025).

Vanchukhina, L. I., Leybert, T. B., Ergasheva, S. T., Khalikova, E. A., & Khanafieva, I. R. (2022). Integration of the higher education systems of Russia and the Republic of Uzbekistan in training for the digital economy. In E. G. Popkova & B. S. Sergi (Eds.), *Digital education in Russia and Central Asia* (*Education in the Asia-Pacific Region: Issues, Concerns and Prospects,* Vol. 65). Springer. https://doi.org/DOI: 10.1007/978-981-16-9069-3_1

ADDITIONAL READING

Asni, N., & Agustia, D. (2022). Does corporate governance induce green innovation? An emerging market evidence. *Corporate Governance (Bradford), 22*(7), 1375–1389. DOI: 10.1108/CG-10-2021-0389

Bing, T., & Li, M. (2019). Does CSR signal the firm value? Evidence from China. *Sustainability (Basel), 11*(15), 4255. Advance online publication. DOI: 10.3390/su11154255

Bolton, P., & Kacperczyk, M. (2021). Do investors care about carbon risk? *Journal of Financial Economics, 142*(2), 517–549. DOI: 10.1016/j.jfineco.2021.05.008

Chircop, J., Tarsalewska, M., & Trzeciakiewicz, A. (2023). Learning to be green: Accounting comparability and environmental violations. *The British Accounting Review, 101240*, 101240. Advance online publication. DOI: 10.1016/j.bar.2023.101240

Dewi, H. F., Anggara, T. C., & Lindrianasari, . (2024). The Impact of Green Accounting and Integrated Reporting on Financial and Market Performance. *IOP Conference Series. Earth and Environmental Science, 1324*(1), 012090. Advance online publication. DOI: 10.1088/1755-1315/1324/1/012090

Hutabarat, F. (2024). Effect of Green Accounting, Leverage, Firm size on Firm Value with Profitability as Intervening Variable. *International Journal of Professional Business Review, 9*(4), e04612. DOI: 10.26668/businessreview/2024.v9i4.4612

Khan, S., & Gupta, S. (2024). The interplay of sustainability, corporate green accounting and firm financial performance: A meta-analytical investigation. Sustainability Accounting. *Management and Policy Journal, 15*(5), 1038–1066. DOI: 10.1108/SAMPJ-01-2022-0016

Yang, M. (2023). Green investment and e-commerce sales mode selection strategies with cap-and-trade regulation. *Computers & Industrial Engineering, 177*, 109036. DOI: 10.1016/j.cie.2023.109036

KEY TERMS AND DEFINITIONS

Circularity: Activities of companies aimed at supporting the product supply chain that can be further recycled without producing waste.

Costs of organization of e-business: All types of costs connected with the organization of the processes of the company's activities in the electronic form.

E-business: Organization of any processes of financial and economic activities of the company with the use of digital technologies.

Green accounting: Accounting on the items of expenditures, income, and operations regarding the achievement of the company's sustainable development.

Investment attractiveness: Parameters of companies' activities that ensure investors' interest in financing these subjects.

Measures in the sphere of sustainable development: Measures to ensure the achievement of the company's goals in the environmental, social, and economic spheres.

Sustainable development: Functioning of companies given the priority of achievement of goals in the sphere of ecologization and support of social stability and economic effectiveness.

Chapter 6
Digital Green Accounting in the Marketing Mix of E-Business for Its Sustainable Development

Fazilat Abdullaeva
https://orcid.org/0009-0007-8114-4805
Tashkent State University of Economics, Uzbekistan

Nazgul Kutusheva
https://orcid.org/0000-0003-2155-6772
Osh State University, Kyrgyzstan

Sirengul Zholdubaeva
https://orcid.org/0009-0009-2862-1793
Osh State University, Kyrgyzstan

Anna Aleksandrovna Tubalets
https://orcid.org/0000-0002-8616-2603
Kuban State Agrarian University Named After I.T. Trubilin, Russia

ABSTRACT

This paper elaborates on the scientific and practical problem of using digital green accounting in the marketing mix of e-business companies in support of sustainable development, reduction of negative environmental impact, and stimulation of decarbonization. Theoretical foundations of e-business, evolution of the marketing mix, and integration of digital green accounting into business processes are analyzed. It is revealed that, in the conditions of digitalization, the marketing mix transforms, acquiring better flexibility and innovativeness, actively integrating environmental

DOI: 10.4018/979-8-3693-8362-9.ch006

values into its structure, and using the potential of digital technologies. In these conditions, information acquires the status of a strategic asset of the company, which raises the competitiveness and sustainability of the e-business company. It is established that an important tool capable of ensuring objectivity, relevance, and the comprehensive character of information is green accounting.

INTRODUCTION

Sustainable development forms the current paradigm of modern economic relations. Its principles are based on the UN Sustainable Development Goals, adopted in 2015 (United Nations, 2015), and are implemented through the corresponding concepts within social responsibility of business, ESG management, climate responsibility, and the circular economy. According to F. Ross, the main priorities of sustainable development in the economy are environmental and climate responsibility, energy efficiency, social equality, and justice, as well as support of the balance between economic, social, and environmental goals (Ross, 2019). They influence strategic priorities, institutional processes, and interaction between business, environment, and stakeholders.

In the conditions of large-scale digital transition, the influence of the provisions of sustainable development on business is also subject to transformation. This is connected primarily with the digitalization of business models, the formation of digital sectors in the economy, and the development of new market needs. As a result of digital transformation, e-business gradually acquires the features of a separate sector of the economy, which has clear differences compared to traditional economic activities. It is based on the use of information and communication technologies, Internet connection, electronic devices, sensors, and information systems, which allow economic agents to satisfy their economic interests. This involves flexibility, scalability, personalization, a high level of automatization of processes, decentralization, and the importance of communication channels and marketing.

Marketing activities in the structure of e-business perform a special role. They are not only a separate function but also an integrating element, which combines different aspects of the interaction of e-business companies, stakeholders, and the market. According to this, marketing in the ecosystem of digital business performs the role of a certain platform, within which the Sustainable Development Goals are implemented, communications with consumers are done, and mechanisms of influence on their consumer preferences and decisions are formed. From the position of sustainable development, marketing performs an ambiguous function: it is a tool for implementing the strategy of sustainable development of the company and is transformed under its influence. Thus, marketing tools ensure the corresponding positioning of the company in the market, perform environmentally-targeted pricing, facilitate optimization of logistics chains, promote the values of sustainable development in the environment of stakeholders, minimize the environmental impact of marketing activities, ensure transparency and reliability of communications, and take into account the social influence of their activities on targeted audiences.

In this context, a special role is assigned to information support of marketing processes. The need to ensure reliability and transparency of communications requires the creation of a comprehensive system of monitoring, accounting, and reporting on environmental aspects of e-business companies' activities. The tools of green accounting allow integrating environmental, social, and economic factors into accounting mechanisms and reflecting them through the non-financial reporting of companies (Dwianika et al., 2024). The application of digital tools allows for a significant increase in the quality of accounting and transparency of reported processes. Thus, the issue of using digital green accounting in the marketing mix of e-business to support sustainable development forms a relevant scientific and practical task, the resolution of which significantly raises the value of using marketing tools due to quality information support and transparency.

The research methodology is based on the system and complex approaches, which allow integrating the methodological apparatus of different scientific spheres, including e-business, digitalization, marketing, cybernetics, accounting, and reporting. The research is based on the concepts of sustainable development, social and climate responsibility, ESG management, and modern marketing theories. It involves the use of the methods of analysis, synthesis, retrospective analysis, comparison, observation, and generalization.

The main value of the work is development of tools to integrate environmental metrics into digital accounting systems of e-business companies, which allows raising the transparency of business processes, optimizing environmental indicators of marketing activities, and ensuring the correspondence of the company's strategy to the Sustainable Development Goals.

BACKGROUND

Relevance of the outlined problems is manifested in different spheres, which cover the marketing mix, development of e-business, growth of the trends of sustainable development, support of green accounting in the conditions of digitalization, and integration of the above processes within one system. The evolution of the marketing mix, which underwent several stages of transformation according to market demands, requires adaptation to the conditions of e-commerce (Dominici, 2024) and processes of digitalization and environmental influences (Goi, 2024).

Previous attempts to reconsider the number and structure of the marketing mix are an important conceptual basis for understanding the mechanism of marketing and its influence on business and public processes (Yudelson, 1999). Thus, attempts to expand the number of the elements of the marketing mix up to 10P (Denney-Stone, 2017) or 7I (Bhatia et al., 2024) allow reconsidering the mechanisms of the influence of marketing and taking into account their interaction with digital technologies and environmental aspects, which are integrated into each element of the marketing mix (Taneja and Bala, 2024).

In the context of ecologization of e-business, its foundations were considered from the position of the complex formation of the electronic sector (Wigand, 1997), identification of its essence and reserves for raising effectiveness (Chaffey and Ellis-Chadwick, 2019), formation of the relevance of integration processes aimed at the digitalization of marketing to achieve long-term competitiveness (Chaffey and Smith, 2022), and assessment of the impact of e-commerce on the ecological situation which requires the implementation of efficient tools of green accounting for monitoring and control of indicators in e-business (Bladelius and Volmerdal, 2021) with the use of digital technologies (Rosário and Dias, 2023).

The concept of green accounting involves the integration of environmental factors in the traditional systems of bookkeeping, which are manifested in e-business (Dwianika et al., 2024), facilitating ecologization of business processes, growth of trust to stakeholders, and increase in the competitive positions of companies (Fronda, 2024), reveal effective methodologies and tools of environmental accounting (Iacob (Zavincu) et al., 2023), use digitalization of green accounting to raise its precision and speed with simultaneous integration with other sub-systems of management (Soraya et al., 2024), and include marketing strategies aimed at support of the sustainable development of e-business (Allayarov and Yakubov, 2024).

Digitalization of green accounting offers an expansion of its potential for the successful integration of environmental indicators into managerial reporting and marketing communications. The focus is on the use of ESG (Environmental, Social, Governance) management in the interaction with digital technologies (Xu et al., 2022), which includes collection, processing, and analysis of ESG data for the formation of the basis for digital green accounting (Ali and Khalid, 2025), ensures integration of ESG metrics into the system of managerial accounting to involve responsible investments (Ergasheva et al., 2023), facilitates the creation of green supply chains based on environmental technologies (Popkova et al., 2024a), and substantiates the perspectives of automatization of corporate accounting and reporting (Popkova et al., 2024b).

Large-scale integration of digital green accounting in the marketing mix of e-business envisages the use of various metrics, digital technologies, and methodologies to ensure the development of companies in the direction of sustainable development. The study of the above processes covers the issues of using blockchain technologies and digital marketing to build trust in green projects (Al-Ababneh et al., 2025), the application of quantitative methods of assessing the carbon footprint of digital technologies, which are used in marketing communications and business technologies (Lannelongue et al., 2021), integration of the principles of the circular economy into the practice of green accounting and the marketing mix of e-business (Bjørnbet & Skaar, 2024), adaptation of business models and accounting systems to the needs of the green economy (Zhang et al., 2022), integration of environmental indicators into the system of managerial reporting (Ngwakwe and Ambe, 2016), and rethinking of economic models and formation of the conceptual basis for the development of digital green accounting as a tool of ensuring sustainable development of e-business (Ross, 2019).

Generalization of the theoretical foundation of the problem of development of green accounting in the marketing mix of e-business for sustainable development shows that integration of digital green accounting into the marketing mix of e-business is a promising direction of development, which combines environmental values, digital technologies, and elements of the marketing mix to achieve the Sustainable Development Goals. Transformation of the marketing mix in this context ensures favorable conditions for the active implementation of the methods of green accounting, the use of ESG metrics and reporting in the information systems of e-business. Thus, the purpose of this paper is theoretical substantiation and development of practical recommendations for implementing digital green accounting in the marketing mix of e-business to ensure its sustainable development in the conditions of current global trends and market demands. Achievement of this goal involves resolution of a range of tasks, which include the retrospective analysis of the evolution of the marketing mix, which is transformed under the influence of digitalization, substantiation of the role of marketing in the integration of market trends and internal processes of e-business, identification of the role of information as a strategic resource in the system of marketing communications, determination of the essence, specifics, and functional capabilities of green accounting from the position of marketing activities of e-business companies, determination of current environmental metrics and their coordination with the elements of the marketing mix in the conditions of digital environment, and assessment of the synergetic effect from the combination of digital technologies and mechanisms of green accounting in the context of raising competitiveness and value of e-business companies.

The methodological basis of the research is determined by the totality of theories and concepts, combined within the system and the complex interdisciplinary approach, which combines different scientific spheres: cybernetics, marketing, economics, entrepreneurship, ecology, accounting, reporting, etc. The key value-based and methodological provisions are here considered in the context of the concepts of sustainable development, ecologization, and decarbonization, which are combined with ESG management, current marketing concepts, and trends of the economy's digitalization. The methodological tools of the research cover general scientific and special methods, which include the table method, analysis, synthesis, retrospective and historical analysis, abstraction, observation, comparison, and generalization.

MAIN FOCUS OF THE CHAPTER

The evolution of e-business, as a separate economic category, dates back to the 1960s -1970s and is connected with the invention of the first attempts at the computerization of business processes, in particular, the systems of electronic data exchange. However, its full use began in the 1990s (Wigand, 1997). This period saw the emergence of the first Internet stores, electronic payment systems, online auctions, and other elements, which formed the basis of modern e-business. Its active development started in the 2000s, when the Internet speed increased substantially, the population's digital literacy grew, and the development of technical infrastructure allowed making Internet technologies generally accessible (Chaffey and Ellis-Chadwick, 2019).

Companies' transition to the electronic form of doing business became a result of a range of factors, which include the following:

– Economic advantages, which include reduction of transaction costs, connected with refusal from certain physical operations, optimization of logistics, and effective stock management (Chaffey and Ellis-Chadwick, 2019);
– Technological conditions, which formed due to active digitalization;
– Social drivers connected with the change in consumer behavior and formation of the culture of online interaction;
– Globalization processes, which allowed integrating business environments and markets of different countries and continents.

Additional factors of the active development of e-business were its ability for scaling, the network effect, the ability to personalize offers, the transformation of business processes, and access to global markets (Chaffey and Smith, 2022). At present, e-business is a complex phenomenon, which evolved from simple forms of automatization to integrated digital ecosystems, and has a large market, technological, and social power. An important feature of e-business is its ability for scaling and adaptation, which grows with the development of digital technologies and globalization. The availability of online systems and platforms allows ensuring quick access to the global market and dynamic interaction with consumers, supporting quality communication, and translating own values among a wide range of economic agents.

Extensive capabilities of e-business are implemented through its sub-systems and functions, which, among others, cover marketing activities. In this context, marketing is integrated with digital solutions and raises the effectiveness of business. Online environment ensures the possibility for personalized marketing communication, detailed analytics based on big data, flexible communication channels, etc. Each element of the marketing mechanism acquires special qualities, which are transformed under the influence of digital technologies and strengthen the strategic opportunities of e-business in the conditions of sustainable development.

The marketing mix is an integrated managerial model, which characterizes different components of marketing activities within a unified system. The initial structure of the marketing mix was formed in the 1960's. It included four key elements (4p) – product, price, place, and promotion – which fully conform to the context of the manufacturer. This structure of the marketing mix reflected all main components of the company's activities in the commodity market in the conditions of the marketing concept. Gradual transition to the concept of total quality management (Yudelson, 1999), the concept of marketing relations, and digital context led to the necessity for reconsidering the elements of the marketing mix to check their correspondence to new conditions (Dominici, 2024). Thus, the initial structure of the marketing mix was changed and supplemented.

At present, the most traditional concept of the marketing mix is 7p, which, apart from the above four elements, includes three new elements: people, process, and physical evidence (Goi, 2024). This expansion was connected with the evolution of the market environment and changes in consumer behavior. The non-material character of services and the related specifics led to an increase in the role of employees (people), who determine the quality of services and processes and require management in the conditions of the growth of competition; as well as the material state and physical evidence, which allowed strengthening the substantiation of the quality of non-material services. Additional elements of the marketing mix also became the drivers of the formation of the personalized approach, automatization, and digitalization of marketing, as well as an increase in the value of the brand as an element of trust to the product or trademark. Thus, the expansion of the marketing mix up to 7p became a result of consideration of market trends and transformation and led to the emergence of new business models, development of digitalization, and growth of the role of customer experience.

Today, in the conditions of digitalization, the list of the elements of the marketing mix is constantly supplemented and improved. Scholars and practitioners strive towards the consideration of new trends in the market development and flexibility of marketing tools. In this context, there is the marketing mix 10p, which includes packaging, pictures, and personality (Denney-Stone, 2017); and the electronic marketing mix (4Ps + 3Ps) + 3S 2P 2C), which, apart from the above 4+3P, integrates digital elements, such as site design, security, sales promotion (3S), personalization, privacy (2P) and Customer Service and Community (2C) (Taneja and Bala, 2024).

In today's world, the utilitarian approach to the purchase has a reduced role. Competing for demand, manufacturers and sellers expand qualitative features of products and means of their presentation, using new elements. In these conditions, the design of the web-site and presentation of the product, safety, personalization, and privacy, as well as additional service and community, form new equal values for the consumer and determine new edges of competition. In these conditions, e-business combines marketing tools and business models, actively interacting with the market.

The high level of dynamics of the market environment and high rates of implementation of new technologies form an environment in which any innovations quickly lose their relevance and require reconsideration. In these conditions, it is important to offer mechanisms that can solve marketing functions by completely new terms and with the corresponding feedback from the market. A completely new, alternative view of the marketing mix in the conditions of the digital economy is the transition from classical 7P to innovative I7, within which increasing demands of consumers are satisfied more fully and flexibly (Table 1).

Table 1. Characteristics of the elements of the marketing mix of e-business within the transition from 7P to I7

Element of 7P	Element of I7	Description of the element of I7
product	insightful product	Studying the demand based on digital tools allows meeting the various personalized needs of consumers
price	inventive prices	Based on analysis of demand, rivals, and consumer behavior, digital companies can use flexible pricing and take into account all aspects of consumer behavior
place	integrated placement and distribution	Modern channels of product distribution combine physical and digital forms, forming omnichannel mechanisms of the interaction with buyers and integrating with flexible logistics tools
promotion	interactive promotion	Consumers stop being passive recipients of marketing information and become active participants in marketing communications through the digital tools of marketing
people	influencers	The role of people from outside of companies, who can actively communicate with communities and influence their behavior through social networks and other communication channels, grows

continued on following page

Table 1. Continued

Element of 7P	Element of I7	Description of the element of I7
process	insights	Orientation towards business processes is modernized through integration with data analytics, marketing studies, and CRM systems, which allows for maximum consideration of changes in consumer preferences and interests
physical evidence	impressions	In the conditions of the digital market, physical evidence plays a smaller role, giving way to the emotional image of the product, which is formed under the influence of design, packaging, interactive content, and digital presence.

Source: Compiled by the authors based on (Bhatia et al., 2024)

Transformation of the marketing mix and an increase in its innovativeness conform to the general challenges and capabilities of the digital economy. In these conditions, big data analytics, personalization of sales, and the use of integrated marketing strategies and omnichannel approaches allow for the significant expansion of the capabilities of e-business and the strengthening of its interaction with current global processes. At that, the marketing mix performs a dual role, being an active tool of influence on the market and, at the same time, being in its context. Thus, on the one hand, it has a large potential for ensuring large-scale changes in the economy and social relations; on the other hand, it is in the context of institutional processes of the type of ecologization of business, climate responsibility, sustainable development, etc.

Transformations that are reflected in Table 1 characterize these changes, which take place in each of the seven elements. Thus, the transition to insightful products and inventive prices due to better analytics and personalization is one of the effective tools for preventing overproduction, integrated placement and distribution facilitate optimization of logistics and reduction of the carbon footprint, interactive promotion and impressions reduce physical presence of advertising on material carriers and allow attracting consumers with the minimum material influence on the environment. Influencers allow using respectable channels for translating the required messages, which reduces the need for intense advertising campaigns and involves the use of reputation as a factor of promotion of common values of mankind, and insights are the tools of detailed analytics on the influence of each element of e-business not only on internal processes but also on stakeholders and environment.

The close connection between the elements of the marketing mix and the market, stakeholders, and global processes determines the objective direction for its development in the context of the achievement of a higher level of sustainability. This vision is implemented through a direct perception of marketing as a tool of interaction with the external environment, as well as through the corresponding manifestations of certain elements of the marketing mix. Given this, the marketing policy of the company cannot be oriented only towards the internal demands of the company. It is always coordinated with external trends, which cover not only economic but also social and environmental contexts. Thus, the current state of the marketing mix of the companies of e-business is largely coordinated with the trends of globalization, digitalization, sustainable development, and climate and social responsibility (Rosário and Dias, 2023; Zhang et al., 2022; Xu et al., 2022). Within the system approach, the interaction between the marketing mix and the current global trends involves their integration with internal values and strategy and further retransmission in the environment of consumers and stakeholders (Fig. 1).

Figure 1. Integrated system of the marketing mix of e-business in the interaction with global trends

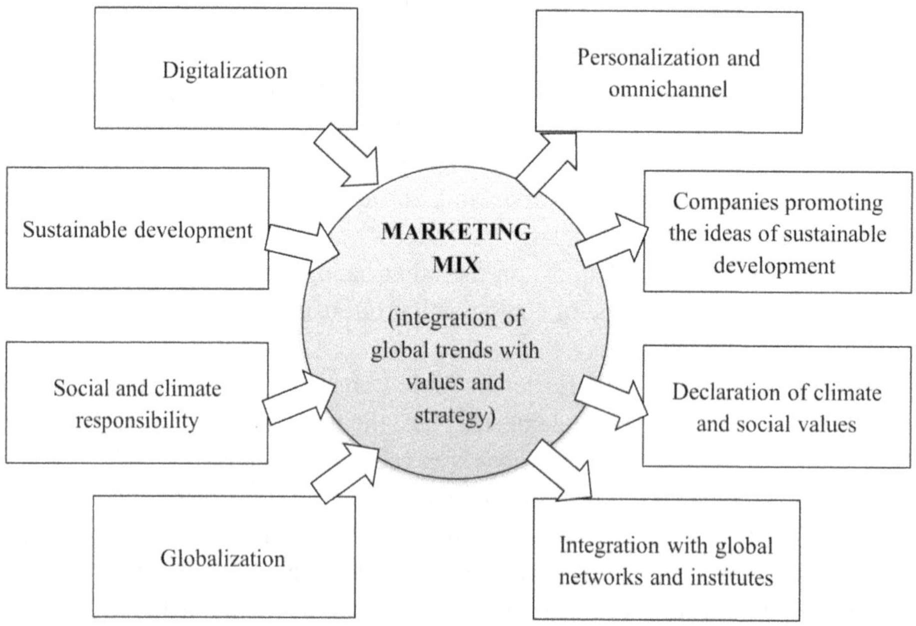

Source: Created by the authors

Thus, the open system of the marketing mix integrates global trends and transforms them into its values, which are manifested through the corresponding strategic elements. As a result, digitalization is realized through the wide application of digital tools and the development of omnichannel and personalization of sales; social and climate responsibility – through the declaration of the corresponding values and goals in the environment of stakeholders and the market; globalization – through integration with global networks and institutions; and the concept of sustainable development – through promoting the appropriate goals and values in the market.

Managing the system of such interconnections through the marketing mix requires the corresponding information policy. The role of information in these conditions is not limited to passive collection of data and monitoring. Its task determines the initial data required for decision-making and achievement of the necessary results. Information is an important element of marketing communication and thus has to conform to a range of demands, which include objectivity, complexity, relevance, and effectiveness. Objectivity of information is a reflection of its reliability and forms trust to the source of marketing communications through which such messages are translated. Complexity characterizes the width of coverage of processes and completeness of information that is translated on behalf of the digital company. Relevance points to a clear understanding of the real value of information and the ability to form the corresponding sample for presentation in the environment of stakeholders. Effectiveness, as a demand for information, points to the necessity for comparing the costs of receiving data and the advantages the company may receive as a result of using this information.

In the conditions of institutionalization of the above global trends, the information about environmental and social aspects of the activities of the e-business company grows and acquires the status of not an auxiliary element of marketing communications but a strategic resource, which influences the company's competitiveness. This change in the status of non-financial information about the company is predetermined by an increase in environmental awareness of consumers and stakeholders, as well as the growth of regulatory demands for the ecologization of business and publication of non-financial reporting. Given this, the formation of a complex system of information support of sustainable development of e-business companies becomes especially relevant.

One of the effective tools that can ensure quality information support of marketing communications of e-business in the sphere of sustainable development is green (environmental) accounting. It includes a symbiosis of accounting methodologies (bookkeeping, managerial, financial, environmental, etc.), and, in the interaction with digital technologies, it forms additional value for the company, which conforms to global trends and public transformations.

Green accounting is a comprehensive approach to bookkeeping, which takes into account environmental and social factors and integrates them into the system of financial reporting (Soraya et al., 2024). It is a special means of reporting about efforts performed by companies to protect the environment, reduce CO_2 emissions, and decrease environmental risks (Fronda, 2024). Green accounting is a system of collection, processing, analysis, and provision of information about the environmental activities of the company, the reporting of which is not envisaged by the provisions and standards of bookkeeping.

Environmental accounting offers e-business companies large advantages, which allow raising corporate transparency and reporting, improving the company's reputation, strengthening trust in it, and ensuring an increase in the company's value and improvement of the level of its competitiveness. An important aspect of green accounting is its influence on the system of company management. Due to this, companies can determine the environmental implications of their activities and manage them according to the declared goals and values (Soraya et al., 2024).

Implementation of digital green accounting in the marketing activities of e-business companies has several stages. First off, there comes a complex audit of environmental parameters of the company's marketing activities, based on the concept of life cycle. Based on the result of the audit, the need for specialized infrastructure is established; it includes programs, devices, and tools, which ensure the collection, processing, and analysis of environmental information. The collected information is assessed based on the developed system of indicators (KPI). The effectiveness of marketing measures is identified, as well as their environmental impact on consumers, products, or the market. The use of information systems and platforms allows integrating the elements of green accounting and marketing analytics, which, in turn, forms conditions for comprehensive support of the system of managerial decision-making.

Using the tools of digital green accounting within marketing strategies involves the use of appropriate quantitative methods to reflect the processes of the environmental impact of the marketing tools on the environment in the absolute or relative value. There is no unified clear methodology that can fully cover the aspects of the environmental influence of marketing activities. However, similar to other aspects, under the condition of comparing marketing indicators with the indicator of environmental contribution, it is possible to assess the level of influence of a certain marketing tool on the state of ecology.

From the position of the complex approach, the tools of environmental accounting could be applied to the elements of the marketing mix, determining the parameters of influence on the environment and facilitating the sustainable development of e-business. The key metrics of this connection are presented in Table 2.

Table 2. Characteristics of environmental metrics of the elements of the marketing mix from the position of digital green accounting of e-commerce companies

Elements of the marketing mix	Environmental metrics of green accounting of the elements of the marketing mix	Influence of digital technologies
product	Tracking the environmental or carbon footprint of the product, assessment of resource- or energy efficiency	Using sensors and IoT devices for online monitoring, using blockchain for data transparency
price	Assessing the volume of deductions for ecological activities in the structure of cost and price of the product, return on environmental investments (costs) from the position of environmental bonus (profit) within a certain period	Using AI and big data algorithms to assess environmental costs and using digital platforms for complex consideration of all aspects of dynamic pricing
place	Environmental assessment of distribution channels, assessment of environmental and carbon footprint of e-business logistics	Using big data analytics and digital systems of logistics management for the optimization of routes and reduction of emissions
promotion	Verification of marketing environmental statements, the carbon footprint of materials of marketing campaigns, the environmental footprint of customers during interaction with the elements of product promotion	Using digital tools to control information channels, and social networks, and check reporting
people	Assessment of environmental competencies of personnel	Using the platforms of online training, creating a digital community, etc.
process	Resource efficiency and environmental friendliness of business processes from the position of carbon footprint, energy consumption, circularity, etc.	Automatization of processes based on ERP/CRM systems, using digital twins to optimize resources and ensure the flexibility of the reaction system
physical evidence	Assessment of energy efficiency and material intensity of the elements of physical environment in marketing	Using smart technologies for digital visualization of environmental indicators

Source: Compiled by the authors based on (Allayarov and Yakubov, 2024; Bjørnbet and Skaar, 2024; Iacob (Zavincu) et al., 2023; Ngwakwe and Ambe, 2016)

Integrating with modern digital tools, the above environmental metrics offer substantial advantages for environmental accounting of marketing activities of e-business companies. The main effects that emerge in the process of such interaction are manifested in the form of an increase in transparency of reporting, optimization of resources, and improvement of strategic planning. The main challenges of this integration lie in the necessity to attract large funds, ensure cyber security, and ensure standardization for coordination of the system of environmental accounting and its universalization.

In the conditions of digitalization, additional institutionalization of green accounting takes place. It is based on a synergetic combination of the capabilities of digital technologies and mechanisms of environmental accounting. Within this combination, special attention is paid to the following functional elements:

- Determining the volume of the environmental impact of digital activity, which assesses the carbon footprint of the digital infrastructure (data centers, servers, network equipment, etc.) (Lannelongue et al., 2021);
- Monetized reflection of positive and negative effects of e-business companies on the environment, which calculates the value indicators of environmental pollution or support of ecologization of business (Bladelius and Volmerdal, 2021);
- Integration of ESG metrics into the system of indicators of marketing activities, which allows for the comprehensive assessment of the success of using the elements of the marketing mix for sustainable development (Ali and Khalid, 2025);
- Digital verification of environmental results and statements, ensures trust to the company's marketing policy due to the use of the blockchain technology (Al-Ababneh et al., 2025).

SOLUTIONS AND RECOMMENDATIONS

The quick development of digital technologies against the background of growth of environmental challenges leads to the necessity for active implementation of innovative approaches for the integration of tools of green accounting and the marketing mix in e-business companies. The efforts that can ensure an increase in the competitive positions in the sphere of e-business based on sustainable development must be aimed not only at the technical coordination of accounting and marketing processes but also at the formation of the corresponding information system, a combination of the influence of digital, marketing, and accounting tools, the conceptual transformation of approaches to the marketing mix, etc. According to this, the main directions of the development of digital green accounting in e-business based on sustainable development must include the following solutions:

- Development and implementation of environmental metrics in the system of bookkeeping and marketing, which involves the formation of a unified methodology of assessing the environmental influence of marketing measures, integration of ESG indicators in the system of managerial decision-making, and the use of digital technologies to ensure precision and objectivity of measuring the impact of marketing activities on ecology, climate situation, and effectiveness of resources use;

- Integration of digital technologies into the system of environmental accounting, which requires the use of modern information platforms created based on big data, AI, the Internet of Things, blockchain, etc. This will allow for the quick accumulation and processing of relevant information and the formation of a constant flow of information about environmental accounting for effective use in current marketing communications;
- Transformation of models of the marketing mix according to market demands and global trends, which requires flexible application of the 4P and 7P models with possible transition to the I7 concept, which can provide better innovativeness to the elements of the marketing mix and ensure effective use of digital technologies in interactive marketing communications in the context of sustainable development;
- Improvement of information support of managerial decisions in the sphere of marketing of e-business companies, which envisages the creation of a systematized information platform based on green accounting, which is combined with the elements of the marketing mix and allows optimizing not only internal processes but also external communications with stakeholders in the context of retranslation of values of sustainable development of e-business companies.

FUTURE RESEARCH DIRECTIONS

The problem of integration of digital technologies and green accounting in the sphere of marketing activities of e-business has been rather poorly studied, which leads to the existence of a wide range of issues for discussion and further research. Attention should be paid to the issues of using digital innovative platforms for the collection, processing, and analysis of environmental data connected with marketing activity. This will allow raising the transparency of information support of sustainable development and stimulating the implementation of new indicators and metrics of environmental effectiveness of the marketing mix elements.

Apart from this, the issue of unification of green accounting methodology is very interesting. Achievement of this goal will allow standardization of the tools for measuring the environmental influence of marketing elements, form, and procedure of non-financial reporting, as well as integration of parallel systems of ESG metrics into the systems of decision-making at e-business companies. Special attention should be paid to development of the algorithms of using AI and big data technologies, which have a large potential for raising environmental resilience and sustainability. Thus, future studies should be aimed at the formation of integrated models that combine the potential of digital technologies, green accounting, e-business, and marketing to achieve the Sustainable Development Goals.

CONCLUSIONS

In the conditions of growth of the paradigm of sustainable development and active digitalization, innovative business models, which are based on active communications and thorough information basis, have the largest potential for achieving success and ensuring complex favorable influence on the development of human civilization. E-business is one of the drivers of digital development. It combines the capabilities of digital technologies, innovative entrepreneurship, and close interaction with consumers and stakeholders. Rational usage of communication channels of e-business requires the use of effective tools, which can actively interact with the market, reveal its trends, and retranslate the values and messages of the company.

Marketing is a factor that can integrate market trends with the internal processes and strategy of the company and ensure their harmonious combination with current business models. Marketing tools are dynamic; they change depending on market trends and transformations. Market influence can be tracked by the example of the marketing mix – integrated managerial model, which unifies different components of the marketing mechanism into one system. Thus, the evolution of the marketing mix from the initial 4p to 7p, and then to 10p, reflects the change in consumer demands and market situation from basic elements that are peculiar for product manufacturers to more flexible and detailed components that reflect current trends and market needs. In the conditions of e-business, the transformation of the marketing mix from the classical 7p to innovative 7i, which takes into account the market dynamics and its marketing flows and ensures comprehensive use of the potential of digital technologies, becomes more popular.

Marketing mechanisms of e-business companies are closely integrated with the external environment and function in the conditions of the global context. According to this, marketing integrates global trends of digitalization, social and climate responsibility, and sustainable development into its values and strategies and retranslates them on behalf of the company in the market. In these conditions, information ceases to be a passive element and acquires the status of a strategic resource which can strengthen the company's competitiveness. Increased demands regarding objectivity, complexity, relevance, and effectiveness are set for this information. An important tool of information support of marketing communications in these conditions is accounting tools, in particular, green (environmental) accounting. Its functional range is determined by the environmental marketing activities of e-business companies. Within green accounting, these activities are assessed for verification, level of influence on the targeted audience, influence on the environmental situation, etc. Due to the close integration of green accounting with digital technologies, companies receive effective tools for communication with stakeholders in the context of market demands and global trends.

Implementing digital green accounting into marketing activities takes place in several stages, which include complex audit, the creation of infrastructure, the development of the system of indicators, and their integration into the information system. A relevant task here is the coordination of environmental metrics with the elements of the marketing mix. The synergy of combining the potential of digital technologies and mechanisms of green accounting allows forming new functional elements, which effectively track the environmental impact of digital activity of e-business companies, provide opportunities for monetization of environmental effects, integrate ESG metrics into the company's information system, and facilitate the digital verification of environmental results. Combined with the tools of the marketing mix, the digitalization of green accounting ensures an increase in corporate transparency, improves the image of digital companies, strengthens trust in them, and ensures an increase in competitiveness and growth of value.

REFERENCES

Al-Ababneh, H., Alkhudierat, N., Barhoush, F., Almajali, A., Ibragimkhalilova, T., & Mugableh, M. (2025). Using blockchain and digital marketing to build trust in green projects. *E3S Web of Conferences*, 614, 1016. https://doi.org/DOI: 10.1051/e3sconf/202561401016

Ali, H., & Khalid, T. (2025). Integrating ESG metrics and sustainability reporting into strategic decision-making for enhanced risk management and regulatory compliance in a globalized economy. ResearchGate. DOI: 10.13140/RG.2.2.19762.11207

Allayarov, S. A., & Yakubov, M. A. (2024). The role of green accounting in digital business marketing: A sustainable development perspective. American. *Journal of Open University Education, 1*(8). https://scientificbulletin.com/index.php/AJOUP

Bhatia, K., Singhal, P., & Mishra, N. (2024). The evolved marketing mix - How innovation is transforming the 7 Ps. URL: https://www.researchgate.net/publication/385551868_The_Evolved_Marketing_Mix_-_How_Innovation_is_Transforming_the_7_Ps. (Accessed: 03.03.2025)

Bjørnbet, M., & Skaar, C. (2024). Framework for life cycle assessment-based circular business model development. *In Sustainable business models* (pp. 4-1–4-15). https://doi.org/DOI: 10.4324/9781032693415-4

Bladelius, J., & Volmerdal, K. (2021). The environmental impact of e-commerce: A comparative analysis of CO_2e emissions in e-commerce and traditional retailing (Bachelor's thesis, Jönköping University). DiVA Portal. URL: https://www.diva-portal.org/smash/get/diva2:1574619/FULLTEXT01.pdf (Accessed: 01.03.2025)

Chaffey, D., & Ellis-Chadwick, F. (2019). Digital marketing: Strategy, implementation and practice. *Pearson.* URL: https://books.google.com.ua/books?hl=uk&lr=&id=-1yGDwAAQBAJ&oi=fnd&pg=PA1&dq=Chaffey,+D.,+%26+Ellis-Chadwick,+F.+(2019)&ots=XjTl6TnI46&sig=ZPi-8kL4iRpHZWuEBzphFNuoqRo&redir_esc=y#v=onepage&q=Chaffey%2C%20D.%2C%20%26%20Ellis-Chadwick%2C%20F.%20(2019)&f=false (Accessed: 03.03.2025)

Chaffey, D., & Smith, P. (2022). *Digital Marketing Excellence: Planning, Optimizing and Integrating Online Marketing* (6th ed.). Routledge., DOI: 10.4324/9781003009498

Denney-Stone, H. (2017). The 10 P's of marketing (2nd edition). *Nudge Marketing.* URL: https://nudgemarketing.com/the-10-ps-of-marketing/ (Accessed: 02.03.2025)

Dominici, G. (2024). From marketing mix to e-marketing mix: A literature overview and classification. *International Journal of Business and Management*, *4*(9), 17–17. DOI: 10.5539/ijbm.v4n9p17

Dwianika, A., Purwanto, E., Suyoto, Y. T., & Pitaloka, E. (2024). Bibliometrics Analysis of Green Accounting Research. *International Journal of Energy Economics and Policy*, *14*(1), 349–358. DOI: 10.32479/ijeep.15055

Ergasheva, S. T., Zinovyeva, I. S., Abdurashitov, A. A., Kopytina, Y. A., & Makarova, T. V. (2023). ESG Investments in Support of the Development of the Green Economy in Russia and Central Asia. *Environmental Footprints and Eco-Design of Products and Processes,* Part F1766, pp. 419-428. DOI: DOI: 10.1007/978-3-031-46525-3_44

Fronda, S. M. (2024). Green accounting: Emerging updates in the accounting industry. *Scrubbed.* URL: https://scrubbed.net/blog/going-green-what-it-means-for-your-businesss-accounting-practices/ (Accessed: 01.03.2025)

Goi, C. L. (2024). A review of marketing mix: 4Ps or more? *International Journal of Marketing Studies*, *1*(1), 2. DOI: 10.5539/ijms.v1n1p2

Iacob, A., Ciobanu, I., & Coman, E. L. (2023). Application Of Environmental Accounting Methods In Business. *Social-Economic Debates*, *12*(1), 1–8.

Lannelongue, L., Grealey, J., & Inouye, M. (2021). Green algorithms: Quantifying the carbon footprint of computation. *Advancement of Science*, *8*(12), 2100707. DOI: 10.1002/advs.202100707 PMID: 34194954

Ngwakwe, C., & Ambe, C. (2016). Business sustainability performance measurement: Eco-ratio analysis. Risk Governance and Control. *Financial Markets & Institutions*, *6*(4), 516–520. Advance online publication. DOI: 10.22495/rgcv6i4siart10

Popkova, E. G., Kaurova, O. V., & Maloletko, A. N. (2024). Introduction. Popkova, E.G., Kaurova, O.V., Maloletko, A.N. (Ed.) Sustainable Cooperation for the Creation of Green Supply Chains Based on Environmental Technologies and Responsible Innovations (Sustainable Civil Infrastructures, Part F3650), *Springer Nature Switzerland*. pp. V-VIII. DOI: DOI: 10.1007/978-3-031-70962-3

Popkova, E. G., Litvinova, T. N., & Zemskova, O. M. (2024), "Smart Automation of Corporate Accounting and Reporting in International Business According to IFRS: Global Premises and Prospects for Russia", Eshov, M.P., Abdurakhmanova, G.K., Burkhanov, A.U., Abdusalomova, N.B. and Ergasheva, S.T. (Ed.) *Development of International Entrepreneurship Based on Corporate Accounting and Reporting According to IFRS* (Advanced Series in Management, Vol. 33A), Emerald Publishing Limited, Leeds, pp. 91-98. https://doi.org/DOI: 10.1108/S1877-63612024000033A011

Rosário, A. T., & Dias, J. C. (2023). The New Digital Economy and Sustainability: Challenges and Opportunities. *Sustainability (Basel)*, *15*(14), 10902. DOI: 10.3390/su151410902

. Ross, F. (2019). Kate Raworth - Doughnut Economics: Seven Ways to Think Like a 21st Century Economist. *Regional and business studies*, 11(2), 81-86. https://doi.org/DOI: 10.33568/rbs.2409

Soraya, B., Nurrochmah, A., & Hwihanus, H. (2024). Business Transformation Towards Sustainability: The Role of Green Accounting in Sustainability Management. *Journal of Environmental Economics and Sustainability*, *1*(3), 1–8. DOI: 10.47134/jees.v1i3.342

Taneja, G., & Bala, A. (2024). Adapting to digital: A review of the e-marketing mix and its evolution beyond the 4Ps. *Zenodo*.https://doi.org/DOI: 10.5281/zenodo.14560872

United Nations. (2015). Sustainable development goals. United Nations. URL: https://sdgs.un.org/goals (Accessed: 01.03.2025)

Wigand, R. (1997). Electronic Commerce: Definition, Theory, and Context. *The Information Society*, *13*(1), 1–16. DOI: 10.1080/019722497129241

Xu, J., She, S., & Liu, W. (2022). Role of digitalization in environment, social and governance, and sustainability: Review-based study for implications. *Frontiers in Psychology*, *13*, 961057. DOI: 10.3389/fpsyg.2022.961057 PMID: 36533022

Yudelson, J. (1999). Adapting McCarthy's Four P's for the Twenty-First Century. *Journal of Marketing Education*, *21*(1), 60–67. DOI: 10.1177/0273475399211008

Zhang, L., Xu, M., Chen, H., Li, Y., & Chen, S. (2022). Globalization, green economy, and environmental challenges: State of the art review for practical implications. *Frontiers in Environmental Science*, *10*, 870271. DOI: 10.3389/fenvs.2022.870271

ADDITIONAL READING

. Abbasabadi, Y., Tehrani, R., & Janani, M. H. (2023). Presentation of a Green Accounting Model in Integrated Reporting Using a Critical Approach: A Model to Replace Integrated Reporting. *Journal of Applied Environmental and Health Research*.https://doi.org/DOI: 10.34172/jaehr.2023.02

Azwin Md Nasir, N., Afiqah Zainuddin, S., Che Nawi, N., Asrul Hery Ibrahim, M., & Hasan, H. (2024). Critical Insights into Green Accounting Research: A Bibliometric Review. In El Khoury, R. (Ed.), *Technology-Driven Business Innovation: Unleashing the Digital Advantage. Studies in Systems, Decision and Control* (Vol. 540). Springer., DOI: 10.1007/978-3-031-62656-2_54

Bernstein, J. (2019). Green Marketing and Sustainable Development. In Leal Filho, W. (Ed.), *Encyclopedia of Sustainability in Higher Education.* Springer., DOI: 10.1007/978-3-030-11352-0_134

Greenham, T. (2010). Green accounting: A conceptual framework. *International Journal of Green Economics*, *4*(4), 333–345. DOI: 10.1504/IJGE.2010.037655

Lisnawati, L., Aryati, T., & Gunawan, J. (2024). Implementation of Digital Innovation on Sustainability Performance: The Moderating Role of Green Accounting in the Industrial Sector. *Eastern-European Journal of Enterprise Technologies*, *127*(13), 59–68. DOI: 10.15587/1729-4061.2024.298639

Özyürek, H. (2024). A Bibliometric Analysis of Green Accounting, Environmental Accounting and Green Business Publications in a Global Perspective. *ICSBT*, *2024*, 115.

Rosalinda, C., Idris, I., & Susanto, P. (2024). Driving SMES towards Green Business: The Impact of Sustainable Marketing Mix on Performance and Loyalty in BNI'S Go Green Movement. *Journal of Ecohumanism*, *3*(7), 4190–4202. DOI: 10.62754/joe.v3i7.4538

Sumiati, A., Susanti, S., Maulana, A., Indrawati, L., Puspitasari, D., & Indriani, R. (2022). Influence of Green Accounting and Environmental Performance on Profitability. In Proceedings of the International Conference on Social, Economics, Business, and Education (ICSEBE 2021). *Advances in Economics, Business and Management Research.* https://doi.org/DOI: 10.2991/aebmr.k.220107.027

Sunarmin, S. (2020). Green Technology Accounting as an Innovation to Reduce Environmental Pollution. *Neraca: Jurnal Akuntansi Terapan*, *1*(2), 135–141. DOI: 10.31334/neraca.v1i2.862

Tjoa, E. V., & Widianingsih, L. P. (2022). Green Accounting, Environmental Performance, and Profitability: Empirical Evidence on High Profile Industry in Indonesia. [RIMA]. *Research in Management and Accounting*, *5*(2), 93–105. Advance online publication. DOI: 10.33508/rima.v5i2.4158

Trisnawati, N. L. D. E., Prabandari, L. P. C., & Budiasni, N. W. N. (2024). Implementasi Green Accounting dan E- Commerce Dalam Pengelolaan Usaha Berbasis Digital Kelompok Remaja LKSA B'Onic. ARSY. *Jurnal Aplikasi Riset Kepada Masyarakat*, *5*(2), 141–149. DOI: 10.55583/arsy.v5i2.1019

KEY TERMS AND DEFINITIONS

Digital accounting: System of bookkeeping that uses digital technologies to collect, process, store, and represent financial and non-financial information and reporting. It is conducted based on automatized accounting processes and involves the possibility of using big data analytics, cloud technologies, and other digital technologies.

Green accounting: System of bookkeeping which tracks environmental impact of economic activities of the company, which covers the use of natural resources, greenhouse gas emissions, and assessment of the environmental impact.

Marketing mix: Integrated model which unifies the components of a marketing mechanism. In its initial form, it includes 4 elements (product, price, place, promotion), and is expanded with the change of the marketing concept and development of the market – up to 7, 10, and more elements, which take into account market demands and dynamics of digitalization of marketing.

E-business: Model of business which is based on the use of information and communication technologies for business operations. It covers online commerce, digital marketing, management of customer relations, online payments, etc.

Digitalization: Process of implementing digital technologies in different spheres of the economy and public life to raise the level of their effectiveness and optimize processes. It is an inseparable component of the digital economy and digital society.

Sustainable development: The concept of socioeconomic development which focuses on well-balanced satisfaction of the needs of the modern generation without any damage and reservations for future generations. It involves the achievement of a balance between the economic, environmental, and social interests of society and business.

ESG metrics: System of indicators that are used to assess the company's activities from the position of environmental, social, and governance effectiveness. They facilitate measuring of non-financial activity of companies and determining their contribution to sustainable development.

Chapter 7

Green Accounting and Digitalization of E-Business for Sustainable Development:

A Methodological Toolkit for Forecasting Enterprise Competitiveness

Aktam U. Burkhanov
https://orcid.org/0000-0003-0108-8852
International School of Finance and Technology, Alfraganus University, Uzbekistan

Ubaydullo G. Gafurov
https://orcid.org/0000-0002-3829-4556
Tashkent State University of Economics, Uzbekistan

Bobir O. Tursunov
https://orcid.org/0000-0002-5004-375X
Tashkent State University of Economics, Uzbekistan

Tuygunoy A. Mamadjanova
https://orcid.org/0009-0009-2305-6123
Termez University of Economics and Service, Uzbekistan

Bunyod Usmonov
https://orcid.org/0000-0001-6453-3832
Tashkent State University of Economics, Uzbekistan

DOI: 10.4018/979-8-3693-8362-9.ch007

ABSTRACT

This research is motivated by the desire to enhance the scientific and methodological support for assessing the current and future competitiveness of entrepreneurship. The research aims to refine the methodological tools for forecasting the competitiveness of enterprises in Uzbekistan. The research examines the empirical experiences of countries with national entrepreneurial competitiveness above the global average, including Uzbekistan in 2025. It demonstrates the limitations and inconsistencies inherent in the current approach to achieving and forecasting the competitiveness of national entrepreneurship in Uzbekistan based on several aspects on marketing tools. The first aspect is an econometric model that links the competitiveness of Uzbek enterprises to their use of marketing tools across the 7P areas in 2025. The second is an optimized forecast of the competitiveness of Uzbek entrepreneurship until 2030. The third one is a set of scientific and practical recommendations for boosting the marketing activity of Uzbek entrepreneurship within the extended 7P framework.

INTRODUCTION

Competitiveness ranks among the top priorities for contemporary economic systems and market players while representing a complex socio-economic concept. In the context of an enterprise, competitiveness is synonymous with market position and signifies the success with which the enterprise defends its interests in a competitive struggle. It is qualitatively expressed through the enterprise's attractiveness as a partner (for procuring its products, investing in its development, and integrating it into broader supply and distribution chains) in comparison with its competitors, that is, with other market players; and quantitatively through overall and export sales, as well as market share and profit (Fang et al., 2024; Kurowska-Pysz et al., 2024; Sai et al., 2025).

The difficulty of ensuring sustainable growth in an enterprise's competitiveness and accurately forecasting it stems from the fact that competitiveness is a dynamic characteristic (subject to significant changes over time) and depends on the enterprise's development potential and the degree to which this potential is realized and on external factors: the actions of competitors and other market players, in other words, the overall market climate (Bogovizet al., 2023).

It should also be noted that competitiveness is largely a subjective attribute, which poses another serious challenge in achieving and forecasting it. This subjectivity is evident in the fact that an enterprise with identical product features and business activities may exhibit varying levels of competitiveness in different markets (Ciambellini et al., 2025).

For example, producing green products and intensifying environmental initiatives may enhance an enterprise's competitiveness in markets with a highly developed environmental culture characterized by eco-conscious consumers, predominantly green investors, and sustainable supply and distribution chains while simultaneously reducing its competitiveness in markets with a moderately developed environmental culture, where market agents are reluctant to incur higher environmental costs when partnering with such an enterprise (Zhao et al., 2025).

Despite these obstacles, the importance of achieving and forecasting enterprise competitiveness cannot be overstated. For market agents deciding whether to collaborate with an enterprise, accounting for its competitiveness is crucial for rationalizing consumer purchasing behavior, for suppliers in enhancing their competitiveness, for creditors and investors in optimizing financial activities, and for state regulators in intensifying economic development (Li et al., 2025).

For the enterprise, ensuring and forecasting its competitiveness is critically important for survival in an aggressive market environment for several reasons. One reason is that an enterprise needs a reliable assessment of its competitiveness at every stage of its life cycle to objectively evaluate its market position and prospects and take timely measures to improve it if necessary. A proper understanding of competitiveness helps the enterprise determine its current life cycle stage and the speed at which these stages are changing (Gou & Wang, 2025).

Another reason is that considering competitiveness is crucial for successful corporate strategic planning and management. Accurate measurement of current and future competitiveness is the cornerstone of reliable informational support for corporate strategic plans, thereby increasing the likelihood of their timely and complete implementation. Additionally, competitiveness plays a pivotal role in launching investment and innovation projects, the attractiveness and necessity of which largely depend on the enterprise's competitive strength (Heriqbaldi et al., 2025).

Furthermore, considering current and forecasted competitiveness is essential when formulating export strategies. A strong position in the domestic market does not guarantee success in the global arena – a venture fraught with risks that can be mitigated by a detailed analysis of competitiveness (Ibrahim et al., 2025). Another consideration is that enterprises must pay close attention to competitiveness when pursuing import substitution and adapting to state policies of free trade or protectionism. Without properly assessing competitiveness or misjudging it, enterprises risk either declining efficiency in a closed economy or facing aggressive competition and price dumping in an overly open market (Anggara et al., 2025).

The foregoing highlights the fundamental importance of achieving and forecasting an enterprise's competitiveness for all market agents in today's economic environment, as well as the significant challenges involved in reliably assessing current and future competitiveness. This represents a pressing scientific and practical problem for entrepreneurship, particularly in Uzbekistan. This is the basis for the relevance of refining the methodological toolkit for forecasting the competitiveness of enterprises in Uzbekistan, which is the research objective.

BACKGROUND

The Existing Approach to Achieving and Forecasting the Competitiveness of National Entrepreneurship in Uzbekistan

In Uzbekistan, considerable attention is devoted to state regulation of the competitiveness of national entrepreneurship. The "Digital Uzbekistan-2030" Strategy (President of the Republic of Uzbekistan, 2025a) provides for measures to stimulate the growth of competitiveness among national entrepreneurial structures. Creating favorable conditions to enhance the competitiveness of Uzbek enterprises has been identified as a primary objective in the President's decree (President of the Republic of Uzbekistan, 2025b).

The current approach to achieving and forecasting the competitiveness of national entrepreneurship in Uzbekistan envisions an active role for the state, with insufficient involvement from entrepreneurial entities. The methodological toolkit for forecasting enterprise competitiveness is based on antitrust regulation, whose economic rationale is to maintain a highly competitive market environment (Ergasheva et al., 2025; Usmonov, B., 2024).

The logic behind forecasting entrepreneurial competitiveness in this context is straightforward: the higher the level of market competition in Uzbek markets, the greater the competitiveness of Uzbek enterprises. The main statistical indicator used in Uzbekistan's established approach for achieving and forecasting national entrepreneurial competitiveness is the conditions for doing business (Kobilov et al., 2023; Tashbaev et al., 2024).

A significant shortcoming of the existing approach is that the mere presence of competition does not guarantee an increase in competitiveness. Only internal mechanisms within the enterprise can trigger the process of enhancing competitiveness; no external regulation (even antitrust measures) can ensure this (Mkrtchyan et al., 2024).

Due to the insufficient activity of Uzbek enterprises in enhancing their competitiveness, its growth potential remains underutilized in Uzbekistan. Moreover, the economic policy of deregulation, rather than promoting import substitution, hinders competitiveness as foreign competitors displace Uzbek enterprises in national markets. Similarly, the state-driven strategy for digital economic development, in the absence of active participation by entrepreneurial structures, only increases the financial burden on the national budget without producing a significant rise in the competitiveness of Uzbek enterprises (Kalieva, 2012).

Consequently, the approach to achieving and forecasting the competitiveness of national entrepreneurship in Uzbekistan requires adjustment through the stimulation of independent initiatives by entrepreneurial structures aimed at boosting their competitiveness (Eshov et al., 2024). Forecasting the competitiveness of Uzbek enterprises should be based on the proactive implementation of corresponding corporate measures, with marketing initiatives being the most promising.

Marketing Toolkit for Achieving and Forecasting Enterprise Competitiveness

The efficacy and promise of marketing tools in achieving and forecasting the competitiveness of entrepreneurial structures have been confirmed by numerous examples, research studies, and publications reflecting successful international experiences. To comprehensively examine these tools, we consider them within the framework of the extended marketing mix—7P:

- P1: Product. In this area, enhancing an enterprise's competitiveness lies in producing and marketing innovative products with new, improved, or unique features that are in demand, thereby increasing their appeal for purchase and consumption (Ratang, 2025; Seddaoui et al., 2025);
- P2: Price. Competitiveness can be improved through increased labor productivity, which lowers production and distribution costs and enables the enterprise to secure and maintain a price advantage in the target market (Goldmann & Knörzer, 2023; Nurjannah et al., 2024);
- P3: Promotion. In this domain, competitiveness may grow through effective branding, including the development and strengthening of global brands for national enterprises, thus enhancing the recognition and appeal of their products worldwide (Almaguer et al., 2025; Przhedetsky et al., 2018);
- P4: Place. In this area, replacing or supplementing traditional offline trade with electronic commerce can boost competitiveness by simplifying the purchasing process, increasing product attractiveness, and expanding the geographic reach and diversity of distribution channels (Barquero-Chaves et al., 2025; Berlilana et al.2025);
- P5: People. The competitiveness of an enterprise can be enhanced by recruiting more qualified and competent employees and providing corporate training to develop targeted skills and foster effective teamwork (Andekina et al., 2024; Petrenko et al., 2024);

- P6: Physical environment. In this area, competitiveness may be increased by reducing the ecological footprint of entrepreneurial activities, essentially through the development of a green economy that improves the physical environment in which these activities occur (Asma Unnisa Begum & Kalpana, 2025; Gyiazov et al., 2023);
- P7: Processes. An enterprise can enhance its competitiveness by either streamlining or optimizing its production and export processes (Litvinova et al., 2017; Neill & Dang, 2025).

A review of the available scientific literature shows that, despite the well-developed marketing toolkit for achieving and forecasting the competitiveness of entrepreneurial structures in various countries, its application in Uzbekistan remains underexplored, representing a gap in the literature. To address this gap, this research poses the research question (RQ): "To what extent does the application of marketing tools in the extended 7P marketing mix influence the competitiveness of Uzbek enterprises?"

Overview of Existing Methods for Forecasting Enterprise Competitiveness and Their Application in Uzbekistan

As a result of an in-depth analysis of the available scientific literature, the authors identified several existing methods for forecasting enterprise competitiveness and their application in Uzbekistan that are widely used in practice. These methods include the following:

- The expert forecasting method involves intuitively formulating forecasts based on available industry reviews, corporate information, and the forecaster's expectations, along with official and informal data on the current and future state of the market and enterprise (Gaurav et al., 2025). Its drawback lies in the subjective nature of the forecasts produced, which reduces their accuracy and reliability (Omanov et al., 2024);
- Historical trend method relies on extending current trends into future periods (Wang et al., 2025). It can utilize qualitative and quantitative information on enterprise activities and market conditions (Zhang et al., 2025). Through comprehensive analysis, the forecaster identifies trends in the evolution of an enterprise's competitiveness over a certain period and assumes that these trends will remain unchanged in the future (Kumar et al., 2025). A significant limitation of this method is that, despite the well-known cyclicality of market economies, business cycles and the life cycles of enterprises are largely unpredictable; subsequent stages often do not repeat but differ markedly from

previous ones (Burkhanov et al., 2024). Consequently, forecasts based on historical trends frequently fail and can be misleading (Yang et al., 2024);

- Statistical forecasting method: This method is primarily associated with the analysis of quantitative data (Fan et al., 2024). Although individual techniques may have specific nuances (Daribekova et al., 2023), the general scientific and economic rationale of this method is universal—it involves identifying patterns in the changes of variables that are incorporated into a comprehensive econometric model, which simplistically reflects the nature of competitiveness and its evolution, including causes and effects while emphasizing the most critical conditions (Yuldashev et al., 2024).

Among these alternatives, the statistical forecasting method is the most preferred due to its objectivity and the high accuracy of its forecasts. However, for its practical application in forecasting the competitiveness of Uzbek enterprises, a detailed and thorough review and analysis of the relevant economic statistics of Uzbekistan is necessary and carried out further in this research.

THE MAIN FOCUS OF THE CHAPTER

Alternative Assessments of the Competitiveness of National Entrepreneurship in Uzbekistan

For the most accurate and objective assessment of entrepreneurial competitiveness, this research employs a statistical forecasting method, the reliability of which is ensured by relying on official international statistics from widely recognized authoritative sources. The research covers the period of 2025, utilizing the latest available statistical data.

The evaluation of the competitiveness of national entrepreneurship in Uzbekistan is conducted by comparing two alternatives: the existing approach to achieving and forecasting competitiveness based on antitrust tools and the proposed new approach based on a marketing toolkit.

To address the research question and measure the extent of the advantages that Uzbek enterprises gain from using marketing tools in the extended 7P marketing mix, the authors selected the econometric methods. The authors applied a correlation analysis to determine the degree of association between entrepreneurial competitiveness (CMP) as assessed by Knowledge for All (2025)), and, on one side, the conditions for doing business (PcGn) as evaluated by the World Bank (2025), which reflect the current approach, and on the other side, the implementation of marketing tools across the 7P areas: P1, P4, P5, and P6, as assessed by UNDP & MBRF (2024), as well as P2, P3, and P7, as evaluated by WIPO (2024).

The research sample includes 15 countries, including Uzbekistan, with approximately equal levels of national entrepreneurial competitiveness. The selection criterion for these countries was CMP scores ranging from 60 to 65 points (Uzbekistan's score is 62.45 points), as indicated in the global ranking by Knowledge for All (2025). This ensures that the data for the sampled countries are comparable, and studying this sample yields results and conclusions that are valid for Uzbekistan.

The highest CMP score in 2025, according to Knowledge for All (2025), is observed in Denmark at 80.62 points. The global average for this indicator is 53.64 points. Accordingly, the economic systems included in the sample of this research can be provisionally classified as countries with national entrepreneurial competitiveness above the global average. Empirical data for the countries in the research sample are presented in Table 1.

Table 1. Statistics for assessing and forecasting the competitiveness of national entrepreneurship in the sample countries in 2025

Country	Economic competitiveness (score 0–100)	Ease of doing business score (100 = best performance)	Firms with products and services new to the market (%)	Labor productivity growth (%)	Global brand value, top 5000 (% GDP)	Trade in digitally deliverable services (% total trade)	Firms constrained with inadequately educated workforce (%)	Ecological footprint per capita (global hectares)	Production and export complexity (score 0–100)
	CMP	PcGn	P1	P2	P3	P4	P5	P6	P7
China	63.93	77.28	0.0	5.4	9.5	43.5	96.6	75.1	76.4
Cyprus	61.98	73.35	68.5	1.8	0.0	70.3	61.9	73.9	52.7
Czech Republic	61.54	76.34	61.7	0.4	2.0	51.3	49.4	56.4	87.1
Estonia	62.07	80.62	50.8	0.2	1.0	51.0	71.2	37.8	68.0
Hungary	60.03	73.42	23.3	1.6	1.5	46.2	61.1	71.1	81.4
India	62.43	71.05	69.1	1.1	5.5	73.0	73.6	96.0	55.1
Indonesia	61.78	69.58	75.4	1.2	2.8	58.6	91.2	90.7	40.7
Malaysia	60.60	81.47	84.2	1.1	9.6	45.2	87.2	68.6	66.9
Moldova	60.67	74.36	57.7	0.5	0.0	30.3	46.6	86.3	43.6
Mongolia	61.47	67.77	91.2	1.3	0.0	24.2	82.4	39.2	12.5
Portugal	63.78	76.47	57.7	1.1	5.1	31.0	35.3	69.3	61.7
Saudi Arabia	62.93	70.87	100.0	-2.1	9.4	24.4	96.8	55.9	58.6
Serbia	63.78	75.65	47.2	2.8	0.0	54.6	67.8	74.3	61.3
Thailand	60.90	80.09	85.8	-0.5	7.9	29.7	97.0	84.5	71.2
Uzbekistan	62.45	69.88	67.2	3.9	0.2	8.6	90.7	87.0	38.6

Source: Developed by the authors based on the materials from the UNDP & MBRF (2024), WIPO (2024), and World Bank (2025)

The results of the correlation analysis obtained by processing the data from Table 1 are illustrated graphically in Figure 1.

Figure 1. Correlation with CMP, %

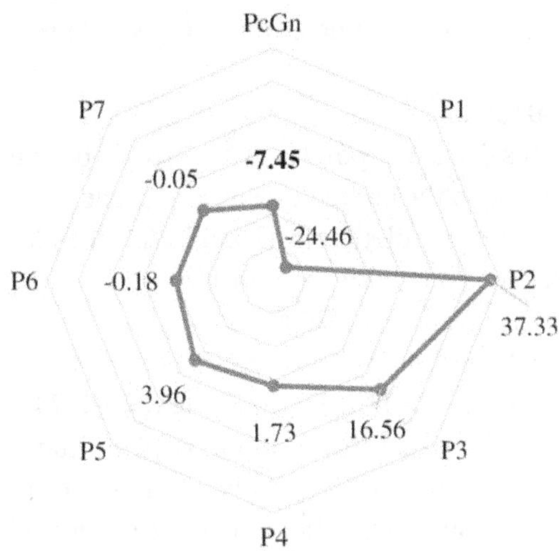

Source: Developed by the authors.

Figure 1 shows that improving the conditions for doing business does not enhance competitiveness in Uzbekistan, as the correlation between CMP and PcGn was positive yet only modest (7.45%). Meanwhile, the use of nearly all marketing tools within the extended 7P marketing mix demonstrated a positive relationship with the competitiveness of Uzbek entrepreneurship. The strongest positive correlation was observed with increased labor productivity (P2: 37.33%) and with the development and strengthening of global brands for national enterprises (P3: 16.56%).

A less pronounced (but still positive) correlation was found between the competitiveness of Uzbek enterprises and the recruitment of more qualified and competent employees, along with their corporate training (P5: 3.96%); the replacement or supplementation of traditional offline trade with e-commerce (P4: 1.73%); reducing the environmental footprint of entrepreneurial activities (P6: -0.185%); and simplifying production and export processes (P7: -0.05%). In contrast, the production and marketing of innovative products showed a negative association with the competitiveness of Uzbek enterprises.

Economic and Mathematical Model of Competitiveness of National Entrepreneurship in Uzbekistan

The authors used regression analysis to develop two alternative econometric models of entrepreneurial competitiveness in countries with a CMP above the global average in 2025. The first model relates the competitiveness of Uzbek enterprises to antitrust regulation:

CMP=63.6125-0.0216PcGn (1)

Model (1) indicates that a one-point improvement in business conditions leads to a 0.0216-point decrease in the competitiveness of Uzbek enterprises, highlighting the inefficacy of antitrust regulation in Uzbekistan. The alternative is the second model, which relates the competitiveness of Uzbek enterprises to their implementation of marketing tools across the 7P areas:

CMP=63.766+0.0005P1+0.362P2+0.157P3+

0.006P4-0.016P5-0.014P6-0.015P7, multiple R=0.5174 (2)

Model (2) demonstrates that the systemic implementation of marketing tools within the extended 7P marketing mix explains 51.74% of the competitiveness of Uzbek entrepreneurship. Specifically, a 1% increase in the production and marketing of innovative products (P1) raises competitiveness by 0.005 points; a 1% increase in labor productivity (P2) raises it by 0.362 points; a 1% increase in the strength of global brands among the top 5000 national enterprises (P3) raises it by 0.157 points; and a 1% increase in the share of e-commerce in foreign trade processes (P4) raises it by 0.006 points.

Conversely, a 1% reduction in the share of employees with inadequate education (P5) increases competitiveness by 0.016 points; a 1-unit decrease in the environmental footprint of entrepreneurship (P6) increases it by 0.014 points; and a one-point simplification of production and export processes (P7) increases it by 0.015 points.

Thus, the marketing toolkit more comprehensively explains the competitiveness of Uzbek entrepreneurship and offers broader opportunities for its forecasting. Therefore, this research adopts econometric model (3) of the competitiveness of national entrepreneurship in Uzbekistan as its forecasting basis.

A New Methodological Approach to Forecasting the Competitiveness of National Entrepreneurship in Uzbekistan Based on a Marketing Toolkit

To enhance the scientific and methodological framework for achieving and forecasting the competitiveness of national entrepreneurship in Uzbekistan, the authors proposed a new methodological approach based on a marketing toolkit and a statistical forecasting method. This approach is designed as a preferable alternative that overcomes the shortcomings of the existing antitrust-based method, which has demonstrated a limited contribution to the competitiveness of Uzbek entrepreneurship in 2025.

In the authors' approach, the areas of the extended marketing mix (7P) are ranked according to their importance in attaining and forecasting the competitiveness of Uzbek enterprises. The 7P areas are listed below in order of decreasing significance, along with the percentage differences between the results achieved by Uzbek enterprises and the sample arithmetic means:

- P2: Labor productivity growth (the result achieved in Uzbekistan is 3.90%, which exceeds the sample average of 1.32% by 195.45%);
- P3: Strengthening the global brands of the top 5000 national enterprises (the result in Uzbekistan is 0.20% of GDP, which is 94.50% below the sample average of 3.63% of GDP);
- P4: Development of e-commerce and the increase in its share in foreign trade (the result in Uzbekistan is 8.60%, which is 79.90% below the sample average of 42.79%);
- P6: Reduction of the environmental footprint of entrepreneurial activities (the result in Uzbekistan is 87.00 global hectares, which is 22.41% worse than the sample average of 71.07 global hectares);
- P7: Simplification of production and export processes (the result in Uzbekistan is 38.60 points, which is 33.89% better than the sample average of 58.39 points);
- P5: Reduction in the share of employees with inadequate education (the result in Uzbekistan is 90.70%, which is 22.70% below the sample average of 73.92%);
- P1: Production and marketing of innovative products (the result in Uzbekistan is 67.20%, which is 7.26% above the sample average of 62.65%).

Thus, the strengths of the competitiveness of Uzbek enterprises in 2025 lie in their outstanding performance in key areas of the extended marketing mix, such as rapid labor productivity growth (P2) and the simplification of production and export processes (P7). In the other 7P areas, achievements are modest and require further improvement. This conclusion reinforces the predictive potential of the new methodological approach and reflects the prospects for enhancing the competitiveness of national entrepreneurship in Uzbekistan.

SOLUTIONS AND RECOMMENDATIONS

In accordance with the new methodological approach for forecasting the competitiveness of national entrepreneurship in Uzbekistan based on a marketing toolkit, an authors' forecast of this competitiveness within the framework of the Digital Uzbekistan Economy Development Strategy until 2030 (President of the Republic of Uzbekistan, 2025a) has been retained to test the developed approach. The forecast is shown in Figure 2.

Figure 2. Forecast of competitiveness of Uzbek entrepreneurship based on marketing methodological tools

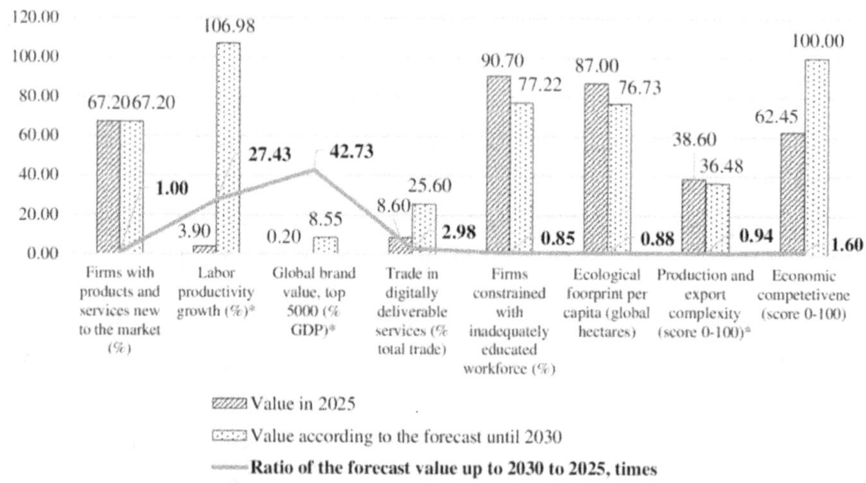

Source: Developed by the authors.

The forecast in Figure 2 is an optimization forecast because it reflects the potential to maximize the competitiveness of Uzbek enterprises through the optimization of their marketing activities in accordance with the model (2). According to this forecast, to increase the competitiveness of Uzbek entrepreneurship by 1.60 times (from 62.45 points in 2025 to 100.00 points by 2030), the following scientific and practical recommendations are proposed to enhance marketing activities within the extended 7P framework:

- P1: Maintain the share of produced and marketed innovative products at 67.20%;
- P2: Accelerate labor productivity growth by 27.43 times (from 3.90% in 2025 to 106.98% by 2030);

- P3: Strengthen the global brands of the top 5,000 national enterprises by 42.73 times (from 0.20% of GDP in 2025 to 8.555% of GDP by 2030);
- P4: Replace traditional offline trade with e-commerce, increasing its share in foreign trade processes by 2.98 times (from 8.605% in 2025 to 25.60% by 2030);
- P5: Attract more qualified and competent employees and provide corporate training, along with reducing the share of employees with inadequate education by 0.85 times (from 90.70% in 2025 to 77.22% by 2030);
- P6: Reduce the environmental footprint of entrepreneurial activities by 0.88 times (from 87.00 global hectares in 2025 to 76.73 global hectares by 2030);
- P7: Simplify production and export processes by 0.94 times (from 38.60 points in 2025 to 36.48 points by 2030).

Thus, the successful testing in Uzbekistan has demonstrated the broad potential of the enhanced methodological toolkit for forecasting enterprise competitiveness, encompassing the prediction of future competitive states and the provision of recommendations for achieving them through increased marketing activity.

Future Research Directions

The enhanced methodological toolkit for forecasting enterprise competitiveness, despite its successful testing on the example of Uzbek entrepreneurship in terms of assessing competitiveness in 2025 and forecasting it through 2030, requires further development. Particularly, it is recommended to re-examine the identified discrepancies in the relationship between the competitiveness of Uzbek enterprises and the conditions for doing business under the current approach, as well as with the production and marketing of innovative products and HR marketing under the new approach.

To clarify the true relationship between the statistical indicators CMP and PcGn in model (1), as well as between CMP and P1 and P5 in model (2), additional qualitative, especially case-based, studies are needed. Such studies should illuminate the practical experience of achieving and evolving the competitiveness of specific Uzbek enterprises over the years and explain the impacts of market conditions and marketing activities on this competitiveness.

It should also be noted that the results obtained in this research are valid only for countries with national entrepreneurial competitiveness above the global average – those with CMP scores between 60 and 65 points, including Uzbekistan, where CMP equals 62.45 points. Consequently, future research should pay attention to the experiences of other countries.

The experiences of countries with high (CMP exceeding 65 points) and low (CMP below 40 points) national entrepreneurial competitiveness, as well as those with competitiveness at the global average level (CMP from 50 to 60 points) and below the global average (CMP from 40 to 50 points), merit independent research. For each of these categories of national entrepreneurial competitiveness, it is necessary to develop an individual econometric model similar to model (2), which will allow for highly accurate forecasts of competitiveness in accordance with the authors' approach.

CONCLUSION

The results presented in this research contribute to the scientific findings of Anggara et al. (2025), Bogoviz et al. (2023), Ciambellini et al. (2025), Fang et al. (2024), Gou and Wang (2025), Heriqbaldi et al. (2025), Ibrahim et al. (2025), Kurowska-Pysz et al. (2024), Li et al. (2025), Sai et al. (2025), and Zhao et al. (2025), thereby complementing the concept of achieving and forecasting enterprise competitiveness. A comparative analysis of the alternative methodological toolkit for forecasting enterprise competitiveness, considering the results of its testing on Uzbek enterprises, is presented in Table 2.

Table 2. Alternative methodological toolkit for forecasting enterprise competitiveness and its testing in Uzbekistan

<table>
<tr><th rowspan="2">Approach</th><th rowspan="2">Toolkit within the approach</th><th rowspan="2">Representation in the published literature</th><th colspan="2">Relationship to the competitiveness of enterprises (CMP)</th></tr>
<tr><th>Correlation, %</th><th>Regression</th></tr>
<tr><td rowspan="2">Existing approach</td><td rowspan="2">PcGn: business environment</td><td rowspan="2">Ergasheva et al. (2025), Eshov et al. (2024), Kalieva (2012), Kobilov et al. (2023), Mkrtchyan et al. (2024), Tashbaev et al. (2024)</td><td>7.45</td><td>-0.021</td></tr>
<tr><td colspan="2">controversial</td></tr>
<tr><td rowspan="14">Proposed approach – marketing approach in the expanded 7P marketing mix</td><td rowspan="2">P1: production and realization of innovative products</td><td rowspan="2">Ratang (2025), Seddaoui et al. (2025)</td><td>-24.46</td><td>0.0005</td></tr>
<tr><td colspan="2">controversial</td></tr>
<tr><td rowspan="2">P2: growth of labor productivity</td><td rowspan="2">Goldmann and Knörzer (2023), Nurjannah et al. (2024)</td><td>37.33</td><td>0.362</td></tr>
<tr><td colspan="2">strong positive</td></tr>
<tr><td rowspan="2">P3: formation and strengthening of global brands of national enterprises</td><td rowspan="2">Almaguer et al. (2025), Przhedetsky et al. (2018)</td><td>16.56</td><td>0.157</td></tr>
<tr><td colspan="2">strong positive</td></tr>
<tr><td rowspan="2">P4: replacing or supplementing traditional offline commerce with e-commerce</td><td rowspan="2">Barquero-Chaves et al. (2025) Berlilana et al. (2025)</td><td>1.73</td><td>0.006</td></tr>
<tr><td colspan="2">moderate positive</td></tr>
<tr><td rowspan="2">P5: attracting more qualified and more competent employees to the company's team, as well as their corporate training</td><td rowspan="2">Andekina et al. (2024), Petrenko et al. (2024)</td><td>3.96</td><td>-0.016</td></tr>
<tr><td colspan="2">controversial</td></tr>
<tr><td rowspan="2">P6: reducing the ecological footprint of entrepreneurship</td><td rowspan="2">Asma Unnisa Begum and Kalpana (2025), Gyiazov et al. (2023)</td><td>-0.18</td><td>-0.014</td></tr>
<tr><td colspan="2">weak positive</td></tr>
<tr><td rowspan="2">P7: simplification of production and export</td><td rowspan="2">Litvinova et al. (2017)Neill and Dang (2025)</td><td>-0.05</td><td>-0.015</td></tr>
<tr><td colspan="2">weak positive</td></tr>
</table>

Source: Developed by the authors.

Based on the summarized data from Table 1, the conclusions drawn in this research are as follows. Unlike Ergasheva et al. (2025), Eshov et al. (2024), Kalieva (2012), Kobilov et al. (2023), Mkrtchyan et al. (2024), Tashbaev et al. (2024) the existing approach to achieving and forecasting the competitiveness of national entrepreneurship in Uzbekistan has limited capabilities and yields contradictory results, as the conditions for doing business (PcGn) demonstrated a positive correlation (7.45%) and a negative regression (-0.0021) with the competitiveness of Uzbek enterprises in 2025.

In its place, a new methodological approach for forecasting the competitiveness of national entrepreneurship in Uzbekistan is proposed based on a marketing toolkit. The authors' approach considers the following findings:

- A strong positive relationship between the competitiveness of Uzbek enterprises in 2025 and labor productivity growth (correlation with P2: 37.33%, regression with P2: 0.362 – confirming the findings of Goldmann and Knörzer (2023) and Nurjannah et al. (2024)), as well as the development and strengthening of global brands among top 5000 national enterprises (correlation with P3: 16.56%, regression with P3: 0.157 – confirming the findings of Almaguer et al. (2025) and Przhedetsky et al. (2018));
- A moderate positive relationship between the competitiveness of Uzbek enterprises in 2025 and the replacement or supplementation of traditional offline trade with e-commerce (correlation with P4: 1.73%, regression with P4: 0.006 – in contrast to the findings of Barquero-Chaves et al. (2025) and Berlilana et al., 2025);
- A weak positive relationship between the competitiveness of Uzbek enterprises in 2025 and the reduction of the environmental footprint of entrepreneurial activities (correlation with P6: -0.18%, regression with P6: -0.014 – in contrast to the findings of Asma Unnisa Begum and Kalpana (2025) and Gyiazov et al. (2023)), as well as the simplification of production and export processes (correlation with P7: -0.05%, regression with P7: -0.015 – in contrast to the findings of Litvinova et al. (2017) and Neill and Dang (2025));
- A contradictory relationship between the competitiveness of Uzbek enterprises in 2025 and HR marketing (correlation with P5: 3.96%, regression with P5: -0.016 – in contrast to Andekina et al. (2024) and Petrenko et al. (2024)), as well as with the production and marketing of innovative products (correlation with P1: -24.46%, regression with P1: 0.0005 – in contrast to Ratang (2025) and Seddaoui et al. (2025)).

The newly developed methodological approach for forecasting the competitiveness of national entrepreneurship in Uzbekistan, based on a marketing toolkit, comprises the following:

1. An econometric model of the relationship between the competitiveness of Uzbek enterprises and their implementation of marketing tools across the 7P areas in 2025;

2. An optimization forecast of the competitiveness of Uzbek entrepreneurship using the marketing toolkit through 2030;
3. A set of scientific and practical recommendations to enhance the marketing activities of Uzbek entrepreneurship across the extended 7P framework for implementing the forecast.

The practical significance of the new approach lies in its potential to adjust and improve the effectiveness of state regulation of national entrepreneurial competitiveness when stimulating the growth of national entrepreneurial structures and creating favorable conditions for enhancing the competitiveness of Uzbek enterprises, as directed by the President of the Republic of Uzbekistan (2025a; 2025b). The implementation of the new approach and the proposed recommendations in practice will enhance forecasting accuracy and more fully realize the growth potential of national entrepreneurship competitiveness in Uzbekistan through 2030

REFERENCES

Almaguer, J., Felix, R., & Harmeling, C. M. (2025). Emoji marketing: Toward a theory of brand paralinguistics. *International Journal of Research in Marketing*, *42*(1), 95–112. DOI: 10.1016/j.ijresmar.2024.06.002

Andekina, R., Rakhmetova, R., Kaliyeva, S., & Maxyutova, A. (2024). Entrepreneurial universities of the Republic of Kazakhstan: The essence and features of development. *Scientific Herald of Uzhhorod University. Series. Physics (College Park, Md.)*, *55*(55), 2690–2700. DOI: 10.54919/physics/55.2024.269an0

Anggara, A. A., Aryoko, Y. P., Dewandaru, R. O., Kharismasyah, A. Y., & Fatchan, I. N. (2025). Does maintaining resources, diversification, and internationalization matter for achieving high firm performance? A Sustainable competitiveness strategy for China Taipei firms. *Sustainability (Basel)*, *17*(4), 1576. DOI: 10.3390/su17041576

Asma Unnisa Begum, I., & Kalpana, R. (2025). Social media marketing effort in impacting the intention of purchase of green cosmetics by Indian consumers. *International Review of Management and Marketing*, *15*(2), 189–199. DOI: 10.32479/irmm.17391

Barquero-Chaves, G., Leiva, J. C., & Mora-Esquivel, R. (2025). Competitive domestic markets and marketing capabilities: The mediating effect of online presence in SMEs. *International Journal of Business Environment*, *16*(1), 19–38. DOI: 10.1504/IJBE.2025.143092

Berlilana, B., Hariguna, T., & El Emary, I. M. M. (2025). Enhancing digital marketing strategies with machine learning for analyzing key drivers of online advertising performance. *Journal of Applied Data Sciences*, *6*(2), 817–827. Retrieved March 13, 2025, from https://bright-journal.org/Journal/index.php/JADS/article/view/658. DOI: 10.47738/jads.v6i2.658

Bogoviz, A. V., Nosirov, J. T., Litvinova, T. N., & Ostrovskaya, V. N. (2023). Environmental Taxation as an Incentive to ESG Management of Green Business in Russia and Central Asia. In Popkova, E. G., & Sergi, B. S. (Eds.), *ESG Management of the Development of the Green Economy in Central Asia. Environmental Footprints and Eco-design of Products and Processes*. Springer., DOI: 10.1007/978-3-031-46525-3_8

Burkhanov, A. U., Kurbonbekova, M. T., Usmonov, B., & Nizomiddinov, J. Z. (2024), "Assessment of the Financial Sustainability of Enterprises: The Case of Uzbekistan", Eshov, M.P., Abdurakhmanova, G.K., Burkhanov, A.U., Abdusalomova, N.B. and Ergasheva, S.T. (Ed.) *Development of International Entrepreneurship Based on Corporate Accounting and Reporting According to IFRS (Advanced Series in Management, Vol. 33B)*, Emerald Publishing Limited, Leeds, pp. 215-223. DOI: 10.1108/S1877-63612024000033B027

Ciambellini, G., D'Adamo, I., Gastaldi, M., & Smol, M. (2025). Sustainability and competitiveness: Economic analysis of a photovoltaic plant with storage in an Italian textile company. *Innovation and Green Development*, *4*(2), 100209. DOI: 10.1016/j.igd.2025.100209

Daribekova, N. S., Sanovich, M. A., Savelyeva, N. K., Dugina, T. A., & Smetanina, A. I. (2023). Roadmap for the transition from digital agriculture to agriculture 4.0 based on deep learning in the economy of the future by 2030. In Popkova, E. G., & Sergi, B. S. (Eds.), *Food security in the economy of the future: Transition from digital agriculture to agriculture 4.0 based on deep learning* (pp. 123–130). Palgrave Macmillan., DOI: 10.1007/978-3-031-23511-5_13

Ergasheva, S. T., Razikova, G. S., Umarova, M. A., Nabixodjayev, A. A., & Salikhodjaeva, U. A. (2025). Labor market development in the Republic of Uzbekistan: Implications for quality. *International Journal of Qualitative Research, 19*(1), 183–198. DOI: 10.24874/IJQR19.01-12

Eshov, M. P., Abdurakhmanova, G. K., Burkhanov, A. U., Abdusalomova, N. B., & Ergasheva, S. T. (2024), "Contribution of Corporate Accounting and IFRS Reporting to Improving International Business Management: Introduction", Eshov, M.P., Abdurakhmanova, G.K., Burkhanov, A.U., Abdusalomova, N.B. and Ergasheva, S.T. (Ed.) *Development of International Entrepreneurship Based on Corporate Accounting and Reporting According to IFRS (Advanced Series in Management, Vol. 33A)*, Emerald Publishing Limited, Leeds, pp. 1-3. DOI: 10.1108/S1877-63612024000033A029

Fan, L., Song, Z., Mao, W., Mao, W., Luo, T., Wang, W., & Cao, F. (2024). Change is safer: A dynamic safety stock model for inventory management of large manufacturing enterprise based on intermittent time series forecasting. *Journal of Intelligent Manufacturing*. Advance online publication. DOI: 10.1007/s10845-024-02442-y

Fang, T. M., Ahmad, N. H., Halim, H. A., Iqbal, Q., & Ramayah, T. (2024). Pathway towards SME competitiveness: Digital capability and digital business model innovation. *Technology in Society*, *79*, 102728. DOI: 10.1016/j.techsoc.2024.102728

Gaurav, A., Gupta, B. B., Bansal, S., & Psannis, K. E. (2025). Bankruptcy forecasting in enterprises and its security using hybrid deep learning models. *Cyber Security and Applications*, *3*, 100070. DOI: 10.1016/j.csa.2024.100070

Goldmann, S., & Knörzer, M. (2023). Technology advancement propels work productivity: Empirical efficiency potential determination in marketing and sales. *MDE. Managerial and Decision Economics*, *44*(4), 1962–1977. DOI: 10.1002/mde.3793

Gou, X., & Wang, S. (2025). How does the anti-trust policy stimulate firms' product market competitiveness? Evidence from the implementation of the Anti-trust Law. *Finance Research Letters*, *77*, 107062. DOI: 10.1016/j.frl.2025.107062

Gyiazov, A. T., Gamulinskaya, N. V., Markeev, S. A., & Popkova, Z. V. (2023). Case experience of conducting climate-responsible entrepreneurship in the digital economy markets in Russia. In Popkova, E. G. (Ed.), *Smart green innovations in industry 4.0* (pp. 97–109). Springer., DOI: 10.1007/978-3-031-45830-9_11

Heriqbaldi, U., Esquivias, M. A., Lau, W., & Cesilia, A. F. (2025). Export promotion programs and firm performance: Linking knowledge, commitment, and market strategy to enhance competitiveness. *Journal of Open Innovation*, *11*(1), 100479. DOI: 10.1016/j.joitmc.2025.100479

Ibrahim, A. A., Ahmad, S. Z., & Abu Bakar, A. R. (2025). Impact of competitive intelligence on firm sustainable competitiveness and performance: Strategic design collaboration's mediating role. *Management Research Review*, *48*(2), 231–257. DOI: 10.1108/MRR-04-2024-0280

Kalieva, S. A. (2012). Integration capacity of Kazakhstan and Russia. *Ekonomika regiona* [Economy of Regions], *4*, 227-233. DOI: 10.17059/2012-4-27

Knowledge for All. (2025). *Economic competitiveness: Country ranking*. Retrieved March 13, 2025, from https://www.knowledge4all.com/ranking?Id=59&Color=A1A881

Kobilov, A. U., Bozorov, J. R., Rajabov, Sh. B., Abdulakhatov, M. M., & Sapaev, I. B. (2023). Development of the digital economy in the Republic of Uzbekistan. *E3S Web of Conferences, 402*, 08038. DOI: 10.1051/e3sconf/202340208038

Kumar, A., Shankar, A., Shaik, A. S., Jain, G., & Malibari, A. (2025). Risking it all in the metaverse ecosystem: Forecasting resistance towards the enterprise metaverse. *Information Technology & People*, *38*(1), 198–218. DOI: 10.1108/ITP-04-2023-0374

Kurowska-Pysz, J., Czart, P., & Kot, S. (2024). Familiness as a determinant of competitiveness of family businesses – The organisational effectiveness-based approach. *Journal of Competitiveness*, *16*(2), 182–209.

Li, W., Liu, X., & Zhou, L. (2025). The role of digital finance in enhancing export competitiveness: Insights from China's listed companies. *Finance Research Letters*, *71*, 106376. DOI: 10.1016/j.frl.2024.106376

Litvinova, T. N., Kulikova, E. S., Kuznetsov, V. P., & Taranov, P. M. (2017). Marketing as a determinant of the agricultural machinery market development. In Popkova, E. (Ed.), *Overcoming uncertainty of institutional environment as a tool of global crisis management* (pp. 465–471). Springer., DOI: 10.1007/978-3-319-60696-5_59

Mkrtchyan, T. M., Rashidov, R. R., Krutilin, A. A., & Tazhiyev, R. O. (2024). Regulation and enforcement of human rights, transparency, data protection, ethics of technology, and data use in the context of digital transformation. In Popkova, E. G. (Ed.), *Digital inclusiveness: Bridging the divide in the digital economy* (pp. 75–86). World Scientific Publishing., DOI: 10.1142/9789811270826_0007

Neill, S., & Dang, L. (2025). The integration of entrepreneurial marketing processes and controls. *Journal of Research in Marketing and Entrepreneurship*. DOI: 10.1108/JRME-06-2024-0138

Nurjannah, N., Yunus, M. H., Nurimansjah, R. A., & Erwina, E. (2024). Total quality management and productivity performance of SMEs: The moderating effect of marketing strategy. *Quality - Access to Success*, *25*(199), 272–278. DOI: 10.47750/QAS/25.199.30

Omanov, S., Usmonov, B., & Tashbaev, B. (2024), "Improving the Analysis of Profitability Indicators of Joint-Stock Company", Eshov, M.P., Abdurakhmanova, G.K., Burkhanov, A.U., Abdusalomova, N.B. and Ergasheva, S.T. (Ed.) *Development of International Entrepreneurship Based on Corporate Accounting and Reporting According to IFRS (Advanced Series in Management, Vol. 33A),* Emerald Publishing Limited, Leeds, pp. 213-219. DOI: 10.1108/S1877-63612024000033A025

Petrenko, Y. S., Burkhanov, A. U., Bukalerova, L. A., & Ustenko, V. S. (2024). Counter-Cyclical Approach to Change Management in Banks for the Sustainable Development of the Financial System. *Global Journal of Flexible Systems Managment*, *25*(S1, Suppl 1), 31–47. DOI: 10.1007/s40171-023-00362-z

President of the Republic of Uzbekistan. (2025a). *Decree "On approval of the Strategy 'Digital Uzbekistan-2030' and measures for its effective implementation"* (October 5, 2020 No. DP-6079 as amended on November 14, 2024). Tashkent, Uzbekistan. Retrieved March 13, 2025, from https://online.zakon.kz/Document/?doc_id=39012756

President of the Republic of Uzbekistan. (2025b). *Decree "On additional measures for further development of competitive environment and reduction of state participation the economy"* (July 6, 2020 No. DP-6019, in the edition of the Decrees of the President of the Republic of Uzbekistan from March 17, 2022 No. DP-89, July 6, 2023 No. DP-108). Tashkent, Uzbekistan. Retrieved March 13, 2025, from https://base.spinform.ru/show_doc.fwx?rgn=138760

Przhedetsky, Y. V., Przhedetskaya, N. V., Przhedetskaya, V. Y., Bondarenko, V. A., & Borzenko, K. V. (2018). The role of social-ethical marketing and information and communication technologies in response to challenges of oncology. *European Research Studies*, *21*(Special Issue 1, SI1), 377–386. DOI: 10.35808/ersj/1188

Ratang, W. (2025). Entrepreneurship, market orientation and marketing performance in culinary business: Mediating effects of innovation and competitive advantage. *Journal of Information Systems Engineering & Management*, *10*(5s), 234–243. DOI: 10.52783/jisem.v10i5s.608

Sai, F., Zhu, G., Qin, Z., & Zheng, L. (2025). Linking technological relatedness to firm innovation: The moderating roles of environmental dynamism, competitiveness and enterprise life cycle. *Baltic Journal of Management*, *20*(1), 52–71. DOI: 10.1108/BJM-08-2024-0435

Seddaoui, R., Abdullah, S. S., Ahmad, S., & Gorundutse, A. H. (2025). Influence of marketing innovation and advanced technologies on firm performance: The case of Algeria. *Journal of Advanced Research in Applied Sciences and Engineering Technology*, *48*(2), 183–196. DOI: 10.37934/araset.48.2.183196

Tashbaev, B., Usmonov, B., & Omanov, S. (2024), "Analysis of Public Debt Policy and Its Effectiveness in Uzbekistan", Eshov, M.P., Abdurakhmanova, G.K., Burkhanov, A.U., Abdusalomova, N.B. and Ergasheva, S.T. (Ed.) *Development of International Entrepreneurship Based on Corporate Accounting and Reporting According to IFRS (Advanced Series in Management, Vol. 33B)*, Emerald Publishing Limited, Leeds, pp. 191-195. DOI: 10.1108/S1877-63612024000033B024

UNDP & MBRF. (2024). Global Knowledge Index 2024. Retrieved March 13, 2025, from https://www.undp.org/arab-states/publications/global-knowledge-index-2024

Usmonov, B. (2024), "Evaluation of Efficiency of Capital Management in Joint-Stock Companies in the Chemical Sector: The Case of Uzbekistan", Eshov, M.P., Abdurakhmanova, G.K., Burkhanov, A.U., Abdusalomova, N.B. and Ergasheva, S.T. (Ed.) *Development of International Entrepreneurship Based on Corporate Accounting and Reporting According to IFRS (Advanced Series in Management, Vol. 33B),* Emerald Publishing Limited, Leeds, pp. 67-74. DOI: 10.1108/S1877-63612024000033B009

Wang, L., Chen, L., Jin, S., & Li, C. (2025). Forecasting the green behaviour level of Chinese enterprises: A conjoined application of the autoregressive integrated moving average (ARIMA) model and multi-scenario simulation. *Technology in Society*, *81*, 102825. DOI: 10.1016/j.techsoc.2025.102825

WIPO. (2024). *Global Innovation Index 2024: Unlocking the promise of social entrepreneurship* (17th ed.). Geneva, Switzerland: WIPO. Retrieved March 13, 2025, from https://www.wipo.int/web-publications/global-innovation-index-2024/assets/67729/2000%20Global%20Innovation%20Index%202024_WEB3lite.pdf

World Bank. (2025). *Ease of doing business score (0 = lowest performance to 100 = best performance).* Retrieved March 13, 2025, from https://data.worldbank.org/indicator/IC.BUS.DFRN.XQ?view=chart

Yang, C., Yan, J., & Wang, G. (2024). Time series trends forecasting for manufacturing enterprises in the digital age. *Journal of Organizational and End User Computing*, *36*(1), 1–22. DOI: 10.4018/JOEUC.345242

Yuldashev, T. K., Qodirov, N. N., Eshov, M. P., & Abdurakhmanova, G. K. (2024). Optimal control problems for the Whitham type nonlinear differential equations with impulse effects. In: Azimov, D. (Ed.), *Proceedings of the IUTAM Symposium on Optimal Guidance and Control for Autonomous Systems 2023* (pp. 205-217). Cham, Switzerland: Springer. DOI: 10.1007/978-3-031-39303-7_25

Zhang, Y., Wang, J., Sun, J., Sun, R., & Qin, D. (2025). Power load forecasting system of iron and steel enterprises based on deep kernel–multiple kernel joint learning. *Processes (Basel, Switzerland)*, *13*(2), 584. DOI: 10.3390/pr13020584

Zhao, J., Hu, P., & Cui, L. (2025). Economic and non-economic impact of digital transformation on ehnterprise competitiveness: Evidence from Chinese-listed companies. *Technology Analysis and Strategic Management*, 1–17. Advance online publication. DOI: 10.1080/09537325.2025.2467927

ADDITIONAL READING

Amer, A. D. A., Korshunova, E., Saady, W. A., & Wang, H. (2025). Navigating the competitive landscape: A comprehensive model to evaluate competitiveness for enterprises in electromechanical systems engineerings. *Brazilian Business Review*, *22*, e20231674. DOI: 10.15728/bbr.2023.1674.en

Budiman, N. A., Mulyani, S., Fithri, D. L., Gunawan, B., & Nugraha, F. (2025). Business model canvas and competitiveness on financial performance of MSMEs. *Journal of Lifestyle and SDG's Review*, *5*(1), e01617. DOI: 10.47172/2965-730X.SDGsReview.v5.n01.pe01617

Díaz-Cruces, E., Rocasolano, M. M., & Colmenárez, P. J. M. (2025). Corporate sustainability: A strategic pillar for sustainable development and business competitiveness. *European Public and Social Innovation Review*, *10*, 1–18. DOI: 10.31637/epsir-2025-795

Inegbedion, H. E., Thikan, P. R., David, J. O., Ajani, J. O., & Peter, F. O. (2024). Small and medium enterprise (SME) competitiveness and employment creation: The mediating role of SME growth. *Humanities & Social Sciences Communications*, *11*(1), 11. DOI: 10.1057/s41599-023-02434-y

Li, C., Yang, G., Cai, W., & Shi, H. (2025). Enterprise digital transformation and green competitiveness: Opportunity or crisis? *Finance Research Letters*, *77*, 107051. DOI: 10.1016/j.frl.2025.107051

Meier, A., Eller, R., & Peters, M. (2025). Creating competitiveness in incumbent small- and medium-sized enterprises: A revised perspective on digital transformation. *Journal of Business Research*, *186*, 115028. DOI: 10.1016/j.jbusres.2024.115028

Naz, M., Maroof, Z., Naheed, R., & Jawad, M. (2025). Climate bond issuance and enterprise EESM competitiveness: Steps toward environmental and climate-responsible development. *Journal of Cleaner Production*, *493*, 144769. DOI: 10.1016/j.jclepro.2025.144769

Nkwinika, S. E. R., & Obokoh, L. O. (2025). Business skills, corporate governance, and competitiveness of small businesses in South Africa. *International Review of Management and Marketing*, *15*(1), 159–167. DOI: 10.32479/irmm.17064

Tao, X., & Cai, W. (2025). The impact of digital finance on export competitiveness: Evidence from Chinese manufacturing enterprises. *Finance Research Letters*, *73*, 106629. DOI: 10.1016/j.frl.2024.106629

Wang, Z., Gao, L., & Wang, W. (2025). The impact of supply chain digitization and logistics efficiency on the competitiveness of industrial enterprises. *International Review of Economics & Finance*, *97*, 103759. DOI: 10.1016/j.iref.2024.103759

KEY TERMS AND DEFINITIONS

Enterprise competitiveness: its market position, the success with which the enterprise defends its interests in competitive struggles, qualitatively expressed by its attractiveness as a partner (for purchasing its products, investing in its development, and integrating into joint supply and distribution chains) compared to competitors (i.e., other market players) and quantitatively measured by overall and export sales, market share, and profit.

Achieving enterprise competitiveness: improving the market position as a dynamic characteristic of the enterprise by realizing its development potential and optimizing external factors, namely, the actions of competitors and other market players (i.e., the overall market conditions).

Assessment of enterprise competitiveness: determining the current market position of an enterprise in comparison with competitors, considering the subjectivity inherent in that an enterprise with identical product qualities and business activities may exhibit varying levels of competitiveness across different markets.

Forecasting enterprise competitiveness: formulating well-founded projections regarding the future competitiveness of an enterprise.

State regulation of the competitiveness of national entrepreneurship: stimulating the growth of national entrepreneurial structures' competitiveness and creating favorable macroeconomic conditions for this purpose.

Antitrust toolkit for forecasting entrepreneurial competitiveness: antitrust regulation aimed at maintaining a highly competitive market environment that naturally incentivizes the growth of national enterprises' competitiveness.

Marketing toolkit for achieving and forecasting the competitiveness of entrepreneurial structures: the manifestation of these structures' initiatives and the active implementation of corresponding corporate marketing measures, particularly within the extended marketing mix (7P), to enhance their competitiveness.

Expert forecasting method for enterprise competitiveness: the intuitive formulation of forecasts based on available industry reviews, corporate information, the forecaster's expectations, and official and unofficial data on the current and future state of the market and enterprise, albeit characterized by the subjective nature of the resulting forecasts.

Forecasting enterprise competitiveness based on past experience: extending current trends into future periods using qualitative and quantitative information about the enterprise's activities and market conditions, from which the forecaster, through comprehensive analysis, identifies trends in the evolution of the enterprise's competitiveness over a given period that is then assumed to persist unchanged in the future.

Statistical method for forecasting enterprise competitiveness: the predominant analysis of quantitative data to identify patterns in the changes of variables, which are integrated into a comprehensive econometric model that simplistically reflects the nature of competitiveness and its evolution, including causes and effects, while emphasizing the most critical conditions.

Chapter 8 The Development and Enhancement of a Balanced Scorecard System in Management Accounting of an Enterprise

Ibroximjon Tursunaliyev
https://orcid.org/0009-0004-3267-6213
Tashkent State University of Economics, Uzbekistan

Ikram Davletov
https://orcid.org/0000-0002-8311-7890
Tashkent State University of Economics, Uzbekistan

Golib Tashmanov
https://orcid.org/0000-0002-4885-3286
Tashkent State University of Economics, Uzbekistan

Jaloliddin Suyunov
https://orcid.org/0009-0003-4689-162X
Tashkent State University of Economics, Uzbekistan

Rustam Xolpulotov
https://orcid.org/0009-0003-6662-1715
Tashkent State University of Economics, Uzbekistan

DOI: 10.4018/979-8-3693-8362-9.ch008

ABSTRACT

A popular strategic management tool for converting an organization's vision and strategy into attainable goals and performance indicators is the Balanced Scorecard (BSC). Traditionally, the BSC has focused on four primary perspectives: financial, customer, internal processes, and learning and growth. However, as business environments evolve and organizations face increasing pressures to maintain operational excellence, manage costs efficiently, and adhere to regulatory requirements, it has become necessary to enhance the traditional BSC framework. This research proposes developing and enhancing the BSC system by incorporating two additional perspectives: quality and compliance and cost management. Organizations are empowered to align strategic objectives across departments and make well-informed decisions thanks to this improved BSC framework.

INTRODUCTION

In today's fast-paced and increasingly complex business environment, organizations are confronted with the challenge of measuring and managing performance across multiple dimensions. Traditional financial metrics (e.g., profit margins, return on investment (ROI), and revenue growth) have long been the cornerstone of performance evaluation in management accounting. However, these metrics often fail to provide a comprehensive view of an organization's overall health, particularly in relation to its long-term strategic goals, innovation, customer satisfaction, and internal capabilities. As a result, organizations are seeking more holistic approaches to performance measurement that incorporate financial and non-financial metrics.

To address this issue, Robert Kaplan and David Norton introduced the Balanced Scorecard (BSC) in the early 1990s as a tool for strategic management. The BSC provides a comprehensive framework that integrates internal processes, customer perspectives, learning and growth initiatives, and financial outcomes. A more accurate evaluation of short-term outcomes and long-term viability is made possible by this multifaceted approach, which enables firms to match their performance measurement systems with their strategic objectives.

Over the years, the BSC has been widely adopted by businesses, nonprofits, and government agencies worldwide. However, its development and implementation have often been met with challenges, especially when attempting to adapt the BSC framework to an organization's specific needs and changing external environments. The importance of management accounting in assisting with strategic decision-making and performance enhancement only increases as companies continue to change. In this regard, companies looking to improve the alignment between strategy creation and execution must build and improve the BSC system in management accounting.

BACKGROUND

In the early 1990s, Robert Kaplan and David Norton created the Balanced Scorecard (BSC) to overcome the limitations of traditional performance assessment approaches. At that time, most businesses relied heavily on financial metrics to evaluate their success. Although these metrics provided an understanding of past performance, they frequently failed to capture the non-financial elements essential for achieving long-term objectives (e.g., customer satisfaction, operational efficiency, and organizational learning).

Over time, the BSC became widely recognized as a flexible tool for aligning an organization's strategic goals with quantifiable results. It emphasizes the following four primary perspectives:

- Financial: Evaluates financial performance and profitability;
- Customer: Measures customer satisfaction and loyalty;
- Internal processes: Monitors operational efficiency and process enhancements;
- Learning and growth: Focuses on employee development, innovation, and organizational culture.

However, as industries evolved and businesses faced increasing challenges (e.g., globalization, technological advancements, and regulatory demands), the original four perspectives of the BSC began to show some limitations. Particularly, industries like metal production, which operate in highly competitive and regulated environments, require a more tailored approach to performance measurement.

For companies like "Uzmetkombinat" JSC, operating in the metal production sector comes with unique challenges, including the following:

- Maintaining high product quality to meet customer demands and industry standards;
- Complying with strict regulations at local, regional, and international levels;
- Controlling costs amidst fluctuating raw material and energy prices;
- Balancing immediate financial targets with long-term growth and sustainability.

These challenges highlight the need for a more comprehensive performance measurement framework. Enhancing the BSC with two additional perspectives (quality and compliance and cost management) can better address the specific needs of metal producers.

1. Quality and compliance perspective:
    - Focuses on producing reliable, high-quality products while adhering to industry regulations;
    - Helps build trust with customers and reduces risks associated with non-compliance.
2. Cost management perspective:
    - Prioritizes efficient use of resources, waste reduction, and process optimization;
    - Aligns cost-control measures with the company's strategic objectives to ensure profitability.

This research aims to improve the traditional BSC by tailoring it to the unique demands of metal producers like "Uzmetkombinat" JSC. By adding new perspectives, the enhanced BSC offers the following:

- A more detailed and relevant view of organizational performance;
- Improved alignment of strategic goals with day-to-day operations;
- Practical tools for managing costs, maintaining quality, and ensuring compliance.

Ultimately, the enhanced BSC framework provides organizations with a powerful tool for decision-making and strategic planning, helping them thrive in an increasingly complex and competitive global market.

The main focus of this chapter is to explore how the Balanced Scorecard (BSC) framework can be developed and enhanced to better serve industries like metal production, particularly in the field of management accounting. It examines the limitations of the traditional BSC model and highlights the need for a more customized approach that has emerged to address the complex and evolving challenges of contemporary business environments.

Key areas covered are as follows:

1. Identifying the gaps in the traditional BSC:
    - This section begins by exploring the foundational four perspectives of the BSC (financial, customer, internal processes, and learning and

growth) and highlights their effectiveness as a framework for performance management;
  - However, it points out that this traditional model often falls short in addressing specific industry needs, such as adhering to compliance standards, ensuring quality, and maintaining rigorous cost control measures.
2. The rationale for enhancing the BSC:
   - This section introduces the concept of expanding the BSD by incorporating two additional perspectives:
     - Quality and compliance: Focused on ensuring organizations adhere to regulatory standards, maintain high product quality, and build customer trust;
     - Cost management: To optimize resource allocation, control costs, and align these efforts with the company's broader goals. These enhancements aim to fill the gaps in the traditional framework and make it more relevant to industries with complex operational and regulatory demands.
3. Relevance to metal producers:
   - The chapter focuses on the unique challenges faced by companies like "Uzmetkombinat" JSC, such as ensuring high-quality production, adhering to strict regulations, and maintaining cost efficiency in a competitive market;
   - It explains how these challenges create a need for a more customized performance measurement framework.
4. Benefits of an improved BSC framework:
   - The enhanced BSC offers a more comprehensive approach to performance management by including non-financial metrics like quality control, compliance tracking, and cost efficiency;
   - It supports better decision-making, fosters strategic alignment across departments, and promotes continuous improvement in key areas.
5. Real-world application:
   - The chapter provides practical examples and insights into how the enhanced BSC can be applied in manufacturing and metal production industries;
   - It also discusses how "Uzmetkombinat" JSC can implement this updated framework to address its strategic and operational goals effectively.

The objective of this chapter is to illustrate the necessity for the traditional BSC to adapt and show how incorporating the quality and compliance and cost management perspectives can enhance its effectiveness and comprehensiveness. By aligning performance measurement with industry-specific needs, this enhanced

BSC framework can help organizations navigate contemporary challenges, improve decision-making, and achieve short-term and long-term success.

Literature Review

The BSC is grounded in several key theoretical concepts, particularly those related to strategic management, performance measurement, and organizational alignment. One of the core concepts is strategy execution, which refers to the alignment of the BSC with an organization's strategic goals. According to Kaplan and Norton (1996), the BSC provides a mechanism for aligning operational activities with strategic priorities. It encourages organizations to assess performance beyond financial indicators, emphasizing critical areas that drive future growth (e.g., customer satisfaction, operational efficiency, and employee development). Furthermore, the BSC is aligned with the concept of performance management. Neely et al. (1995) argue that performance management systems should measure outcomes and focus on leading indicators that drive future performance. The BSC addresses this by linking lagging financial outcomes with leading indicators from other perspectives. Incorporating the BSC into management accounting signifies a transition from conventional, finance-centric performance measurement systems to a more holistic and balanced approach to performance management. Management accounting traditionally focused on cost management, budgeting, and financial reporting (Anthony, 1965). However, as organizations became more complex, there was a growing need for performance systems that could address non-financial factors, such as customer satisfaction and internal process efficiency (Kaplan & Norton, 1992).

Gimbert, Bisbe, and Mendoza (2010) highlight that the BSC offers management accountants a way to integrate non-financial measures into their decision-making processes. In doing so, it provides a more holistic view of organizational performance. Chenhall and Langfield-Smith (2007) emphasize the role of the BSC in helping organizations to better allocate resources, monitor key performance indicators (KPIs), and ensure alignment between daily operations and long-term strategy. For instance, a manufacturing company might evaluate cost efficiency through financial metrics. It also monitors customer satisfaction (customer perspective) and internal operational efficiency (process perspective) to identify areas for enhancement. The addition of the Learning and Growth perspective allows the BSC to address long-term organizational capabilities and innovation, fostering a forward-looking approach to performance management. The BSC has seen widespread application across sectors, including private businesses and public organizations, with numerous case studies highlighting its success. In the private sector, Niven (2002) discusses how companies in industries (e.g., manufacturing, retail, and services) have effectively implemented the BSC to align their operational outcomes with strategic goals.

For instance, Matos and Hall (2007) shows that the BSC helped Royal Dutch Shell better align its global operations with its strategic goals of growth and sustainability.

In the public sector, the BSC has been used to improve service delivery and accountability. Marr and Schiuma (2003) explore how local government agencies in the UK adapted the BSC to monitor performance, focusing on customer satisfaction and internal process efficiency, rather than just financial performance. This was particularly beneficial in areas like healthcare, where the public value and stakeholder engagement were critical. Kaplan and Norton (2001) also explored how the BSC can be adapted to fit non-profit organizations. They argued that in non-profits, where financial measures are often secondary, the BSC helps align mission-driven goals with performance measurement (e.g., impact on beneficiaries and the efficiency of operations). While the BSC has been widely adopted, its implementation is not without challenges. One of the primary criticisms of the BSC is its complexity and the difficulty of defining meaningful and actionable metrics across the four perspectives (Malina & Selto, 2001). Developing the right set of KPIs that align with strategic goals can be a daunting task, especially in large or decentralized organizations.

Ittner and Larcker (2003) argue that the challenge of alignment between the various perspectives of the BSC can lead to difficulties in translating strategic objectives into specific actions. For instance, organizations may struggle to balance short-term financial objectives with long-term customer or learning and growth goals. They also suggest that the BSC can sometimes become a checklist of disconnected metrics, rather than a tool that genuinely drives strategy. Another key challenge highlighted in the literature is the need for customization of the BSC to specific organizational contexts. Neely et al. (2002) argue that the BSC does not follow a universal template; its successful implementation typically involves customizing the framework to align with the organization's distinct features, industry context, and strategic objectives. Customization can involve revising the perspectives, changing the KPIs, or integrating additional performance measures related to sustainability, innovation, or digital transformation.

In recent years, organizations have faced new challenges with digital transformation and data integration. The advent of big data and advanced analytics has led to calls for enhancing the BSC to include real-time data collection and analysis (Dubey et al., 2019). Integrating real-time analytics can help businesses respond faster to market changes. It requires significant changes to data infrastructure and systems. To address the evolving needs of organizations, researchers have proposed various enhancements to the BSC, especially with the advent of new technologies. Sydow et al. (2020) argue that the integration of big data and predictive analytics into the BSC could provide organizations with more actionable insights, enabling them to anticipate changes in customer demand or operational inefficiencies before they occur. In a similar vein, Chavan (2009) highlights how contemporary enterprise resource planning (ERP) systems and performance dashboards enhance BSC implementation by simplifying data collection, increasing data accuracy, and offering managers real-time performance insights. This integration enhances decision-making while enabling ongoing monitoring and refinement of the BSC.

Another enhancement that has gained traction in recent years is the integration of sustainability metrics within the BSC framework. With a growing emphasis on corporate social responsibility (CSR) and sustainable practices, the BSC can be tailored to incorporate environmental, social, and governance (ESG) performance metrics (Epstein & Roy, 2001). This adaptation enables businesses to meet increasing stakeholder demands for transparency regarding their environmental and social impact.

In conclusion, the BSC has established itself as a powerful tool in management accounting, providing organizations with a holistic framework to align their strategic goals with quantifiable results. Despite its widespread adoption, there remain challenges in its implementation and use, particularly in terms of complexity, customization, and integration with advanced technologies. This literature review has highlighted the evolution of the BSC from a simple performance measurement tool to a more dynamic, technology-driven system. The next chapter will build upon these insights by exploring the methodology for enhancing the BSC within contemporary management accounting practices, with a focus on integrating new technologies and improving alignment with organizational strategy.

Methodology

Data-collection, observational, and grouping approaches were used in the study.

Information from the State Statistics Committee of the Republic of Uzbekistan, the joint-stock corporation "Uzmetkombinat," as well as Uzbek library catalogs and online resources, are used in relation to the study issue. Additionally, databases of international organizations, scholarly articles, information-analytical bulletins, government reports, and Internet resources are used.

RESULTS AND DISCUSSION

In the manufacturing industry, the BSC is often used to balance cost control with operational efficiency and product quality (Kaplan, 1990). Manufacturing companies use the internal process perspective to focus on production efficiency, waste reduction, and cycle time improvements. The customer perspective focuses on key factors such as product quality, delivery timelines, and customer satisfaction. In addition, manufacturing companies utilize the learning and growth perspective to prioritize investments in employee training and advanced technology, aiming to improve production capabilities.

A prominent example is the metal production industry, where companies have adopted the Balanced Scorecard (BSC) to streamline production costs and improve operational efficiency. These firms track financial metrics such as cost per ton of metal produced, while also monitoring scrap reduction rates and energy efficiency under the internal process perspective. The customer perspective focuses on customer satisfaction with product quality and delivery timelines.

Moreover, to improve efficiency, it is necessary to include two more perspectives for BSC. The first additional perspective is the quality and compliance perspective. This perspective is particularly significant for metal-producing companies, given their emphasis on maintaining product quality, ensuring regulatory compliance, and adhering to strict industry standards. In the metal industry, quality issues can lead to significant financial losses, safety risks, and reputational damage. This perspective focuses on ensuring that processes and products meet rigorous internal and external standards, as well as ensuring compliance with regulatory requirements.

This perspective centers on maintaining high product standards, meeting customer specifications, and adhering to industry regulations. It ensures the company produces reliable and high-quality metal products while complying with legal and regulatory frameworks, which is essential for maintaining customer trust, minimizing waste, and avoiding penalties (Table 1).

Table 1. Application of Quality and Compliance Perspective in "Uzmetkombinat" JSC

Perspective	Objectives	Key Performance Indicators (KPIs)	Strategic goals:
Quality and Compliance **perspective**	Provide products or services that reliably fulfill or surpass customer expectations	Product quality metrics	• Strive to be an acknowledged industry leader in quality and compliance, establishing standards of excellence • Ensure complete adherence to all relevant local, regional, and international regulations to prevent non-compliance penalties or legal complications • To consistently meet or exceed customer expectations by delivering high-quality products and services, thereby improving customer loyalty and market share
	Meet all relevant regulatory and legal requirements within the industry	Process quality control	
	Cultivate a culture focused on continuous improvement in processes, products, and systems	Regulatory compliance	
	Guarantee that external suppliers and vendors adhere to quality and compliance standards	Supplier quality management	
	Maintain a high level of customer satisfaction while upholding stakeholder trust	Customer satisfaction with quality	

Source: Developed by the authors

Tata Steel emphasizes quality control in its manufacturing processes by adopting Six Sigma and TQM methodologies to minimize defects and improve product consistency. Tata Steel has been ISO 9001 certified, showcasing its commitment to quality standards. ArcelorMittal, one of the world's largest steel producers, has implemented a robust quality management system, ensuring that its steel products meet stringent specifications for industries like automotive, construction, and infrastructure. ArcelorMittal also complies with multiple global standards, such as ASTM and EN norms, for ensuring product quality. Nucor Corporation, a leading steel manufacturer in the USA, follows stringent quality control procedures in its production processes. Nucor's focus on innovation and process improvement allows it to maintain high-quality standards while reducing waste and improving efficiency, making it a leader in sustainable steel production.

The benefits from including the quality and compliance perspective are as follows:

1. Improved product reliability: Ensures products meet customer expectations and perform reliably in various applications (e.g., automotive, construction, and aerospace);
2. Regulatory risk mitigation: Minimizes the risk of fines, legal issues, or product recalls due to non-compliance with standards and regulations;
3. Cost savings: Reduces costs associated with rework, scrap, and waste by ensuring that quality is built into every stage of the process;
4. Customer loyalty: High product quality and consistent compliance with standards lead to greater customer trust and repeat business.

Tizroo et al. (2017) examined how integrating Quality Management Systems (QMS) with the BSC framework can improve strategic alignment in the steel industry. It discusses the benefits of including quality and compliance metrics within the BSC to drive performance and operational excellence. For metal producers, integrating QMS with BSC allows for a more comprehensive approach to managing quality and compliance. The study illustrates how metal companies can incorporate quality metrics into their BSC to enhance performance tracking and improve overall quality management. The case study highlights improved alignment between strategic goals and quality objectives in the steel industry, demonstrating the effectiveness of combining QMS with the BSC framework.

Shin et al. (2018) introduce a quality scorecard tailored for Industry 4.0, discussing its application in modern manufacturing environments. It provides a framework for aligning quality and compliance goals with strategic objectives and explores how this integration can enhance performance measurement. Metal producers can benefit from incorporating quality metrics into their BSC to ensure that quality and compliance are aligned with strategic goals. The research provides practical insights into measuring and managing quality within manufacturing environments, with a specific focus on the metals industry. It highlights that integrating quality metrics into the Balanced Scorecard improves performance management and accountability for manufacturing companies, including those operating in the metal sector.

Bukh et al. (2002) examine the integration of Intellectual Capital (IC) and the Balanced Scorecard (BSC) as performance management systems in a software company. The research explores how incorporating quality and compliance perspectives into the BSC framework can strengthen organizational performance and strategic alignment. It also provides the analysis of how these developments in quality management can be effectively applied within the BSC for metal-producing companies. It highlights the benefits of incorporating quality and compliance metrics to drive strategic performance. The review consolidates findings from multiple studies, demonstrating how merging quality management with the BSC can result in enhanced performance outcomes and better strategic alignment.

Sahraen (2020) examined the incorporation of compliance and risk management into the Balanced Scorecard framework, focusing on heavy industries like metal production. It provides insights into how compliance metrics can be integrated with strategic objectives to enhance overall performance. For metal-producing companies, incorporating compliance into the BSC ensures that regulatory requirements and risk management are aligned with strategic goals. The paper explores practical methods for incorporating these elements into performance measurement. It presents evidence from heavy industries, illustrating that embedding compliance and risk management into the BSC enhances performance management and ensures better regulatory compliance.

Shin et al. (2018) presented a practical approach to using the BSC for quality improvement in metal production. It details how quality and compliance metrics can be effectively integrated into the BSC to drive improvements and ensure alignment with strategic objectives. Metal producers can use the insights from this article to incorporate quality improvement metrics into their BSC, enhancing their ability to monitor and manage quality and compliance in production processes. The paper provides case studies and examples from the metal industry demonstrating the effectiveness of using the BSC for quality improvement.

Moreover, the cost management perspective is an essential addition to the BSC, especially in the metal industry, where controlling costs can significantly impact profitability. This perspective focuses on managing and optimizing costs throughout the production process, from raw material procurement to final product delivery. Incorporating cost management into the BSC ensures that cost control initiatives are closely aligned with strategic objectives, enabling cost efficiency to support and reinforce broader organizational goals (Table 2).

Table 2. Application of Cost Management perspective in "Uzmetkombinat" JSC

<table>
<tr><th>Perspective</th><th>Objectives</th><th>Key Performance Indicators (KPIs)</th><th>Strategic Goals:</th></tr>
<tr><td rowspan="6">Cost and management perspective</td><td>To attain cost control and enhance profitability.</td><td>Cost of goods sold (COGS)</td><td rowspan="6">• Cost management perspective
• Maximize profitability through cost control
• Achieve resource optimization
• Maintain quality while reducing costs</td></tr>
<tr><td>To consistently identify and eliminate activities and processes that do not add value.</td><td>Operational efficiency</td></tr>
<tr><td>To improve the efficiency of resource usage, including labor, materials, and energy.</td><td>Cost variance analysis</td></tr>
<tr><td>To maximize the value extracted from raw materials while minimizing waste and cost.</td><td>Material utilization</td></tr>
<tr><td>To develop pricing strategies that balance customer value and profitability.</td><td>Supplier costs</td></tr>
<tr><td>To minimize these costs while ensuring optimal stock levels to meet customer demand.</td><td>Inventory management costs</td></tr>
</table>

Source: Developed by the authors

Integrating a cost management perspective into the BSC offers several benefits for metal-producing companies. These benefits stem from the enhanced ability to manage and optimize costs while aligning them with strategic objectives.

The benefits of integrating cost management perspective into the balanced scorecard are as follows:

1. Enhanced cost control:
    - Improved visibility: Provides a clear view of cost drivers and variances, enabling better control over production and operational costs;
    - Early detection: Helps in identifying cost overruns and inefficiencies early, allowing for timely corrective actions.
2. Alignment with strategic objectives:
    - Strategic cost management: Aligns cost management efforts with broader business goals, ensuring that cost control supports overall strategy and competitive positioning;
    - Focus on key areas: Facilitates prioritizing cost management efforts in areas that most significantly influence strategic objectives (e.g., lowering production costs or optimizing material usage).
3. Improved financial performance:
    - Cost reduction: Enables cost reduction by improving budgeting, forecasting, and control, thereby directly enhancing profitability;
    - Cost efficiency: Improves cost efficiency by streamlining resource allocation, minimizing waste, and enhancing operational processes.
4. Better decision-making:

- Informed decisions: Provides accurate and timely cost data, supporting informed decision-making related to pricing, investment, and operational changes;
- Scenario analysis: Allows for scenario planning and analysis to assess the financial impact of different cost management strategies and operational decisions.

5. Increased accountability:
    - Responsibility assignment: Assigns cost management responsibilities to relevant departments or individuals, fostering accountability and ownership;
    - Performance measurement: Tracks and measures cost-related performance metrics, encouraging departments to adhere to budgetary constraints and efficiency goals.
6. Enhanced operational efficiency:
    - Process optimization: Identifies opportunities for process improvements and cost-saving measures, leading to more efficient production operations;
    - Resource utilization: Optimizes the use of resources, such as raw materials and labor, to reduce costs and improve overall production efficiency.
7. Better risk management:
    - Cost risk assessment: Helps assess and mitigate risks related to cost fluctuations, such as changes in raw material prices or energy costs;
    - Contingency planning: Supports the development of contingency plans to manage unexpected cost increases or financial challenges.
8. Improved competitive position:
    - Cost advantage: Achieves a cost advantage over competitors by maintaining lower production costs, enabling competitive pricing strategies;
    - Market responsiveness: Enhances the ability to respond to market changes and price fluctuations effectively, maintaining competitiveness in the industry.
9. Alignment with financial goals:
    - Budget adherence: Ensures that cost management aligns with financial goals (e.g., achieving target profit margins or maintaining cost-to-revenue ratios);
    - Performance incentives: Links cost management performance with financial incentives, driving better adherence to cost control measures.
10. Enhanced reporting and transparency:
    - Comprehensive reporting: Provides detailed cost-related reports and analysis, enhancing transparency and communication of cost performance across the organization;

- Stakeholder communication: Improves communication with stakeholders by providing clear insights into cost management and its impact on financial performance.

Kaplan and Anderson (2022) discussed the integration of strategic cost management (SCM) with the BSC framework. It highlights how companies can use the BSC to manage costs strategically, ensuring that cost control is aligned with long-term business objectives and financial performance. Metal producers can leverage SCM techniques integrated with BSC to align cost management with strategic goals, optimize production costs, and improve overall financial performance. Case studies demonstrate improved cost management and financial outcomes in industries, including metals, through the integration of SCM and BSC.

Drury (2018) explored how cost management techniques can be effectively integrated into the Balanced Scorecard to enhance performance measurement. It offers valuable insights into cost control, variance analysis, and cost-benefit evaluation in manufacturing environments. Metal manufacturers can utilize these approaches to improve cost efficiency, analyze cost variances, and optimize resource allocation by integrating cost management into their BSC framework. The research includes examples from manufacturing industries showing how integrating cost management into the BSC leads to better performance measurement and cost control.

Bataineh et al. (2019) examined how operational efficiency can be enhanced through the BSC by focusing on cost management. It provides practical examples of how manufacturing companies, including metal producers, can use the BSC to monitor and control production costs. The paper's insights are applicable to metal production, where controlling operational costs and improving efficiency are crucial for maintaining competitive advantage and profitability. The research features case studies and quantitative data demonstrating the beneficial effects of the BSC on operational efficiency and cost management within manufacturing industries.

In summary, the cost management perspective within the BSC is vital for metal producers to efficiently manage production costs, optimize resource utilization, and align cost control initiatives with strategic goals. The recent literature highlights various approaches and benefits of integrating cost management into the BSC framework, providing practical insights and evidence from the metal industry and other manufacturing sectors. This integration helps enhance overall performance, improve financial outcomes, and maintain competitive advantage.

Solutions and Recommendations

To address the challenges identified and enhance the BSC system for "Uzmetkombinat" JSC, the following practical solutions and recommendations are proposed:

1. Expand the traditional balanced scorecard framework:
    - Add new perspectives: Introduce the quality and compliance perspective to ensure that products meet high standards, regulations are followed, and customer expectations are consistently met;
    - Incorporate the cost management perspective to focus on controlling costs, reducing waste, and ensuring resources are used efficiently while supporting the company's strategic goals.
    - Customize KPIs: Develop specific KPIs tailored to the metal industry (e.g., energy efficiency metrics, scrap reduction rates, and compliance-related indicators).
2. Leverage advanced technology:
    - Adopt ERP systems: Implementing ERP software enables streamlined data collection and provides managers with accurate, real-time information, facilitating more informed and effective decision-making;
    - Leverage AI and predictive analytics: Utilize AI-powered tools to forecast trends, detect inefficiencies, and support proactive, data-driven decision-making;
    - Interactive dashboards: Provide managers with user-friendly dashboards that display performance metrics in real time, making it easier to track progress across all perspectives.
3. Foster a culture of continuous improvement:
    - Implement quality management systems: Adopt frameworks like Total Quality Management (TQM) or Six Sigma to minimize defects, improve processes, and maintain high product quality;
    - Invest in employee development: Provide training programs to equip employees with knowledge of cost management, compliance requirements, and the significance of their roles in achieving strategic objectives;
    - Establish feedback mechanisms: Encourage regular feedback and performance reviews to ensure alignment with strategic objectives and identify areas for improvement;
4. Align efforts across the organization:
    - Encourage cross-department collaboration: Break down silos by fostering open communication and cooperation between departments, ensuring that all teams work towards shared goals;
    - Integrate strategic goals: Link short-term operational objectives with the company's long-term vision to create consistency and avoid conflicting priorities.
5. Address metal industry-specific needs:
    - Optimize costs: Focus on controlling production costs by monitoring raw material usage, improving energy efficiency, and reducing waste;

- Strengthen compliance and risk management: Create specialized teams to monitor regulations and ensure the company consistently meets industry standards and avoids legal or financial penalties;
- Enhance customer satisfaction: Leverage customer feedback to improve product quality, optimize delivery timelines, and strengthen relationships with customers.

6. Continuously monitor and refine the enhanced BSC:
   - Regular updates: Schedule periodic reviews of the BSC framework to ensure it remains relevant to the company's evolving needs and industry changes;
   - Adjust KPIs and goals: Update metrics and objectives as market conditions shift or new challenges emerge, ensuring the framework stays dynamic and effective.

To conclude, by expanding the BSC to include additional perspectives, adopting advanced technology, and promoting a culture of continuous improvement, "Uzmetkombinat" JSC can strengthen its performance management system. These solutions will help the company meet immediate challenges and position itself for sustainable growth, improved efficiency, and long-term success in the competitive metal production industry.

Future Research Directions

To further advance the application and effectiveness of the BSC in management accounting, particularly for industries like metal production, the following research directions are recommended (Table 3).

Table 3. Future Research Directions for the BSC

Focus Area	Research Direction	Objective
Emerging technologies	Explore AI and machine learning for real-time data analysis in the BSC	Enhance predictive decision-making and proactive strategy formulation
	Use big data to identify trends and refine performance metrics	Improve accuracy and relevance of performance insights
	Investigate blockchain for enhancing compliance and transparency	Strengthen trust and accountability in quality and compliance processes
Industry-specific needs	Develop KPIs tailored for metal producers and similar industries	Align performance measurement with industry-specific challenges and goals
	Adapt the BSC for small and medium enterprises (SMEs)	Make the framework scalable and practical for smaller organizations

continued on following page

Table 3. Continued

Focus Area	Research Direction	Objective
Expanding perspectives	Integrate sustainability and ESG metrics into the BSC	Align organizational performance with environmental and social goals
	Explore a dedicated risk management perspective	Address uncertainties like market volatility and supply chain disruptions
Global and cultural impact	Study how cultural and regional factors influence BSC implementation	Ensure the BSC is adaptable for global and diverse organizational settings
	Investigate BSC use in managing global supply chains	Optimize cost, quality, and compliance in complex supply networks
Organizational Behavior	Assess the impact of the BSC on employee motivation and engagement	Foster a stronger connection between individual contributions and organizational goals
	Study leadership roles in successful BSC adoption	Enhance strategic alignment and support for the BSC framework
Real-Time Applications	Explore dynamic BSC models that adapt to changing business environments	Enable continuous performance monitoring and decision-making
	Use IoT and smart manufacturing systems to update BSC in real-time	Enhance responsiveness to operational changes and challenges
Long-Term Impact	Conduct longitudinal studies on the BSC's long-term effects on performance	Understand sustained impacts on financial, operational, and strategic outcomes
	Compare traditional and enhanced BSC models across industries	Identify the added value of integrating new perspectives like quality and cost management

Source: Developed by the authors

CONCLUSION

The BSC has served as a vital performance management tool, enabling organizations to translate their strategic objectives into measurable actions across four core perspectives: financial, customer, internal processes, and learning and growth. However, in the context of today's enterprises, the business landscape has become increasingly complex; organizations are required to expand their approach to ensure they remain competitive, compliant, and efficient. This need for a more comprehensive view of performance has led to the enhancement of the traditional

BSC model by integrating two additional perspectives: quality and compliance and cost management.

By incorporating these two perspectives, enterprises can ensure alignment with strategic objectives and foster a more holistic approach to organizational management. The quality and compliance perspective focuses on ensuring that operational and product quality meet industry standards, regulatory requirements, and customer expectations. This perspective is crucial for mitigating risks, enhancing product integrity, and improving customer satisfaction, while the cost management perspective focuses on efficient resource allocation, effective cost control, and maximizing profits while maintaining quality and delivering a positive customer experience.

Enhancing the BSC by incorporating the quality and compliance perspective alongside the cost management perspective provides a more holistic and integrated approach to management accounting. This transformation allows businesses to monitor and enhance financial performance and the quality of their products, services, and operations while ensuring compliance with industry standards and regulations. These additional perspectives provide a more comprehensive framework that strengthens strategic decision-making, fosters continuous improvement, and positions organizations for long-term success in an increasingly complex and competitive global marketplace.

Incorporating these perspectives into the BSC provides a holistic view of organizational performance that balances cost-efficiency with quality, compliance, and long-term profitability, ultimately empowering organizations to achieve short-term goals and long-term strategic success.

REFERENCES

Anthony, R. N. (1965). *Planning and control systems: A framework for analysis*. Harvard University Press.

Bataineh, A., Al-Shwiyat, Z., & Alrjoub, A. (2019). The effect of using balanced scorecard (BSC) on reducing production costs in the Jordanian industrial companies. *The Journal of Business and Retail Management Research, 13*(3), 190–200. DOI: 10.24052/JBRMR/V13IS03/ART-17

Bukh, P. N., Johansen, M. R., & Mouritsen, J. (2002). Multiple integrated performance management systems: IC and BSC in a software company. *Singapore Management Review, 24*(3), 21–33.

Chavan, M. (2009). The balanced scorecard: A new challenge. *Journal of Management Development, 28*(5), 393–406. DOI: 10.1108/02621710910955930

Chenhall, R. H., & Langfield-Smith, K. (2007). Multiple perspectives of performance measures. *European Management Journal, 25*(4), 266–282. DOI: 10.1016/j.emj.2007.06.001

Drury, C. (2018). *Management and cost accounting* (10th ed.). Andover, UK: Cengage Learning. Retrieved March 12, 2025, from https://www.cengage.uk/c/management-and-cost-accounting-12e-drury-tayles/9781473791244/

Dubey, R., Gunasekaran, A., Childe, S. J., Blome, C., & Papadopoulos, T. (2019). Big data and predictive analytics and manufacturing performance: Integrating institutional theory, resource-based view and big data culture. *British Journal of Management, 30*(2), 341–361. DOI: 10.1111/1467-8551.12355

Epstein, M. J., & Roy, M. J. (2001). Sustainability in action: Identifying and measuring the key performance drivers. *Long Range Planning, 34*(5), 585–604. DOI: 10.1016/S0024-6301(01)00084-X

Gimbert, X., Bisbe, J., & Mendoza, X. (2010). The role of performance measurement systems in strategy formulation processes. *Long Range Planning, 43*(4), 477–497. Retrieved March 12, 2025, from https://merit.url.edu/en/publications/the-role-of-performance-measurement-systems-in-strategy-formulati-4. DOI: 10.1016/j.lrp.2010.01.001

Ittner, C. D., & Larcker, D. F. (2003). Coming up short on nonfinancial performance measurement. *Harvard Business Review, 81*(11), 88–95. PMID: 14619154

Kaplan, R. S. (1990). *Measures for manufacturing excellence.* Harvard Business School Press.

Kaplan, R. S., & Anderson, S. R. (2022). The impact of strategic cost management on financial performance: The role of balanced scorecard. *Harvard Business Review, 100*(3), 72–83.

Kaplan, R. S., & Norton, D. P. (1992). The balanced scorecard: Measures that drive performance. *Harvard Business Review, 70*(1), 71–79. PMID: 10119714

Kaplan, R. S., & Norton, D. P. (1996). *The balanced scorecard: Translating Strategy into Action.* Harvard Business School Press.

Kaplan, R. S., & Norton, D. P. (2001). *The strategy-focused organization: How balanced scorecard companies thrive in the new business environment.* Harvard Business School Press. DOI: 10.1108/sl.2001.26129cab.002

Malina, M. A., & Selto, F. H. (2001). Communicating and controlling strategy: An empirical study of the effectiveness of the balanced scorecard. *Journal of Management Accounting Research, 13*(1), 47–90. DOI: 10.2308/jmar.2001.13.1.47

Marr, B., & Schiuma, G. (2003). Business performance measurement – Past, present and future. *Management Decision, 41*(8), 680–687. DOI: 10.1108/00251740310496198

Matos, S., & Hall, J. (2007). Integrating sustainable development in the supply chain: The case of life cycle assessment in oil and gas and agricultural biotechnology. *Journal of Operations Management, 25*(6), 1083–1102. DOI: 10.1016/j.jom.2007.01.013

Neely, A., Adams, C., & Kennerley, M. (2002). *The performance prism: The scorecard for measuring and managing business success.* Harlow, UK: Financial Times Prentice Hall.

Neely, A., Gregory, M., & Platts, K. (1995). Performance measurement system design: A literature review and research agenda. *International Journal of Operations & Production Management, 15*(4), 80–116. DOI: 10.1108/01443579510083622

Niven, P. R. (2002). *Balanced scorecard step-by-step: Maximizing performance and maintaining results.* John Wiley & Sons.

Sahraen, A. N. (2020). Risk mitigation using integration enterprise risk management and balanced scorecard model: A case study in a consulting services company in Indonesia. *Spektrum Industri, 18*(1), 73–85. DOI: 10.12928/si.v19i1.17830

Shin, W. S., Dahlgaard, J. J., Dahlgaard-Park, S. M., & Kim, M. G. (2018). A quality scorecard for the era of Industry 4.0. *Total Quality Management & Business Excellence, 29*(9-10), 959–976. DOI: 10.1080/14783363.2018.1486536

Sydow, J., Schreyögg, G., & Koch, J. (2020). On the theory of organizational path dependence: Clarifications, replies to objections, and extensions. *Academy of Management Review, 45*(4), 717–734. DOI: 10.5465/amr.2020.0163

Tizroo, A., Esmaeili, A., Khaksar, E., Šaparauskas, J., & Mozaffari, M. M. (2017). Proposing an agile strategy for a steel industry supply chain through the integration of balance scorecard and Interpretive Structural Modeling. *Journal of Business Economics and Management, 18*(2), 288–308. DOI: 10.3846/16111699.2017.1279683

KEY TERMS AND DEFINITIONS

Key Performance Indicators (KPIs): specific metrics that help track progress toward achieving business objectives, ensuring performance is measurable and actionable.

Quality and compliance perspective: a proposed addition to the BSC that highlights the importance of meeting quality standards, regulatory requirements, and minimizing risks.

Cost management perspective: another enhancement to the BSC that focuses on controlling costs, minimizing waste, and ensuring resources are used efficiently while aligning with business goals.

Strategic goals: long-term objectives that guide an organization's efforts, ensuring they align with its mission and vision.

Operational efficiency: the ability to deliver high-quality products or services while minimizing resource use and reducing inefficiencies.

Performance metrics: measurable indicators that show how well an individual, team, or organization is achieving specific objectives.

Total Quality Management (TQM): a management philosophy dedicated to the continuous improvement of product and service quality by emphasizing process optimization and prioritizing customer satisfaction.

Compliance metrics: indicators that measure whether an organization is meeting legal, regulatory, or industry-specific standards.

Sustainability metrics: measures that assess a company's impact on environmental, social, and governance (ESG) factors, often tied to long-term goals.

Strategic alignment: ensuring that all resources, actions, and processes within an organization are directed toward achieving its strategic goals.

Chapter 9
Econometric Analysis of Factors Affecting the Competitiveness of Industrial Enterprises

Aktam U. Burkhanov
https://orcid.org/0000-0003-0108-8852
Alfraganus University, Uzbekistan

Bobir O. Tursunov
https://orcid.org/0000-0002-5004-375X
Tashkent State University of Economics, Uzbekistan

Bunyod Usmonov
https://orcid.org/0000-0001-6453-3832
Tashkent State University of Economics, Uzbekistan

Tuygunoy A. Mamadjanova
https://orcid.org/0009-0009-2305-6123
Termez University of Economics and Service, Uzbekistan

Mavluda Sh. Akhmedova
https://orcid.org/0009-0000-9582-4843
International School of Finance and Technology, Uzbekistan

ABSTRACT

The motivation for this research stemmed from the need to strengthen the scientific and methodological support for the new wave of industrialization of Uzbekistan's economy, ensuring its active participation in the Fifth Industrial Revolution. This

DOI: 10.4018/979-8-3693-8362-9.ch009

research conducts an econometric analysis of the factors influencing the competitiveness of industrial enterprises and develops recommendations for optimizing the impact of these factors on Uzbekistan's industrial production with examination of leading international practices. The paper's uniqueness is that it introduces, for the first time, a three-dimensional classification of the macroeconomic factors affecting the global competitiveness of Uzbek industrial enterprises. In the proposed classification, the first dimension pertains to the area of management, the second to the magnitude of the regression coefficient and the corresponding nature of its impact on global industrial competitiveness, and the third to the favorability of the factor's effect on the global competitiveness of Uzbekistan's industrial production.

INTRODUCTION

Like the world's leading industrial economies, Uzbekistan actively participates in industrial revolutions, currently experiencing the Fourth and Fifth Industrial Revolutions concurrently (Xu et al., 2025). The paramount importance of an industrial economic upsurge for the Uzbek economic system is emphasized at the highest governmental level and enshrined in the "Uzbekistan – 2030" strategy (President of the Republic of Uzbekistan, 2024). However, on its path to industrial growth, Uzbekistan encounters serious obstacles that hinder this progress, slow the pace of industrial revolutions, and prevent the realization of an unprecedented "economic miracle" in the 21st century.

The fundamental cause of these obstacles lies in the outdated approach to state regulation of industrial entrepreneurship in Uzbekistan. The current method, implemented today, was formulated in the last century and fails to account for the specific architecture of the contemporary global economic system (Amin & Cumming, 2025). Among the most significant shortcomings of the traditional approach still in use is, first, its adherence to the principle of absolute free international trade. The restrictions imposed by the WTO have undermined this principle, rendering it obsolete and placing the affected countries at a disadvantage in international trade (Sun et al., 2025).

Guided by this principle, the government of Uzbekistan seeks to eliminate foreign trade barriers, a policy that encourages the influx of foreign corporations into Uzbek national industrial markets. These corporations engage in price dumping and fierce competition, while Uzbek companies face trade barriers abroad in their export endeavors. Consequently, Uzbekistan's foreign trade policy, modeled after leading developed nations, should transition from free trade to protectionism to support the development of domestic industrial production and the export of its products. Therefore, regulatory efforts should focus on fostering industrial production in Uzbekistan rather than merely removing trade barriers (Guo et al., 2025; Usmonov, B. 2024).

Second, a significant drawback is the inefficiency of state financing for the modernization of the industrial economy, which perpetuates technological lag (Zhang et al., 2025). aspiring to secure a leading position among the participants of the Fourth and Fifth Industrial Revolutions, is keen on the innovative development of its industrial economy. To this end, instead of imposing state mandates, deregulation and market self-regulation should be promoted to stimulate industrial innovation (Opoku, 2025). Government initiatives such as state orders, subsidies, grants, and tax incentives for industrial enterprises do not provide the necessary flexibility for these market agents and tend to stifle their innovative initiatives (Su & Zhao, 2025).

Third, a critical shortcoming is the narrow focus of state regulators on boosting industrial development through increased sales, with insufficient attention paid to the quality of manufactured and marketed industrial products. The efforts by public authorities in Uzbekistan to stimulate the national economy's industrial upsurge primarily consist of integrating the country into global transport routes and logistics networks, as well as pursuing external trade integration to improve customs conditions for industrial exports (Singh & Cohen, 2025). However, favorable conditions for placing industrial products on the global market cannot ensure (and do not guarantee) their active export sales without the requisite technical characteristics and innovative features demanded in today's marketplace (Pinheiro, 2025).

Thus, a new approach to state regulation of industrial entrepreneurship is needed in today's world, including in Uzbekistan, one that focuses on unlocking the potential to enhance the competitiveness of the country's industrial products. To develop this practically needed new approach, it is essential to delineate the set of macroeconomic factors that determine the competitiveness of the production entities in Uzbekistan's industrial economy. Therefore, this research aims to conduct an econometric analysis of the factors influencing the competitiveness of industrial enterprises in Uzbekistan's economy, select the key factors among them, and identify opportunities to optimize their impact to drive an industrial upsurge in the Uzbek economy.

BACKGROUND

The fundamental basis of this research is the theory of industrial economics, which acknowledges that recent industrial revolutions have given a powerful new impetus to economic upsurges, creating conditions for the acceleration and expansion of industrial growth (Awode & Oduola, 2024; Iqbal et al., 2024; Li et al., 2024, 2025; Piechucka et al., 2024; Wang et al., 2025).

However, to realize this potential, it is essential to ensure the high global competitiveness of industrial enterprises. The primary indicator used to measure this global competitiveness – data for which can be obtained from official international statistics – is the share of industrial value added in GDP (IdCp) (Jakob & Mehling, 2025; Mariotti, 2024; Oyewo et al., 2025; Sandoval-Caraveo et al., 2024; Tao & Cai, 2025; Wismansyah et al., 2024).

A detailed and substantive review of the previously published research on this topic, conducted in this research, has identified the leading macroeconomic factors affecting the global competitiveness of industrial enterprises. An original classification of these factors by the area of management is proposed. The production management factors include the following:

- Design of unique industrial prototypes (PF_1) (Liu et al., 2025; Patiño & Maya, 2025);
- Diversification of national industrial production (PF_2) (Tashbaev et al., 2024; Inshakova et al., 2021);
- Green attributes of industrial products in accordance with the ISO 14001 environmental standard (PF_3) (Huang et al., 2025; Salahodjaev et al., 2023);
- Technical qualities of industrial products in accordance with the ISO 9001 quality standard (PF_4) (Astanakulov et al., 2022; Nosirov et al., 2023);
- The technical complexity of domestically produced and exported industrial products (PF_5) (Burkhanov et al., 2024; Kim et al., 2024).

The economic rationale for examining these factors is to determine what specific attributes of industrial products define their global competitiveness and how industrial production can be organized to maximize these attributes. The innovation management factors are as follows:

- Creation of high-performance jobs in the country's industrial sector (IF_1) (Andekina et al., 2024; Vanchukhina et al., 2022);
- The share of national industrial enterprises that attract research personnel and leverage their R&D talents (IF_2) (Andronikidis et al., 2025; Bogoviz et al., 2023);
- Private investment by national industrial enterprises in industrial R&D (IF_3) (Bezrukova et al., 2016; Zheng et al., 2025);
- R&D cooperation between national industrial enterprises and local universities through innovation networks (IF_4) (Hrosul et al., 2021; Laatsit & Johansson, 2025);

- Utilization of foreign-developed intellectual property in industrial production technologies (IF_5) (Kalieva, 2012; Ostrovskaya et al., 2017).

The economic significance of considering these factors lies in establishing the role of human resource management in the innovative development of the country's industrial production, identifying the most effective and preferable sources of funding for industrial innovation (public or private financing), and determining whether the industrial upsurge is driven by indigenous or borrowed innovations.

The literature review concludes that the essence of the competitiveness of industrial enterprises is fairly well defined in the available scientific literature and that a general set of factors influencing this competitiveness is known. Nevertheless, the empirical experience of shaping the global competitiveness of industrial enterprises under the influence of these factors remains insufficiently studied and elaborated, including in Uzbekistan. This presents a gap in the literature.

In light of this gap, the research poses the research question (RQ): "How exactly do macroeconomic factors affect the global competitiveness of industrial enterprises in Uzbekistan?" Addressing this gap and answering the RQ is crucial because identifying the most significant macroeconomic factors is necessary for targeted and highly effective intervention in these factors when implementing state industrial and economic policies in Uzbekistan.

An ambiguous and vague understanding of the impact of macroeconomic factors on the global competitiveness of Uzbek industrial enterprises leads to dispersed efforts and excessive expenditure of financial and non-financial resources, thereby preventing the full realization of Uzbekistan's industrial growth potential. To address this research question, the research conducts an econometric analysis of the factors influencing the competitiveness of industrial enterprises, drawing on international practical experience, including that of contemporary Uzbekistan.

THE MAIN FOCUS OF THE CHAPTER

Factor Analysis of the Global Competitiveness of Industrial Enterprises in the World's Industrially Developed Economies

To conduct an econometric analysis of the factors influencing the competitiveness of industrial enterprises, reliably incorporate Uzbekistan's experience, and obtain results applicable to its economy, this research establishes a special sample of 15 countries with a level of global competitiveness in national industrial entrepreneurship similar to that of Uzbekistan.

The criterion for including countries in the sample was the value of the statistical indicator calculated by the World Bank (2025), namely, the share of industrial value added in GDP (IdCp). In Uzbekistan, IdCp is 30.61%. In the sample, all countries have an IdCp exceeding 30% but below 40%. This selection makes it possible to examine the leading international practices of economies with a well-developed industrial sector (though not exclusively industrialized) that are participating in the Fourth and Fifth Industrial Revolutions, including Uzbekistan. This empirical research is based on statistical data current as of early 2025.

The methodological framework of this research relies on regression analysis, used to conduct a factor analysis of the global competitiveness of industrial enterprises in the sample countries. It establishes the regression relationship of IdCp with a set of ten factors (PF_{1-5} and IF_{1-5}) using data from the statistical report of WIPO (2024). The sample statistics are summarized in Table 1.

Table 1. Global industrial competitiveness and its factors in the sample countries in 2025

Country	Industry (including construction), value added (% of GDP)	Factors of production management					Factors of innovation management				
		Industrial designs by origin, bln. PPP$ GDP	Domestic industry diversification, score 0–100	ISO 14001 environment/ bln. PPP$ GDP	ISO 9001 quality/ bln PPP$ GDP	Production and export complexity, score 0–100	Labor productivity growth, %	Research talent, % in businesses	GERD financed by business, %	University-industry R&D collaboration, score 0–100	Intellectual property payments, % total trade
	IdCp	PF_1	PF_2	PF_3	PF_4	PF_5	IF_1	IF_2	IF_3	IF_4	IF_5
Bangladesh	34.59	0.9	66.6	0.2	0.7	23.8	4.2	0.0	0.0	21.2	0.1
Botswana	34.32	0.1	81.3	0.5	0.4	20.0	0.0	0.0	0.0	13.3	1.5
Egypt	32.12	1.1	90.8	0.8	2.0	39.6	2.3	6.3	3.9	50.3	0.5
Czech Republic	30.42	2.4	90.8	9.9	23.2	87.1	0.4	53.6	1.3	72.0	0.8
Ireland	33.19	0.6	69.6	1.6	4.2	79.3	-0.9	44.4	55.5	70.2	21.4
Kazakhstan	32.33	0.2	61.2	0.5	0.9	31.2	1.8	0.0	47.4	23.9	0.4
Korea, Rep.	31.59	19.0	93.4	5.3	10.5	94.3	0.8	82.6	76.3	69.0	1.6
Mexico	31.56	0.3	87.0	1.0	3.2	71.7	-1.4	50.6	17.0	42.5	0.9
Nigeria	32.58	0.9	0.0	0.1	0.6	2.4	-1.2	0.0	0.0	15.0	0.4
Paraguay	32.36	0.0	0.0	0.3	4.6	31.9	0.1	0.0	0.2	11.0	0.1
Peru	33.86	0.2	85.5	2.9	5.3	21.3	-0.1	0.0	0.0	22.8	0.9
Slovakia	32.86	1.7	74.1	8.5	17.8	79.9	1.4	30.6	45.7	27.2	0.7
Thailand	32.89	2.6	93.0	3.2	9.2	71.2	-0.5	60.8	80.8	54.2	1.8

continues on following page

Table 1. Continued

Country	Industry (including construction), value added (% of GDP)	Factors of production management					Factors of innovation management				
		Industrial designs by origin, bln. PPP$ GDP	Domestic industry diversification, score 0–100	ISO 14001 environment/ bln. PPP$ GDP	ISO 9001 quality/ bln PPP$ GDP	Production and export complexity, score 0–100	Labor productivity growth, %	Research talent, % in businesses	GERD financed by business, %	University-industry R&D collaboration, score 0–100	Intellectual property payments, % total trade
	$IdCp$	PF_1	PF_2	PF_3	PF_4	PF_5	IF_1	IF_2	IF_3	IF_4	IF_5
Uzbekistan	30.61	0.7	87.8	3.1	4.2	38.6	3.9	12.9	42.4	60.3	0.5
Zambia	35.11	0.8	64.8	0.2	0.5	21.9	-1.8	0.0	0.0	37.3	0.2

Source: Developed by the authors based on the materials from WIPO (2024) and World Bank (2025)

As a result of the econometric processing of the data presented in Table 1, the authors developed an econometric model (1) to represent the relationship between the global competitiveness of industrial enterprises in the world's industrially developed economies, including Uzbekistan, and the selected set of factors in 2025:

$$IdCp = 32.90 + 0.15PF_1 + 0.04PF_2 - 0.70PF_3 + 0.35PF_4 - 0.03PF_5 - 0.19IF_1 - 0.03IF_2 + 0.01IF_3 - 0.05IF_4 + 0.16IF_5, \text{ multiple } R=0.8443 \quad (1)$$

According to model (1), the combined effect of these factors explains 84.43% of the global competitiveness of industrial entrepreneurship in industrially developed economies such as Uzbekistan in 2025. An increase of 1 billion PPP$ GDP in the number of patented industrial prototypes with a unique design used in national industrial production leads to a 0.15% rise in the share of industrial value added in GDP.

Improving the technical qualities of industrial products through an increase of 1 billion PPP$ GDP in the number of funded projects for quality standardization in accordance with ISO 9001 contributes to a 0.35% rise in the share of industrial value added in GDP. A one-point increase in the technical complexity of domestically produced and exported industrial products is associated with a 0.03% decline in the share of industrial value added in GDP.

A 1% growth in the share of high-performance jobs in the country's industrial sector is linked to a 0.19% reduction in the share of industrial value added in GDP. Similarly, a 1% increase in the share of national industrial enterprises that attract research personnel and harness their R&D talents results in a 0.03% decrease in the share of industrial value added in GDP.

An increase of 1% in the share of private investments by national industrial enterprises in the financing of industrial R&D ensures a 0.01% growth in the share of industrial value added in GDP. A one-point improvement in the level of R&D cooperation between national industrial enterprises and local universities through innovation networks is accompanied by a 0.05% decrease in the share of industrial value added in GDP.

Finally, a 1% rise in the share of foreign-developed intellectual property used by national industrial enterprises in industrial production technologies within the structure of the country's foreign trade enables a 0.16% increase in the share of industrial value added in GDP.

Monitoring the Competitiveness of Uzbekistan's Industrial Enterprises in 2025

To develop the most comprehensive understanding of the current state of the competitiveness of Uzbekistan's industrial enterprises in 2025, the authors conducted a general monitoring, the results of which are presented in Figure 1. The economic aspect of the monitoring consists, first, of classifying the macroeconomic factors under consideration based on their obtained regression coefficients, thereby distinguishing between those with positive and negative values.

Second, by means of a comparative analysis, the values (Table 1) of all factor variables in model (1) for Uzbekistan are compared with the arithmetic means of these variables across the entire sample. This yields a three-dimensional classification of macroeconomic factors. The first dimension is the area of management (production or innovation). The second dimension is the value of the regression coefficient and, correspondingly, the nature of its impact on the global competitiveness of industrial production (positive or negative). The third direction is the favorability of the factor's effect on the global competitiveness of industrial production in Uzbekistan (more favorable or less favorable compared to other industrially developed economies in the sample).

Figure 1. Monitoring of competitiveness of industrial enterprises of Uzbekistan in 2025

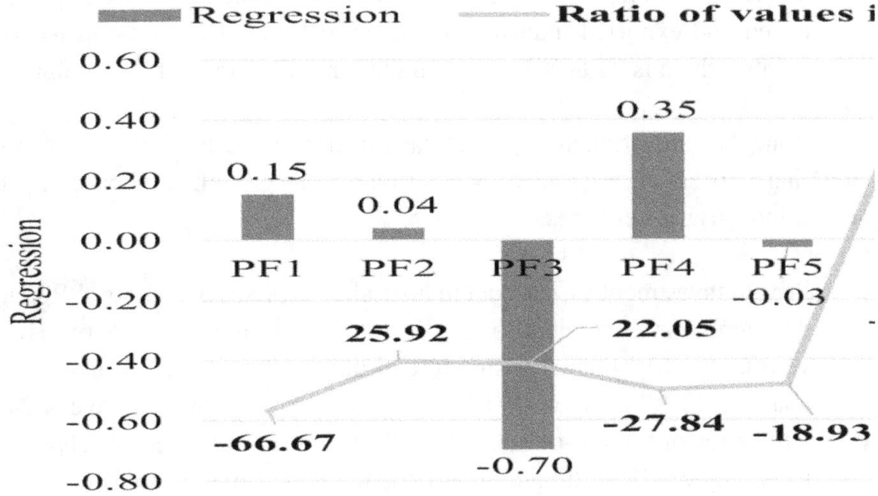

Source: Developed by the authors.

The results of the monitoring shown in Figure 1 indicate that the total positive regression coefficient (0.54) is approximately three times higher than that for innovation management factors (0.17) among production management factors. The arithmetic mean of the ratios of the production management factors' values in Uzbekistan to the sample average was negative, at -13.09%, while for innovation management factors, it was positive, at 111.02%.

Thus, production management factors exert a much greater positive influence on the global competitiveness of industrial enterprises in industrially developed economies, although these factors in Uzbekistan have a less favorable impact compared to the overall sample. Among the production management factors in industrially developed economies, including Uzbekistan, the following contribute to the growth of global competitiveness of industrial enterprises:

- Design of unique industrial prototypes (PF_1): the regression coefficient for this factor is 0.15; the number of patented industrial prototypes with a unique design used in national industrial production in Uzbekistan is estimated at 0.70 billion PPP$ GDP, which is 66.67% lower than the sample average of 2.10 billion PPP$ GDP;
- Diversification of national industrial production (PF_2): the regression coefficient for this factor is 0.04, and the level of diversification in Uzbekistan is estimated at 87.80 points, which is 25.92% higher than the sample average of 69.73 points;

- Technical qualities of industrial products (PF_4): the regression coefficient for this factor is 0.35, and the level of technical complexity of domestically produced and exported industrial products in Uzbekistan is estimated at 4.20 points, which is 27.84% lower than the sample average of 5.82 points.

Among the innovation management factors in industrially developed economies, including Uzbekistan, the following contribute to the growth of global competitiveness of industrial enterprises:

- Private investment by national industrial enterprises in industrial R&D (IF_3): the regression coefficient for this factor is 0.01, and the share of private investments in the financing structure of industrial R&D in Uzbekistan is estimated at 42.40%, which is 71.66% higher than the sample average of 24.70%;
- Utilization of foreign-developed intellectual property in industrial production technologies (IF_5): the regression coefficient for this factor is 0.16, and the share of foreign-developed intellectual property acquired by national industrial enterprises in the structure of the country's foreign trade is estimated at 0.50%, which is 76.42% lower than the sample average of 2.12%.

An Enhanced Approach to State Regulation of the Development of Industrial Entrepreneurship in Uzbekistan

The econometric analysis clarified the set of factors that positively influence the competitiveness of industrial enterprises in industrially developed economies, including Uzbekistan. The developed enhanced approach to state regulation of industrial entrepreneurship in Uzbekistan proposes focusing attention and efforts on these selected macroeconomic factors.

This set primarily includes production management factors such as the design of unique industrial prototypes, diversification of national industrial production, and the technical qualities of industrial products, and secondarily, innovation management factors such as private investments by national industrial enterprises in industrial R&D and the utilization of foreign-developed intellectual property in industrial production technologies.

Among the selected factors, those that exert a favorable influence in Uzbekistan, strengthening the global competitiveness of Uzbek industrial enterprises, are the diversification of national industrial production and private investments in industrial R&D, the levels of which in Uzbekistan exceed those observed in the overall sample of industrially developed economies.

Conversely, the selected factors that have an unfavorable impact on Uzbekistan, contributing to the reduced global competitiveness of Uzbek industrial enterprises, are the design of unique industrial prototypes, the technical qualities of industrial products, and the utilization of foreign-developed intellectual property in industrial production technologies, the levels of which in Uzbekistan are lower than the sample averages for industrially developed economies.

SOLUTIONS AND RECOMMENDATIONS

To develop scientific and practical recommendations for improving state regulation of industrial entrepreneurship in Uzbekistan, the authors' approach includes three alternative scenarios depicting changes in the global competitiveness of Uzbekistan's industrial enterprises based on the impact of selected key macroeconomic factors.

The first scenario is termed "realistic" because it reduces disparities among industrially developed economies. For its quantitative characterization, the arithmetic means from Table 1 are substituted into model (1) to forecast changes in the selected factor variables (PF_1, PF_2, PF_4, IF_3, and IF_5) and the outcome variable (IdCp).

Under this scenario, the following combination and dynamics of the selected macroeconomic factors influencing the global competitiveness of industrial entrepreneurship in Uzbekistan are assumed. Regarding production management factors for Uzbek industrial enterprises, the following changes are envisaged:

- Improvement in the design of unique industrial prototypes by a factor of three: the number of patented industrial prototypes with a unique design used in national industrial production in Uzbekistan increases from 0.70 billion to 2.10 billion PPP$ GDP.;
- A reduction in the diversification of national industrial production by a factor of 0.79, transitioning towards industrial specialization: the diversification level in Uzbekistan decreases from 87.80 points to 69.73 points;
- Enhancement of the technical qualities of industrial products by a factor of 1.39: the technical complexity of domestically produced and exported industrial products in Uzbekistan rises from 4.20 points to 5.82 points.

Regarding innovation management factors for Uzbek industrial enterprises under this scenario, the following changes are assumed:

- A restriction of private investments in industrial R&D by a factor of 0.58: the share of private investments in the financing structure of industrial R&D in Uzbekistan falls from 42.40% to 24.70%;

- A shift towards borrowed industrial technologies, with an increased reliance on them by a factor of 4.24: the share of foreign-developed intellectual property used in industrial production technologies within the country's foreign trade increases from 0.50% to 2.12%.

Under the realistic scenario, the global competitiveness of Uzbekistan's industrial enterprises is projected to grow by a factor of 1.06, with the share of industrial value added in GDP rising from 30.61% to 32.43%.

The second scenario is labeled "pessimistic" because it entails a deterioration in all selected macroeconomic factors in Uzbekistan. For its quantitative characterization, the worst (minimal) values from Table 1 are substituted into model (1) to forecast changes in the selected factor variables (PF_1, PF_2, PF_4, IF_3, and IF_5) and the outcome variable (IdCp).

Under this scenario, the following combination and dynamics of the selected macroeconomic factors influencing the global competitiveness of industrial entrepreneurship in Uzbekistan are assumed. Regarding production management factors for Uzbek industrial enterprises, the following changes are envisaged:

- A complete abandonment of unique industrial prototype design in Uzbekistan: the number of patented industrial prototypes with a unique design used in national industrial production is reduced to zero;
- Narrow specialization of national industrial production in Uzbekistan: the diversification of national industrial production is reduced to zero;
- A simplification of the technical qualities of industrial products by a factor of 0.10: the technical complexity of domestically produced and exported industrial products in Uzbekistan decreases from 4.20 points to 0.40 points.

Regarding innovation management factors for Uzbek industrial enterprises under this scenario, the following changes are assumed:

- A complete abandonment of private investments in industrial R&D in Uzbekistan: the share of private investments in the financing structure of industrial R&D is reduced to zero;
- A shift towards domestic industrial technologies: the share of foreign-developed intellectual property used in industrial production technologies within the country's foreign trade is reduced by a factor of 0.20, falling from 0.50% to 0.10%.

Under the pessimistic scenario, the global competitiveness of Uzbekistan's industrial enterprises is forecast to decline by a factor of 0.84, with the share of industrial value added in GDP decreasing from 30.61% to 25.64%.

The third scenario reflects broad opportunities to optimize the impact of the selected macroeconomic factors for an industrial upsurge in Uzbekistan's economy. This scenario is termed "optimistic" because it achieves in Uzbekistan a macroeconomic situation comparable to that of the leading industrially developed economies in the sample.

For its quantitative characterization, the best—maximum—values of the factor variables from Table 1 are substituted into model (1) to forecast changes in the selected factor variables (PF_1, PF_2, PF_4, IF_3, and IF_5) and the outcome variable (IdCp). For clarity, the recommended optimistic scenario for implementation in Uzbekistan is illustrated in Figure 2.

Figure 2. Recommendations to improve the competitiveness of industrial enterprises in Uzbekistan

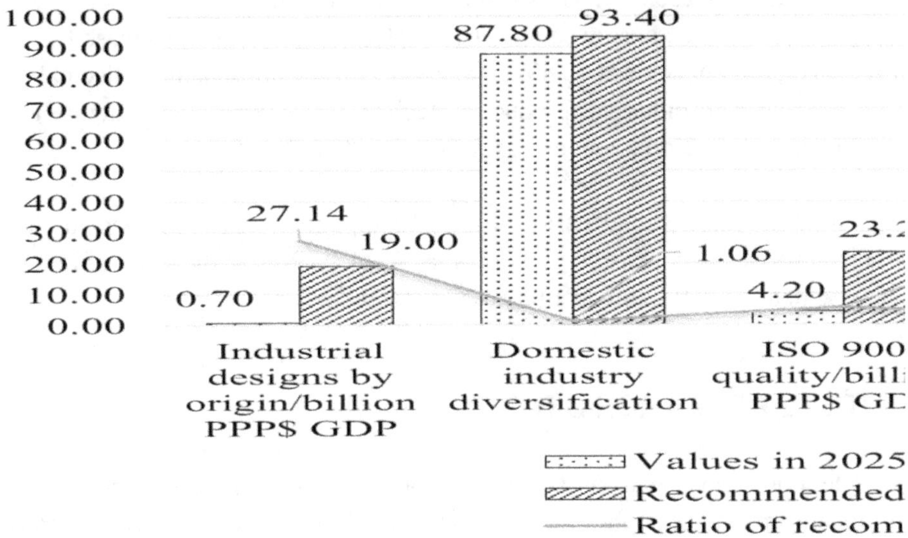

Source: Developed by the authors

As shown in Figure 2, under this scenario, the following combination and dynamics of the selected macroeconomic factors influencing the global competitiveness of industrial entrepreneurship in Uzbekistan are anticipated. Regarding production management factors for Uzbek industrial enterprises, the following changes are projected:

- Enhancement of the design of unique industrial prototypes by a factor of 27.14: the number of patented industrial prototypes with a unique design used in national industrial production in Uzbekistan increases from 0.70 billion PPP$ GDP to 19.00 billion PPP$ GDP;
- An increase in the diversification of national industrial production by a factor of 1.06, moving toward industrial specialization: the diversification level in Uzbekistan rises from 87.80 points to 93.40 points;
- Improvement of the technical qualities of industrial products by a factor of 5.52: the technical complexity of domestically produced and exported industrial products in Uzbekistan increases from 4.20 points to 23.20 points.

Regarding innovation management factors for Uzbek industrial enterprises under this scenario, the following changes are envisaged:

- Strengthening the influx of private investments in industrial R&D by a factor of 1.91: the share of private investments in the financing structure of industrial R&D in Uzbekistan rises from 42.40% to 80.80%;
- A shift towards borrowed industrial technologies, with an increased reliance on them by a factor of 42.80: the share of foreign-developed intellectual property used in industrial production technologies within the structure of the country's foreign trade increases from 0.50% to 21.40%.

Under this optimistic scenario, the global competitiveness of Uzbekistan's industrial enterprises is forecast to grow by a factor of 1.99, with the share of industrial value added in GDP rising from 30.61% to 60.94%.

FUTURE RESEARCH DIRECTIONS

The econometric analysis has enhanced and expanded the scientific explanation of how macroeconomic factors affect the competitiveness of industrial enterprises in industrially developed economies, such as Uzbekistan, where the share of industrial value added in GDP ranges from 30% to 40%. The experience of other groups of countries, classified according to the level of industrial development of their economies, falls outside the scope of this study and remains insufficiently explored.

In light of the above, it is recommended that future research focus on conducting econometric analyses of the impact of macroeconomic factors on the competitiveness of industrial enterprises in other categories of countries, in particular in industrializing economies (with an industrial value added share in GDP below 30%), as well as in economies specializing in industrial production (with an industrial value added share in GDP above 40%).

Moreover, it would be beneficial to complement the quantitative study based on econometric methodology with qualitative research (e.g., using case study methods). Such studies should investigate practical examples and identify the reasons for the negative impact on the global competitiveness of industrial entrepreneurship in Uzbekistan of certain production management factors (e.g., the green attributes of industrial products and the technical complexity of domestically produced and exported industrial products) and certain innovation management factors (e.g., the creation of high-performance jobs in the country's industrial sector, the share of national industrial enterprises that attract research personnel and harness their R&D talents, and the R&D cooperation between national industrial enterprises and local universities through innovation networks).

CONCLUSION

The obtained results continued the series of studies by Awode and Oduola (2024), Iqbal et al. (2024), Jakob and Mehling (2025), Li et al. (2024, 2025), Mariotti (2024), Oyewo et al. (2025), Piechucka et al. (2024), Sandoval-Caraveo et al. (2024), Tao and Cai (2025), Wang et al. (2025), and Wismansyah et al. (2024). They further enriched the theory of industrial economics by filling a gap in the literature, providing an answer to the research question, and explaining precisely how macroeconomic factors influence the global competitiveness of industrial enterprises in modern Uzbekistan (Table 2).

Table 2. Factors of competitiveness of industrial enterprises: existing literature vs. Uzbekistan's experience

Factors of competitiveness of industrial enterprises		Reflections of factors in the literature	Identified influence of factors in Uzbekistan (regression)
Factors of production management	Design of unique industrial samples	Liu et al. (2025) and Patiño and Maya (2025)	positive (0.15)
	Diversification of national industrial production	Tashbaev et al. (2024) and Inshakova et al. (2021)	positive (0.04)
	Green properties of industrialized products	Huang et al. (2025) and Salahodjaev et al. (2023)	negative (-0.70)
	Technical properties of industrial products	Astanakulov et al. (2022) and Nosirov et al. (2023)	positive (0.35)
	Technical complexity of the country's manufactured and exported industrial products	Burkhanov et al. (2024) and Kim et al. (2024)	negative (-0.03)
Factors of innovation management	Creation of highly productive jobs in the country's industrial production facilities	Andekina et al. (2024) and Vanchukhina et al. (2022)	negative (-0.19)
	Share of national industries attracting research personnel and discovering their R&D talents	Andronikidis et al. (2025) and Bogoviz et al. (2023)	negative (-0.03)
	Private investment in industrial R&D by national industries	Bezrukova et al. (2016) and Zheng et al. (2025)	positive (0.1)
	R&D collaboration of national industrial enterprises with local universities based on innovation networks	Hrosul et al. (2021) and Laatsit and Johansson (2025)	negative (-0.05)
	Use of intellectual property objects created abroad for industrial production technologies	Kalieva (2012) and Ostrovskaya et al. (2017)	positive (0.16)

Source: Developed by the authors

The scientific novelty of the obtained results lies in the fact that they have enabled a three-dimensional classification of the macroeconomic factors influencing the global competitiveness of industrial enterprises in modern Uzbekistan. In the author's classification, the first dimension is the area of management (production or innovation). The second dimension is the value of the regression coefficient and, correspondingly, the nature of its impact on the global competitiveness of industrial production (positive or negative). The third dimension is the favorability of the factor's effect on the global competitiveness of industrial production in Uzbekistan (more favorable or less favorable compared to other industrially developed economies in the sample).

The econometric model developed to explain the global competitiveness of industrial enterprises in industrially developed economies, including Uzbekistan, in 2025 holds theoretical significance because it refines and quantitatively measures the influence of each selected macroeconomic factor on competitiveness and narrows the range of factors that positively affect competitiveness.

As shown in Table 2, the positive influence on the global competitiveness of industrial entrepreneurship in Uzbekistan is confirmed for production management factors such as the design of unique industrial prototypes (in agreement with Liu et al. (2025) and Patiño and Maya (2025)), diversification of national industrial production (consistent with Tashbaev et al. (2024) and Inshakova et al. (2021)), and the technical qualities of industrial products (consistent with Astanakulov et al. (2022) and Nosirov et al. (2023) as well as for innovation management factors such as private investments by national industrial enterprises in industrial R&D (consistent with Bezrukova et al. (2016) and Zheng et al. (2025)), and the utilization of foreign-developed intellectual property in industrial production technologies (in agreement with Kalieva (2012) and Ostrovskaya et al. (2017)).

A negative impact on the global competitiveness of industrial entrepreneurship in Uzbekistan has been identified for production management factors such as the green attributes of industrial products (which contradict Huang et al. (2025) and Salahodjaev et al. (2023)) and the technical complexity of domestically produced and exported industrial products (which contradict Burkhanov et al., (2024) and Kim et al. (2024)) as well as for innovation management factors such as the creation of high-performance jobs in the country's industrial sector (contradicting Andekina et al. (2024) and Vanchukhina et al. (2022)), the share of national industrial enterprises that attract research personnel and harness their R&D talents (contradicting Andronikidis et al. (2025) and Bogoviz et al. (2023), and R&D cooperation between national industrial enterprises and local universities through innovation networks (contradicting Hrosul et al. (2021) and Laatsit and Johansson (2025)).

The detailed monitoring of the global competitiveness of Uzbekistan's industrial enterprises in 2025 presented in this article has practical significance, as it has revealed both the strengths (a high level of diversification in national industrial production and substantial private investments in industrial R&D) and weaknesses (insufficiently unique industrial prototype design, weak technical qualities of industrial products, and underutilization of foreign-developed intellectual property in industrial production technologies) of the macroeconomic environment in Uzbekistan, and it has explained the causal relationships affecting the competitiveness of Uzbek industrial enterprises.

The developed enhanced approach to state regulation of industrial entrepreneurship in Uzbekistan has managerial significance, as the approach itself and the corresponding scientific and practical recommendations for optimizing the impact

REFERENCES

Amin, Q. A., & Cumming, D. (2025). Industrial heterogeneity, governance structure and firm value. *European Financial Management, 31*(1), 265–298. DOI: 10.1111/eufm.12497

Andekina, R., Rakhmetova, R., Kaliyeva, S., & Maxyutova, A. (2024). Entrepreneurial universities of the Republic of Kazakhstan: The essence and features of development. *Scientific Herald of Uzhhorod University. Series. Physics (College Park, Md.), 55*(55), 2690–2700. DOI: 10.54919/physics/55.2024.269an0

Andronikidis, A., Kouskoura, A., Kalliontzi, E., & Bakouros, I. (2025). The embeddedness of responsible research innovation in Sabadell's territorial policies: The case of smart specialization in industrial systems. *Journal of Innovation and Entrepreneurship, 14*(1), 8. DOI: 10.1186/s13731-025-00468-x

Astanakulov, O. T., Abdurakhmanova, G. K., Balbaa, M. E., & Goyipnazarov, S. B. (2022). Ensuring the smooth operation of physical technology companies in distributed environments. Proceedings of ICFNDS '22: *The 6th International Conference on Future Networks & Distributed System* (pp. 66-73). New York, NY: Association for Computing Machinery. DOI: 10.1145/3584202.3584213

Awode, S. S., & Oduola, M. O. (2024). The interplay between technological innovation and human capital development in driving industrial productivity and competitiveness in Africa. *Journal of Economic Development, 27*(1), 56–71. DOI: 10.1108/JED-03-2024-0079

Bezrukova, T. L., Gyiazov, A. T., & Bazieva, A. M. (2016). Modeling and forecasting of innovative development of entrepreneurial structures under global competition. *Aktual'ni Problemi Ekonomìki, 182*(8), 344–351.

Bogoviz, A. V., Nosirov, J. T., Litvinova, T. N., & Ostrovskaya, V. N. (2023). Environmental Taxation as an Incentive to ESG Management of Green Business in Russia and Central Asia. In Popkova, E. G., & Sergi, B. S. (Eds.), *ESG Management of the Development of the Green Economy in Central Asia. Environmental Footprints and Eco-design of Products and Processes*. Springer., DOI: 10.1007/978-3-031-46525-3_8

Burkhanov, A. U., Kurbonbekova, M. T., Usmonov, B., & Nizomiddinov, J. Z. (2024), "Assessment of the Financial Sustainability of Enterprises: The Case of Uzbekistan", Eshov, M.P., Abdurakhmanova, G.K., Burkhanov, A.U., Abdusalomova, N.B. and Ergasheva, S.T. (Ed.) *Development of International Entrepreneurship Based on Corporate Accounting and Reporting According to IFRS (Advanced Series in Management, Vol. 33B)*, Emerald Publishing Limited, Leeds, pp. 215-223. DOI: 10.1108/S1877-63612024000033B027

Guo, J., Huang, Z., & Zhou, B. (2025). How does industrial policy affect corporate M&A Activities? *Finance Research Letters*, *75*, 106909. DOI: 10.1016/j.frl.2025.106909

Hrosul, V., Kruhlova, O., Mkrtchyan, T., Zubkov, S., & Timchenko, O. (2021). Enterprise integration and formation of cluster structures in the field of food sector. *Agricultural and Resource Economics*, *7*(2), 119–140. DOI: 10.51599/are.2021.07.02.07

Huang, Z., Li, H., Song, M., & Ma, L. (2025). Intersecting sustainability and governance: The impact of industrial land price distortion on carbon emission efficiency in China. *Applied Geography (Sevenoaks, England)*, *176*, 103510. DOI: 10.1016/j.apgeog.2025.103510

Inshakova, A. O., Sozinova, A. A., & Litvinova, T. N. (2021). Corporate fight against the COVID-19 risks based on technologies of industry 4.0 as a new direction of social responsibility. *Risks*, *9*(12), 212. DOI: 10.3390/risks9120212

Iqbal, M., Kalim, R., & Arshed, N. (2024). Evaluating industrial competitiveness strategy in achieving environmental sustainability. *Competitiveness Review*, *34*(2), 353–369. DOI: 10.1108/CR-12-2022-0191

Jakob, M., & Mehling, M. (2025). Addressing competitiveness concerns of EU exporters with industrial policy: The role of innovation support. *World Trade Review*, 1–20. Advance online publication. DOI: 10.1017/S1474745624000405

Kalieva, S. A. (2012). Integration capacity of Kazakhstan and Russia. *Ekonomika regiona* [Economy of Regions], *4*, 227-233. DOI: 10.17059/2012-4-27

Kim, K., Park, K., Jeon, H. W., & Kremer, G. E. (2024). Design complexity based flexible order dispatching for additive manufacturing production. *International Journal of Production Economics*, *274*, 109307. DOI: 10.1016/j.ijpe.2024.109307

Laatsit, M., & Johansson, G. (2025). Fostering industrial symbiosis in process industries: An innovation policy perspective. *Environmental Technology & Innovation*, *37*, 104027. DOI: 10.1016/j.eti.2025.104027

Li, X., Jiang, X., & Yang, C. (2025). Dynamic evolution of the manufacturing international competitiveness of China and the U.S. against the U.S. Manufacturing Reshoring Policy. *China Journal of Econometrics*, *5*(1), 129–147.

Li, Z., Chen, J., Li, Z., & Zhang, Y. (2024). Strengthen or weaken? How industrial internet platform affects the core competitiveness of manufacturing companies. *Operations Management Research : Advancing Practice Through Research*, *17*(1), 220–232. DOI: 10.1007/s12063-023-00426-4

Liu, Y., Du, H., Wu, Y., & Mo, T. (2025). FPGA accelerated deep learning for industrial and engineering applications: Optimal design under resource constraints. *Electronics (Basel)*, *14*(4), 703. DOI: 10.3390/electronics14040703

Mariotti, S. (2024). "Open strategic autonomy" as an industrial policy compass for the EU competitiveness and growth: The good, the bad, or the ugly? *Economia e Politica Industriale*, *52*(1), 1–26. DOI: 10.1007/s40812-024-00327-y

Nosirov, J. T., Kukaeva, L. I., Hussein, B. A. A., & Ustenko, V. S. (2023). Disclosure of the Export Potential of High-Tech Enterprises in the Context of Industry 4.0 Through Quality Management. *Proceedings on EngineeringSciences*, *5*(S2), 295–310. DOI: 10.24874/PES.SI.02.009

Opoku, R. K. (2025). Resilience capabilities and performance dimensions of manufacturing supply chains in a developing economy. *Business Process Management Journal*. Advance online publication. DOI: 10.1108/BPMJ-07-2024-0577

Ostrovskaya, V. N., Tyurina, Y. G., Konina, O. V., Przhedetskaya, N. V., Pupynina, E. G., & Natsubidze, A. S. (2017). Perspectives of elimination of "institutional gaps" in foreign economic activities of subjects of SME within the global crisis management. In Popkova, E. (Ed.), *Overcoming uncertainty of institutional environment as a tool of global crisis management* (pp. 213–218). Springer., DOI: 10.1007/978-3-319-60696-5_26

Oyewo, B., Tawiah, V., & Alta'any, M. (2025). Determinants and impact of strategy-driven manufacturing accounting techniques on organisational competitiveness: A structural equation modelling approach. *Journal of Accounting and Organizational Change*, *21*(1), 114–142. DOI: 10.1108/JAOC-10-2022-0165

Patiño, E., & Maya, J. (2025). A toolbox of analog form-finding techniques: Experiments for the generation of bioinspired forms in industrial design. *International Journal of Designed Objects*, *19*(1), 41–89. DOI: 10.18848/2325-1379/CGP/v19i01/41-891

Piechucka, J., Sauri-Romero, L., & Smulders, B. (2024). Competition and industrial policies: Complementary action for EU competitiveness. *Journal of Competition Law & Economics, 20*(4), 384–408. DOI: 10.1093/joclec/nhae015

Pinheiro, C. (2025). Relatedness and economic complexity as tools for industrial policy: Insights and limitations. *Structural Change and Economic Dynamics, 72*, 1–10. DOI: 10.1016/j.strueco.2024.09.019

President of the Republic of Uzbekistan. (2024). *Decree of the President of the Republic of Uzbekistan No. DP-37 "On the state program for the implementation of the Strategy 'Uzbekistan – 2030' in the 'Year of support for youth and business'"* (February 21, 2024). Tashkent, Uzbekistan. Retrieved March 10, 2025, from https://lex.uz/uz/docs/6811938

Salahodjaev, R., Djalilov, B., Kobiljonov, I., Otajonov, S., & Kasimova, N. (2023). Industrialization and CO_2 emissions: Accounting for the role of renewable energy in OIC member states. *International Journal of Energy Economics and Policy, 13*(5), 37–43. DOI: 10.32479/ijeep.12544

Sandoval-Caraveo, M. D. C., Surdez-Pérez, E. G., & Lamoyi-Bocanegra, C. L. (2024). Internal and external competitiveness of small industrial companies in COVID-19. *Aibi. Revista de Investigacion Administracion e Ingenierias, 12*(1), 11–17. DOI: 10.15649/2346030X.3434

Singh, D., & Cohen, V. (2025). Socio-economic dimensions and human centricity in Industry 5.0: A study on manufacturing sectors in central and Eastern European economies. *Journal of Economic Studies (Glasgow, Scotland), 52*(2), 254–275. DOI: 10.1108/JES-02-2024-0067

Su, X., & Zhao, Y. (2025). Asymmetric time-frequency risk spillovers between the Fourth Industrial Revolution assets and commodity futures: Is economic policy uncertainty a driving factor? *Global Finance Journal, 64*, 101076. DOI: 10.1016/j.gfj.2025.101076

Sun, D., Dong, J., Gu, X., & Chen, Z. (2025). Scenario simulation and regulation policy optimization of industrial enterprise production water considering scale heterogeneity: A case study in the chemical industry. *Computers & Industrial Engineering, 202*, 110961. DOI: 10.1016/j.cie.2025.110961

Tao, X., & Cai, W. (2025). The impact of digital finance on export competitiveness: Evidence from Chinese manufacturing enterprises. *Finance Research Letters, 73*, 106629. DOI: 10.1016/j.frl.2024.106629

Tashbaev, B., Usmonov, B., & Omanov, S. (2024), "Analysis of Public Debt Policy and Its Effectiveness in Uzbekistan", Eshov, M.P., Abdurakhmanova, G.K., Burkhanov, A.U., Abdusalomova, N.B. and Ergasheva, S.T. (Ed.) *Development of International Entrepreneurship Based on Corporate Accounting and Reporting According to IFRS (Advanced Series in Management, Vol. 33B)*, Emerald Publishing Limited, Leeds, pp. 191-195. DOI: 10.1108/S1877-63612024000033B024

Usmonov, B. (2024), "Evaluation of Efficiency of Capital Management in Joint-Stock Companies in the Chemical Sector: The Case of Uzbekistan", Eshov, M.P., Abdurakhmanova, G.K., Burkhanov, A.U., Abdusalomova, N.B. and Ergasheva, S.T. (Ed.) *Development of International Entrepreneurship Based on Corporate Accounting and Reporting According to IFRS (Advanced Series in Management, Vol. 33B)*, Emerald Publishing Limited, Leeds, pp. 67-74. DOI: 10.1108/S1877-63612024000033B009

Vanchukhina, L. I., Leybert, T. B., Ergasheva, S. T., Khalikova, E. A., & Khanafieva, I. R. (2022). Integration of the Higher Education Systems of Russia and the Republic of Uzbekistan in Training for the Digital Economy. In Popkova, E. G., & Sergi, B. S. (Eds.), *Digital education in Russia and Central Asia* (pp. 3–13). Springer., DOI: 10.1007/978-981-16-9069-3_1

Wang, Z., Gao, L., & Wang, W. (2025). The impact of supply chain digitization and logistics efficiency on the competitiveness of industrial enterprises. *International Review of Economics & Finance*, *97*, 103759. DOI: 10.1016/j.iref.2024.103759

WIPO. (2024). *Global Innovation Index 2024: Unlocking the promise of social entrepreneurship* (17th ed.). Geneva, Switzerland: WIPO. Retrieved March 10, 2025, from https://www.wipo.int/web-publications/global-innovation-index-2024/assets/67729/2000%20Global%20Innovation%20Index%202024_WEB3lite.pdf

Wismansyah, A. R., Kadir, A. R., Baja, S., & Amar, M. Y. (2024). Dynamic capabilities and competitiveness: Relationship among industrial policy, structural transformation, and economic growth in Indonesian regional industries. *Journal of Infrastructure. Policy and Development*, *8*(5), 3773. DOI: 10.24294/jipd.v8i5.3773

World Bank. (2025). *Industry (including construction), value added (% of GDP)*. Retrieved March 10, 2025, fromhttps://data.worldbank.org/indicator/NV.IND.TOTL.ZS?view=chart

Xu, D., Fei, X., Chen, Q., Hong, X., & Shen, G. (2025). Interplay of industrial transformation, diversified governance, and talent gathering on the ruralization of China. *Journal of Urban Planning and Development*, *151*(1), 04024055. DOI: 10.1061/JUPDDM.UPENG-5240

Zhang, Y., Wu, D., Luo, G., Lv, H., Yang, P., Zhou, J., & Liu, L. (2025). The impact of BEV manufacturing on China's economy and environment: An input–output perspective. *Journal of Cleaner Production, 490*, 144773. DOI: 10.1016/j.jclepro.2025.144773

Zheng, X., Huang, J., & Yuan, Z. (2025). Move to innovation: Place-based industrial relocation policy and firm innovation in China. *International Journal of Emerging Markets, 20*(1), 157–186. DOI: 10.1108/IJOEM-08-2022-1299

ADDITIONAL READING

Amin, M. (2025). How does competition from informal firms impact research and development by formal manufacturing small and medium enterprises in the developing and emerging economies? *Kyklos, 78*(1), 45–73. DOI: 10.1111/kykl.12410

Aslam, J., Saleem, A., Lai, K.-H., & Kim, Y. B. (2025). Critical successes factors for the adoption of additive manufacturing: Integrated impact for circular economy model. *Technological Forecasting and Social Change, 213*, 124041. DOI: 10.1016/j.techfore.2025.124041

Bressanelli, G., & Saccani, N. (2025). Prioritizing Circular Economy actions for the decarbonization of manufacturing companies: The C-Readiness tool. *Computers & Industrial Engineering, 201*, 110876. DOI: 10.1016/j.cie.2025.110876

Huang, C., Min Du, A., & Lin, B. (2025). How does the digital economy affect the green transition: The role of industrial intelligence and e-commerce. *Research in International Business and Finance, 73*, 102541. DOI: 10.1016/j.ribaf.2024.102541

Khan, M., Majid, A., & Ahmed, A. (2025). Circular economy practices in manufacturing SMEs: A perspective of environmental management in developing countries. *Sustainable Futures : An Applied Journal of Technology, Environment and Society, 9*, 100418. DOI: 10.1016/j.sftr.2024.100418

Panza, L., & Peron, M. (2025). The role of carbon tax in the transition from a linear economy to a circular economy business model in manufacturing. *Journal of Cleaner Production, 492*, 144873. DOI: 10.1016/j.jclepro.2025.144873

Sun, S., Zhang, M., Liu, L., & Zhou, D. (2025). Synergistic governance efficiency of industrial pollution and CO_2 emissions under the digital economy. *Journal of Environmental Management, 374*, 124148. DOI: 10.1016/j.jenvman.2025.124148 PMID: 39826365

Xu, N., Shahzad, F., & Hu, R. (2025). Unveiling environmental excellence: The confluence of green Industrial Internet of Things, circular economy practices and dynamic capabilities in manufacturing firms. *Journal of Manufacturing Technology Management, 36*(2), 479–503. DOI: 10.1108/JMTM-03-2024-0155

Zhang, H., Sun, Y., Liu, X., & Liu, Y. (2025). Assessing the impact of financial development, eco-innovations on sustainable development: Insights from industrial economies of E7. *Applied Economics*, 1–24. Advance online publication. DOI: 10.1080/00036846.2025.2451989

Zisopol, D. G., Minescu, M., & Iacob, D. V. (2025). A study on the optimization of FDM parameters for the manufacturing of compression specimens from recycled ASA in the context of the transition to the circular economy. *Engineering, Technology &. Applied Scientific Research, 15*(1), 19898–19902. DOI: 10.48084/etasr.9569

KEY TERMS AND DEFINITIONS

Global competitiveness of industrial enterprises: The extent to which national industrial products are exportable, as evidenced by the share of industrial value added in GDP.

Industrial revolutions: Sources of impetus for an industrial upsurge in the economy by creating the conditions necessary for accelerating and expanding this growth.

Industrially developed economies of the world: Countries characterized by high global competitiveness in national industrial entrepreneurship, with well-developed industrial sectors (though not exclusively industrial) and active participation in the Fourth and Fifth Industrial Revolutions.

Innovation management factors: Elements influencing the role of HRM in the innovative development of a country's industrial production, identifying the most effective and preferable sources of financing for industrial innovation (whether public or private), and clarifying whether the industrial upsurge is driven by indigenous or borrowed innovations.

Macroeconomic factors: Factors that emerge at the level of the national economic system and can be regulated by the state.

Production management factors: Elements that determine which specific attributes of industrial products shape their global competitiveness, and how industrial production should be organized to optimize these attributes.

The approach to state regulation of industrial entrepreneurship: A set of fundamental principles and public management tools applied to adjust the business activities of market agents in the industrial economy, thereby enhancing their global competitiveness.

Chapter 10
Sustainable Finance and Impact Investing

Daniele Schilirò
https://orcid.org/0000-0002-2761-5510
University of Messina, Italy

ABSTRACT

The chapter delves into the concept of sustainability in finance, highlighting the primary goal of sustainable finance of directing investments toward sustainable technologies and organizations. Sustainable finance encompasses financial activities and services that adopt ESG criteria into investment decisions and organizational practices. The essay also focuses on the relationship between sustainability and financial performance and shows that, in general, organizations that adhere to fair and sustainable working practices do not experience detrimental effects on profitability. A related theme explores impact investing, which involves making investments that determine positive social or environmental effects while achieving financial returns. Despite the complex challenges of measurement and homogenization at the international level in evaluating the impact of investments on the environment and society, impact investing is growing and delivering results. It has drawn the attention of researchers as it represents the new frontier of ethical and sustainable finance.

INTRODUCTION

This contribution analyzes the concept of sustainability in the financial sector, emphasizing that the primary objective of sustainable finance is to direct investments toward organizations and the technologies they employ, enabling them to promote sustainability in economic, environmental, and social domains. The integration of ESG criteria into investment decisions and organizational practices is the essential

DOI: 10.4018/979-8-3693-8362-9.ch010

purpose of sustainable finance. It also involves enhancing risk management concerning pressing issues in the ESG domains. A closely related theme is the significance of impact investing, which focuses on making investments that generate positive social or environmental outcomes while also achieving financial returns. This approach directs capital into ventures that not only seek profit but also help address the world's most pressing challenges such climate change, resource depletion, and social inequality. Today, impact investing represents the new frontier of ethical and sustainable finance.

The structure of the chapter is as follows: After presenting the context of the study, it examines the issues of sustainability and sustainable finance, focusing on the relationship between sustainability and financial performance. It then explores impact investing, its positive effects, and its challenges. The chapter ends with a conclusion.

BACKGROUND OF THE STUDY

The background of this study is rooted in the growing recognition of sustainability in finance as an essential framework for mitigating the negative impacts of organizations on the environment and society without compromising economic performance. Sustainability has now become mainstream and includes investors with purely financial goals (Edmans and Kacperczyk, 2022). Equally important is the role of impact investments that adhere to ESG criteria and represent the new frontier of ethical and sustainable finance (Gutterman, 2024).

This study adopts a conceptual approach, making its methodology theoretical in nature. The analysis, while largely theoretical, includes a literature review, as well as data derived from reliable secondary data sources provided by international organizations.

The aim of the chapter is to first understand the relationship between sustainable finance and impact investing. The essay also seeks to answer questions such as:

Is sustainable finance outperforming traditional finance?

What is impact investing, and how do impact investments perform in terms of ESG factors, risk, and return? How do investors measure the success of impact investments beyond financial returns?

This chapter provides insights into the concepts of sustainability, sustainable development, sustainable finance, and impact investing, highlighting their interconnections. The analysis of the literature, in particular, helps clarify the potential and the challenges of sustainable finance and impact investing.

MAIN FOCUS OF THE CHAPTER

This chapter focuses on two conceptual constructs: sustainable finance and impact investing, examining both concepts. The study does not claim to provide definitive or exhaustive answers or solutions, given the limited empirical literature on impact investing and the measurement challenges that hinder a clear resolution of the issues examined. However, it aims to contribute to a deeper exploration of these increasingly relevant and significant themes, which influence the environment, organizational practices, market performance, and societal reputation.

SUSTAINABILITY AND SUSTAINABLE FINANCE

Sustainability is a fundamental and broad concept that refers to meeting present needs without compromising the ability of future generations to meet their own (Schilirò, 2019). The World Commission on Environment and Development, in its report *Our Common Future* (Brundtland, 1987), provided a widely recognized definition of sustainability closely related to sustainable development. It emphasized that sustainable development has inherent limitations imposed by the state of technology, social organization on environmental resources, and the biosphere's ability to absorb the effects of human activities.

Sustainable development has emerged as a key concept and goal for both organizations and society, receiving a significant boost in 2015 from the United Nations' 2030 Agenda for Sustainable Development and its 17 SDGs.

Furthermore, Rizzello & Kabli (2020) and Kumar et al. (2022) highlighted the launch of UNDP's SDG Finance Taxonomy, which aims to provide a roadmap for managing the financing and transaction costs of projects aligned with the SDGs, while seeking support from private capital and financial institutions.

The concept of sustainability is more critical today than ever due to growing concerns about climate change, resource depletion, and social inequality. However, progress toward the goals of the 2030 Agenda has been slow and uneven. There remains a significant risk that several of these objectives will not be achieved due to uncertainty and a lack of commitment from governments in many countries, as seen in the implementation of the COP26 agreements in Paris. Millions of people continue to live in extreme poverty, while income inequality—both within and between countries—is rising. Moreover, unsustainable consumption and production models are placing severe strain on the planet's health (Schilirò, 2019). Nevertheless, like climate action, sustainability must remain non-negotiable despite political shifts, as the future of both the planet and humanity is at stake.

In this regard, Ripple et al. (2020) highlighted the urgency and severity of climate change's impact on our planet, particularly due to the excessive consumption associated with a wealthy lifestyle. The authors suggest drastic measures to drive strong political and economic decisions. Additionally, they emphasize several strategies, primarily focusing on the energy sector.

The concept of sustainability has evolved into a rapidly growing, interdisciplinary field of research. Economic sustainability, in particular, encompasses a range of practices and principles designed to sustain long-term economic growth without compromising social or environmental well-being. It involves ethical business practices, corporate social responsibility, and sustainable resource management. Sustainability is increasingly being integrated through ESG factors, which are Environmental, Social, and Governance. These three factors provide a framework for businesses and organizations to manage their operations while balancing profitability with their impact on the planet, society, and governance structures. In other words, ESG factors serve as key pillars and a framework for evaluating an organization's performance in three critical areas. With increasing social pressure and growing environmental concerns, particularly regarding climate change, the world is placing greater emphasis on sustainable practices. As a result, ESG criteria have become essential for investors and organizations.

Furthermore, sustainable development and the achievement of sustainable development goals are closely interconnected with sustainable finance, as the latter also addresses environmental and social challenges. Sustainable development balances economic growth, social inclusion, and environmental protection to ensure long-term prosperity for both people and the Earth. Sustainable development is a suitable approach to addressing the current challenges of the global environmental economy in the context of climate change (Popkova & Sergi, 2023). It benefits a broad range of stakeholders by promoting positive external outcomes in the economy, society, and environment (Schilirò, 2024).

Campbell and Sigalov (2022) emphasize that sustainable finance incentivizes investments that support sustainable development while still generating financial returns.

Zairis et al. (2024) acknowledge the growing presence of sustainable finance in academic research and maintain that the fundamental function of finance is the productive use of available funds. They highlight that sustainable finance offers a framework that integrates ESG criteria into financial activities, services, and business and investment decisions. This framework encompasses various practices and products designed to promote sustainable economic growth, minimize environmental impact, and address social challenges.

Since environmental and social considerations are often intertwined—particularly as climate change tends to exacerbate existing inequalities—the governance of public and private organizations, including management structures and employee relations, is fundamental in ensuring the integration of social and environmental factors into decision-making.

According to Taccuso (2023), sustainable finance applies the concept of sustainable development to financial activities. Its key objective is to create long-term value by employing capital that contributes positively to society and does no harm to the environment. However, several aspects of defining sustainable development require clarification, particularly in determining the boundary between sustainable and 'normal' investments and in categorizing the various types of sustainable investments. The application of ESG criteria to investments involves evaluating complex and interconnected factors. Unfortunately, there is no universally accepted set of standards for measuring ESG performance and, therefore, assessing and comparing different investments and their sustainability.

One of the most extensively studied areas is the relationship between sustainability and financial performance. Finance becomes sustainable when ESG criteria are integrated into the decision-making process within the financial sector (Martiny et al., 2024; Ziolo et al., 2021; Schilirò, 2020a). Montalbon et al. (2007) analyzed environmental management practices to examine their relationship with firm performance. They developed a comprehensive set of these practices and empirically tested their impact on firm performance. Their study confirmed the environmental management practice–firm performance link. While previous research had examined this relationship using a smaller set of practices, this research found a positive association between environmental management practices and multiple firm performance measures, contributing to the evolving field of environmental management. Friede et al. (2015) noted that the search for a relationship between environmental, social, and governance (ESG) criteria and corporate financial performance dates back to the early 1970s. These authors identified generalizable findings and found empirical evidence supporting the validity of ESG investing in business.

Bakken (2021) highlighted the financial sector's significant power in funding sustainability projects, raising awareness of sustainability issues, particularly regarding alternative energy sources and ensuring no detrimental effects on profitability.

Schilirò (2020) also observed that in the post-COVID world, increasingly shaped by digital globalization, finance—mainly through fintech development—plays a vital role. Furthermore, as the climate crisis worsens, the financial sector becomes even more central and attractive. Environmental, social, and governance (ESG) factors are now key considerations in investment strategies and, more broadly, in organizational decision-making.

Atz et al. (2022) assessed the rapid developments of the past five years regarding whether the principle of sustainability leads to better financial performance. They argued that climate change has been a key driver in accelerating corporate efforts and financial products aimed at addressing ESG issues. Their findings have provided strong evidence for corporate managers to justify investments in sustainability as a means of improving corporate financial performance. However, returns from ESG investing showed to be indistinguishable from those of conventional investments, raising the unresolved issue of how to properly measure ESG investing.

Kumar et al. (2022) conducted a large-scale review of sustainable finance performance. Their research utilized big data analytics through machine learning to analyze scholarly research and spanned several major themes in sustainable finance (e.g., climate financing, green financing, impact investing, energy investing, and more). The approach is especially noteworthy given the relevance of applying new technologies in sustainable finance research. Their analysis of performance indicated a preference for qualitative research over quantitative research, attributed to insufficient data and case studies for the latter.

Broom (2022) reported that, in addition to benefiting the planet and promoting a more just and inclusive society, substantial empirical evidence demonstrates that organizations adopting sustainable finance criteria actually yield higher returns for investors. Broom (2022) attributes these positive outcomes to several factors, one of which is shifting customer attitudes. A U.S. survey found that two-thirds of consumers across all age groups prefer to buy from companies that align with their values. Among millennials (aged 18 to 34), this figure rises to 83%. Additionally, a global survey cited by Broom (2022) found that consumers are four to six times more likely to buy from a brand with a corporate purpose they support. Conversely, if a company takes actions they disagree with, three-quarters of respondents indicated they would stop purchasing from that brand and encourage others to do the same.

Moreover, carbon-intensive industries—such as coal, oil, and gas—are facing increasing difficulties and higher costs when raising capital, as major lenders are often reluctant or outright refuse to do business with them. In contrast, companies adopting sustainable practices are more likely to secure contracts, reduce costs by using fewer resources, face less stringent regulations, retain top talent, and avoid financial losses associated with outdated, carbon-intensive processes.

This literature highlights the crucial role of finance in shaping decisions that drive sustainability and impact the environment, the future of human life, and societal inclusivity, while ensuring economic performance and profitability are not neglected. It generally indicates that sustainable finance is more effective than traditional finance.

Companies that follow ESG criteria are more likely to attract customers and employees, seize business opportunities linked to societal trends such as climate change and financial inclusion, and avoid environmental fines or regulatory intervention. Such companies tend to generate high risk-adjusted returns, making them appealing even to investors with purely financial motives (Edmans & Kacperczyk, 2022). Therefore, sustainable finance, which integrates ESG factors into investment strategies, is becoming increasingly prominent and widely adopted. Furthermore, both the private and public sectors must integrate ESG elements into sustainable finance (Schilirò, 2020a). Thus, the relationship between ESG and sustainable finance is indispensable.

Furthermore, the application of ESG criteria significantly impacts finance professionals within organizations. Those who learn (or help develop) how to manage this new approach are likely to help their organizations create more value and, through their daily work, make a substantial positive impact.

The scale of sustainable finance is poised for significant growth in the coming years. Investors and financial institutions are increasingly using ESG criteria to assess risk and identify sustainable growth opportunities. Green finance, climate finance, social finance, sustainable banks, innovation in financial products and services, and regulatory developments are all relevant aspects of sustainable finance.

Green finance is a crucial component of sustainable finance, focusing on environmentally friendly investments and practices that contribute to positive environmental outcomes. It specifically supports environmental projects, such as renewable energy, energy efficiency, pollution prevention, and conservation.

Bhatnagar et al. (2022) highlighted that green finance plays a vital role in addressing climate change and promoting a more sustainable economy. It has also emerged as an instrument for achieving carbon neutrality and fostering sustainable economic growth.

Fu et al. (2023) focused on investments in green and low-carbon solutions to combat climate change, as well as on promoting sustainable economic growth. The authors recommend policy measures to advance green finance and foster sustainable growth by aligning financial incentives with sustainable outcomes, enhancing transparency, and incorporating social equity into green finance initiatives. They also emphasized the necessity of regulatory frameworks to strengthen green finance and support carbon-neutral practices.

Green finance utilizes green bonds and green loans as financial instruments in the credit and capital markets. Specifically, green bonds are debt securities issued by companies, banks, states, and supranational bodies to raise funds for environmentally sustainable and climate-related projects.

In recent years, global companies have significantly increased their green investments, including green bonds, which raise capital for specific environmental initiatives. The proceeds from green bond issuance must be allocated to projects with clear environmental benefits, which should be explicitly described in the issuance prospectus.

Climate finance targets investments that reduce greenhouse gas emissions and support adaptation to climate change's impacts. This includes financing for renewable energy, energy efficiency, and climate resilience projects.

Social finance aims to address social issues such as inequality, inclusive growth, healthcare, education, and community development. Social bonds are bond instruments whose proceeds are used, in whole or in part, to finance new projects with a strong social impact or to refinance existing social initiatives. Another instrument used in social finance is social-impact investing.

Sustainable banks incorporate ESG criteria into their lending, investment, and retail banking services. For this reason, they adopt methodologies for assessing creditworthiness that consider the ESG risks and opportunities of counterparties. Their ESG-aligned activities may include green lending, sustainability-linked lending, and advisory services for sustainable business practices.

Sustainability and ESG criteria drive innovation in financial products and services. Therefore, the development of new financial instruments and services aims to support sustainability, as, for example, sustainability-linked bonds, green mortgages, and microfinance for sustainable projects.

Furthermore, many countries and international bodies are developing regulatory frameworks and standards to promote sustainable finance, such as the EU Taxonomy for Sustainable Activities and the Task Force on Climate-Related Financial Disclosures (TCFD). It is important to remember that the EU taxonomy is a cornerstone of the EU's sustainable finance framework and a key market transparency tool. It helps direct investments to the economic activities most critical for the transition, aligning with the objectives of the European Green Deal (European Commission, 2020).

Sustainable investing involves strategies that consider ESG factors in portfolio selection and management. These can include socially responsible investing (SRI) and impact investing.

However, the boundary between sustainable finance and ESG is often unclear. Typically, sustainable investing is an investment approach that considers ESG factors in portfolio selection. On the other hand, responsible investing is defined as an investment approach that explicitly recognizes the relevance of ESG factors for the investor and the market's long-term health (Roncalli, 2023). In general, ESG investing aims to incorporate extra-financial analysis during asset selection.

As highlighted above, we are increasingly witnessing the growth of sustainable finance, driven substantially by the growing awareness of environmental and social challenges, regulatory changes, investor demand, and the recognition that sustainable practices often lead to better long-term financial performance and risk management.

We acknowledge that no universally accepted framework or set of standards exists for measuring ESG performance. However, ESG scores are widely used to quantify an organization's environmental, social, and governance (ESG) efforts, assigning a numerical value or letter grade to reflect performance in these areas. Investors, rating agencies, and other stakeholders use ESG scores to evaluate an organization's sustainability initiatives and ethical practices. These scores can range from low to high, indicating the extent to which ESG considerations are integrated into operations and decision-making processes. ESG scores are determined based on various metrics and indicators related to environmental, social, and governance factors. These may include data on carbon emissions, energy efficiency, water usage, waste management, employee diversity, labor practices, executive compensation, board diversity, transparency, and ethical business conduct. The specific metrics used vary depending on the ESG scoring methodology or framework applied. Furthermore, organizations often develop tailored ESG metrics based on sector and stakeholder needs. This lack of consistency makes it difficult to accurately assess and compare organizational performance.

Another key aspect of making sustainable finance effective is overcoming the problem of greenwashing. As sustainable finance products now cover a broad range of instruments—from bonds and loans to, more recently, derivatives—they address various aspects of sustainability, including financing ‘green’ and ‘social’ projects and broader sustainability-linked targets across environmental, social, and governance (ESG) matters. Investors are becoming increasingly aware of their portfolios' environmental impacts and prefer to invest in organizations that effectively manage ESG risks and opportunities. The financial market's growing focus on environmental initiatives and sustainable investing is putting increasing pressure on executives, with many feeling compelled to prioritize ESG initiatives. In response, some organizations resort to greenwashing—creating false impressions or making misleading claims about the environmental responsibility of their products and policies.

Greenwashing is common in sustainable finance practices and manifests in various ways, such as in the assessment and verification of ESG objectives, reporting standards and measurement methods, and the lack of reporting obligations and ESG commitments.

To conclude, the lack of standardized metrics, the need for better quality and comparability of ESG data, and the widespread practice of greenwashing are challenges that must be addressed to further advance sustainable finance.

IMPACT INVESTING

The previous section examined key aspects of sustainable finance, including sustainable investing, which involves incorporating ESG factors into investment strategies for portfolio selection and management. In fact, investors have recently concentrated on high-profile sustainability-related themes such as clean tech, infrastructure, affordable housing, energy-efficient real estate, or sustainable forestry.

Gutterman (2024) states that impact investing is one strategy sustainable investors use to consider ESG factors. The term was first used by the Rockefeller Foundation in 2007. Its primary goal is to mitigate the negative effects of business activity on society or the environment (Investopedia, 2025). Impact investing not only considers ESG factors but also intentionally seeks to create positive social or environmental change through the selection and management of investees, including entrepreneurs launching businesses with a clear social or environmental purpose. As Gutterman (2024) explains, impact investing represents an advanced stage of sustainable investing, which originated with the socially responsible investment movement in the 1970s. This movement was characterized by the use of negative, or exclusionary, screening processes designed to avoid specific assets based on environmental, social, and governance (ESG) criteria. These criteria included moral values (e.g., avoiding investments in tobacco or gambling), standards and norms (e.g., human rights considerations), ethical convictions (e.g., opposition to animal testing), and legal requirements (e.g., excluding controversial armaments such as cluster bombs or landmines to comply with international conventions). The next stage introduced 'best-in-class' (positive) screening, which contrasts significantly with negative screening. This approach emphasizes making investment and lending decisions based on the demonstrated high ESG performance of sectors, companies, or projects, as well as adherence to minimum standards of business practice aligned with international norms on climate protection, human rights, working conditions, and anti-corruption measures.

Another definition is provided by UNDP's Istanbul International Center for Private Sector in Development (IICPSD, 2024), who defined impact investing as the deployment of funds into investments that generate a measurable and beneficial social or environmental impact alongside a financial return on investment. It represents an innovative way of boosting the private sector's contribution to sustainable development.

Authors such as Freireich and Fulton (2009), Höchstädter and Scheck (2015), and Gao and Hoepner (2024) characterize impact investing as investments made with the explicit intention of fostering environmental sustainability and yielding both positive social impacts and financial returns.

As mentioned earlier, the gist of impact investing is represented by investments that generate positive environmental or social impacts without neglecting financial returns. Its primary purpose is to deploy capital to drive meaningful social change. This strategy can span various asset classes, including stocks, bonds, mutual funds, and microloans.

Most impact investing is carried out by institutional investors (e.g., hedge funds, private foundations, banks, pension funds, and other fund managers). However, other players (e.g., web-based investment platforms, investor networks) offer opportunities for individuals to participate (Investopedia, 2025).

Impact investments influence various industries, including healthcare, education, clean and renewable energy, and agriculture. Several states and international institutions have also committed to various initiatives to support the expansion of sustainable finance and impact investments. A prominent example is the European Union, which, within the European Green Deal, has introduced requirements for financial products to be labeled "green" or "sustainable," It also created a taxonomy for sustainable economic activities to help establish standards for determining whether an activity qualifies as environmentally sustainable.

To get an idea of the size of the impact investing market, the GIIN (2024) report estimates that over 3,907 organizations currently manage $1.571 trillion USD in impact investing assets under management (AUM) worldwide. To make this estimate, GIIN (2024) uses a comprehensive database of impact AUM managed by organizations deploying an impact investing strategy. It arrives at an estimate of the supply of capital being used for impact investing strategies—essentially defining the size of the market. Market size expansion can be attributed to factors such as the compound annual growth rate (CAGR) of impact AUM, the growth in the supply of capital, and the increasing number of investor organizations. GIIN's data show that larger investors are specifically driving this growth. The major players in the market are institutional asset owners, particularly pension funds, as well as insurance companies and sovereign wealth funds, which are beginning to reshape their portfolios by incorporating impact-driven investments as a strategic priority.

Across a subset of 1,593 organizations, excluding outliers, GIIN (2024) estimates that the average investment portfolio holds $986 million USD in impact AUM, while the median portfolio holds $42 million USD. The report highlights that an outsized proportion of investments is managed in Europe and the U.S., while Asia—along with emerging markets and the Global South—remains underrepresented and underinvested. Impact AUM allocation continues to be disproportionately insufficient to keep pace with the region's growing needs, challenges, and development opportunities. The large SDG financing gap persists. However, while the mismatch remains, the disparity is not as severe as it was previously.

Furthermore, a survey reported by Investopedia (2025) indicated that the majority of impact investors (approximately 67%) seek market-rate returns. In particular, ESG investors prioritize organizations with ethical governance and utilize ESG factors to enhance traditional financial analysis by identifying potential risks and opportunities beyond standard valuations.

According to Investopedia (2025), socially responsible investing (SRI) is distinct from ESG investing. Unlike ESG analysis, which shapes valuations, SRI uses ESG factors to apply negative or positive screens to the investment universe. While SRI is often considered a type of impact investing, it may focus more on avoiding harm, such as through tobacco-related exclusions. Impact investing, in contrast, typically emphasizes generating a positive impact through its investments. Furthermore, SRI is also known as green investing when focused on environmental causes.

Hand et al. (2020) in their *Annual Impact Investor Survey* identified and explained the core elements of impact investing, including intentionality, expectation of financial returns, range of return expectations, asset classes, and impact measurement. In particular, intentionality is a qualifying element and essential to impact investing. Additionally, impact investments target financial returns that range from below market rate to risk-adjusted market rate (with two-thirds of impact investment capital seeking risk-adjusted market rates). Asset classes are varied, including, but not limited to, cash equivalents, fixed income, venture capital, and private equity. Impact investments are not grants; investors expect their investments to generate a financial return on capital or, at a minimum, a return of capital.

A hallmark of impact investing is the investor's commitment to measuring and reporting the social and environmental performance and progress of underlying investments. This ensures transparency and accountability, while also informing the practice of impact investing and contributing to the field's development.

Moreover, Hand et al. (2020) emphasized that financial institutions play a leading role in attracting the most capital within the impact investing market and deploying impact financing to address climate challenges.

The literature on impact investing has focused primarily on private equity and conceptualization (Agrawal & Hockerts, 2021; Andersen & Tekula, 2022; Barber et al., 2021; Gutterman, 2024; Meng et al., 2022; Moran & Ward-Christie, 2022; Roundy et al., 2017).

Fu et al. (2024) also highlighted that green finance is closely related to impact investing. They emphasize that investors are willing to accept lower financial returns in exchange for non-financial benefits that enhance environmental and social performance.

Another contribution in the same direction is Jaya (2024), who explores the intersection of impact investing and green finance, highlighting the role of institutional investors in reshaping financial markets. Adopting a qualitative approach, the author finds that key regulations, such as the EU's SFDR and the TCFD recommendations, support transparency and drive the adoption of sustainable practices. Furthermore, Jaya (2024) observes a positive link between robust ESG performance and financial returns, demonstrating the compatibility of environmental responsibility with profit objectives.

Another interesting study is Chiappini et al. (2023), which analyzes the intersection of research on impact investing and its closely related financial vehicles. The study jointly examines both the literature on impact investing and the literature on the correlated financial products used in the industry. The authors observe that academic research on impact investing generally uses the specific financial mechanism of social impact bonds. However, they argue that, given the complex nature of impact investing it is more useful to adopt a plurality of financial vehicles and, therefore, several financial tools.

Gao and Hoepner (2024) emphasize the important role of impact financing, particularly in generating large-scale impacts. Additionally, impact financing helps bridge the capital gap while advancing sustainable development goals. Their research suggests that incorporating impact considerations into debt financing presents significant potential for financial institutions to achieve both financial and environmental outcomes. Given the financial sector's pivotal role in sustainability, they also find that financial institutions increasingly integrate environmental impacts alongside financial returns as part of their objectives. Gao and Hoepner (2024) also advocate for making impact investing more accessible and mainstream by promoting impact financing, which can address a wide range of institutional needs with more liquid and sustained capital. Furthermore, market regulation is crucial in impact investing. It is an effective tool to oversee and lead financial institutions to integrate environmental considerations and achieve large-scale impact. Gao and Hoepner's empirical study demonstrates that impact financing is an effective model for scaling up impact.

Berk and van Binsbergen (2025), through an empirical investigation that corroborates their theoretical propositions by examining firm changes in ESG status, explore the mechanism linking investor action to its societal impact. In particular, they seek to evaluate the impact of divestiture initiatives in secondary markets by determining whether these initiatives have materially affected the cost of capital. Berk and van Binsbergen (2025) distinguish between primary and secondary markets, emphasizing that achieving social change through the secondary market requires a significantly higher degree of participation compared to the primary market. Their results suggest that, rather than divesting in secondary markets, socially conscious investors should invest in primary markets and leverage their stakes to exercise control rights and influence corporate policy. They conclude that, at current participation levels, the divestiture strategy is unlikely to have a significant impact on the long-term cost of capital for targeted firms. They propose that utilizing primary markets would be more effective for driving social change.

Regarding the literature, empirical research on impact investing remains limited. Existing studies primarily examine this topic within the equity market, often neglecting impact financing in the credit market.

To conclude, impact investing is a strategy used by sustainable investors to consider ESG factors into their decision-making. This strategy not only considers ESG factors but also intentionally seeks positive change.

Among the positive effects, we can mention:

- Social and Environmental Benefits: Impact investing helps fund projects that address global challenges, such as climate change, poverty, and inequality, leading to measurable social and environmental improvements.
- Financial Returns with Purpose: Investors can achieve competitive financial returns while aligning their portfolios with their values and sustainability goals.
- Closing Funding Gaps: It provides the necessary capital to sectors that traditional investments may overlook.
- Encouraging Corporate Responsibility: It encourages companies and financial institutions to integrate Environmental, Social, and Governance (ESG) factors into their business strategies.
- Long-Term Economic Stability: Sustainable investments contribute to long-term economic resilience by reducing risks associated with environmental and social disruptions.

One crucial aspect of impact investing is measurement. Brandenburg (2012) suggests that impact investors can choose from various principles, frameworks, and standards when developing strategies for measuring, managing, and reporting on their investments' impact.

These include the IFC Operating Principles for Impact Management, which constitute a global standard and provide an end-to-end framework of best practices for investors in the design, implementation, and continuous improvement of their impact management systems and processes. They offer a reference point for assessing the impact management systems of funds and institutions while enhancing transparency and accountability in capital markets.

Another key framework is the UN Principles for Responsible Investment, which consist of six principles establishing a global standard for responsible investing.

Additionally, the Global Impact Investment Network's IRIS+ system supports the practice of impact investing by promoting transparency, credibility, and accountability in using impact data for decision-making across the impact investment industry (IRIS, 2024).

As highlighted by Gutterman (2024), the measurement problem is relevant because impact investors must be able to assess their outcomes and demonstrate the achievement of their objectives.

Furthermore, impact investing relies on several impact measurement and management tools to assess and track social and environmental outcomes. These include, among others: Impact Management Project – A guideline to help investors classify and measure their impact investments. ESG and Impact Rating Systems, such as the Global Reporting Initiative (GRI) – A framework for sustainability reporting that helps organizations disclose their ESG performance. Financial and Social Impact Metrics, such as Social Return on Investment (SROI) – A method that quantifies the social value created per dollar invested. Data and Technology-Driven Impact Tools, such as HIP Investor Ratings – A system that rates investments based on their potential for positive impact, and Impact Reporting & Investment Standards (IRIS+ Metrics) – A set of standardized metrics for tracking impact performance over time.

However, the issue remains: for impact investing to move forward and mature as an industry, progress must continue on the harmonization of impact measurement and reporting frameworks.

Therefore, challenges such as impact measurement and standardization persist, as measuring and comparing investments in terms of their impact on society and the environment is a complex task due to the lack of universal standards and methodologies. There are risks of greenwashing, as some companies and funds may exaggerate or misrepresent their impact credentials to attract investment without bringing about real change. This pattern of harmful activity is prevalent in the textile and oil industries. In Asia, for example, the textile industry, a center for global production, frequently causes severe environmental damage, such as water contamination and excessive waste, due to a lack of robust environmental regulations. Likewise, several African countries suffer from the combined negative impacts of the oil industry and the dumping of textile waste from Western countries. These negative environmental activities are not reflected in the companies' reports. Furthermore, there are regulatory and policy uncertainties, as a lack of clear regulations and inconsistent policies across markets can create uncertainty and barriers for impact investors. There are also liquidity constraints, as some impact investments, especially in private markets, may have lower liquidity than traditional investments, making them less attractive to some investors. Finally, a key issue is limited awareness and accessibility, as many investors, especially retail investors, are not fully aware of impact investment opportunities. They also face high minimum investment requirements, which represent barriers to entry.

SOLUTIONS AND RECCOMENDATIONS

The analysis conducted in this chapter on the two key concepts, Sustainable Finance and Impact Investing, does not provide definitive solutions, but it offers some interesting and useful indications.

Firstly, the examination of the literature on sustainable finance indicates that it has the potential to outperform traditional finance. This is because it considers and positively impacts a broader context, encompassing not only economic and financial factors, but also environmental and social ones.

Secondly, impact investing represents a further advancement in sustainable finance. It substantively incorporates ESG criteria and offers positive returns, particularly in environmental terms, despite its inherent risks. The primary challenge lies in accurately measuring impact, effectively managing these initiatives, and avoiding greenwashing practices. These practices deceive stakeholders and ultimately damage the reputation of genuine impact investments. The analysis strongly indicates that a successful impact investing approach prioritizes a long-term strategy, rather than reacting to the frequent fluctuations caused by political and economic uncertainties.

FUTURE RESEARCH DIRECTIONS

The conceptual analysis conducted in this contribution on sustainable finance and impact investing suggests several lines of future research.

In the realm of sustainable finance, crucial areas for future research include the investigation of global standards and frameworks. Additionally, research is needed to enhance ESG data quality. This requires investigations aimed at developing standardized, reliable, and comparable ESG metrics, facilitating globally consistent ESG reporting and bolstering overall data reliability. Furthermore, future analyses should emphasize government policy issues and explore various avenues for implementing reforms that would establish a robust sustainable financial system, particularly in developing countries.

Concerning impact investing, it is crucial to enrich the currently limited empirical research on the subject. Furthermore, future research should tackle the challenge of impact measurement, particularly by developing methodologies to enable comparison of impact across diverse sectors and geographies. It should also aim to enhance policy and regulatory environments. Specifically, research should explore the role of government policies in fostering impact investing and analyze the effects of regulatory frameworks on the expansion of the impact investing market.

CONCLUSION

Sustainable finance and impact investing are related concepts, both aiming to align financial activities with environmental and social goals. Sustainable finance refers to the integration of ESG criteria into financial decision-making across various types of investments, lending, and capital allocation. It encompasses a range of financial instruments and strategies designed to promote long-term economic growth while minimizing negative environmental and social impacts. Sustainable finance encompasses key components such as green bonds, sustainability-linked loans, ESG-focused investment funds, corporate sustainability reporting, and climate risk assessment in financial institutions.

Since sustainability is the core concept of sustainable finance, its main goal is to promote responsible financial practices contributing to global sustainability efforts.

Furthermore, this essay sought to answer the questions concerning the definition of impact investing and the performance of impact investments in terms of ESG factors, risk, and return. Impact investing, a component of sustainable finance, actively seeks to generate measurable positive social or environmental impact in conjunction with financial returns. In contrast to general ESG investing, which primarily focuses on mitigating risks, impact investing intentionally allocates capital to projects, businesses, or funds that yield tangible benefits. By emphasizing specific social or environmental outcomes, such as renewable energy, affordable housing, or healthcare, impact investing necessitates measurable impact reporting. Its core objective is to drive positive change while securing financial returns. Given the scarcity of empirical research and the lack of a universally accepted standard for measuring investment impact, offering a conclusive answer regarding their performance is difficult. Nevertheless, in numerous instances, they appear to achieve positive outcomes.

In conclusion, our analysis of these two essential strategies to implement ESG objectives suggests that sustainable finance provides the framework for integrating ESG considerations into financial decision-making. At the same time, impact investing is a more proactive approach within this framework since it enables direct capital channeling toward projects that drive measurable positive change. In practice, both are essential for achieving global sustainability goals, but impact investing plays a more targeted role in creating direct social and environmental benefits.

REFERENCES

Agrawal, A., & Hockerts, K. (2021). Impact investing: Review and research agenda. *Journal of Small Business and Entrepreneurship*, *33*(2), 153–181. DOI: 10.1080/08276331.2018.1551457

Andersen, K., & Tekula, R. (2022). Value, Values, and Valuation: The Marketization of Charitable Foundation Impact Investing. *Journal of Business Ethics*, *179*(4), 1033–1052. DOI: 10.1007/s10551-022-05159-1

Atz, U., Van Holt, T., Liu, Z. Z., & Bruno, C. (2022). Does Sustainability Generate Better Financial Performance? Review, Meta-analysis, and Propositions. *Journal of Sustainable Finance & Investment*, *13*(1), 802–825. DOI: 10.1080/20430795.2022.2106934

Bakken, R. (2021). What Is Sustainable Finance and Why Is It Important? *Blog Harvard Extension School*, August 09. https://extension.harvard.edu/blog/what-is-sustainable-finance-and-why-is-it-important/#:~:text=What%20Is%20Sustainable%20Finance%20and%20Why%20Is%20It,%E2%80%94%20finance%20chief%20among%20them.%20Enter%3A%20sustainable%20finance

Barber, B. M., Morse, A., & Yasuda, A. (2021). Impact investing. *Journal of Financial Economics*, *139*(1), 162–185. DOI: 10.1016/j.jfineco.2020.07.008

Berk, J. B., & van Binsbergen, J. H. (2025). The impact of impact investing. *Journal of Financial Economics*, *164*(103972), 1–16.

Bhatnagar, M., Taneja, S., & Özen, E. (2022). A wave of green start-ups in India—The study of green finance as a support system for sustainable entrepreneurship. *Green Finance*, *4*(2), 253–273. DOI: 10.3934/GF.2022012

Brandenburg, M. (2012). Impact Investing's Three Measurement Tools, *SSIR*, October 12, 2012. https://ssir.org/articles/entry/impact_investings_three_measurement_tools

Broom, D. (2022). What is sustainable finance and how it is changing the world, *World Economic Forum*, January 20. https://www.weforum.org/agenda/2022/01/what-is-sustainable-finance/

Brundtland, G. H. (1987). Our Common Future: Report of the World Commission on Environment and Development. Geneva, UN-Dokument A/42/427. http://www.un-documents.net/ocf-ov.htm

Campbell, J. Y., & Sigalov, R. (2022). Portfolio choice with sustainable spending: A model of reaching for yield. *Journal of Financial Economics*, *143*(1), 188–206. DOI: 10.1016/j.jfineco.2021.05.018

Chiappini, H., Marinelli, N., Jalal, R. N.-U., & Birindelli, G. (2023). Past, present and future of impact investing and closely related financial vehicles: A literature review, *Sustainability Accounting. Management and Policy Journal*, *14*(7), 232–257. DOI: 10.1108/SAMPJ-09-2022-0471

Edmans, A., & Kacperczyk, M. (2022). Sustainable Finance. *Review of Finance*, *26*(6), 1309–1313. DOI: 10.1093/rof/rfac069

European Commission. (2020). Taxonomy Regulation for climate change mitigation, 18 June, 2020. European Commission. https://finance.ec.europa.eu/sustainable-finance/tools-and-standards/eu-taxonomy-sustainable-activities_en

Freireich, J., & Fulton, K. (2009). *Investing for Social & Environmental Impact. A Design for Catalyzing an Emerging Industry*. Monitor Institute, MA. https://www2.deloitte.com/in/en/pages/financial-services/articles/investing-for-socialandenvironmentalimpact.html

Friede, G., Busch, T., & Bassen, A. (2015). ESG and financial performance: Aggregated evidence from more than 2000 empirical studies. *Journal of Sustainable Finance & Investment*, *5*(4), 210–233. DOI: 10.1080/20430795.2015.1118917

Gao, Y., & Hoepner, A. G. F. (2024). Virtues of impact financing: Do financial institutions benefit from considering the environmental impact on financing decisions? *Journal of Environmental Management*, *359*(120259), 1–14. DOI: 10.1016/j.jenvman.2024.120259 PMID: 38350274

GIIN. (2024). *Sizing the Impact Investing Market 2024*, Global Impact Investing Network. https://thegiin.org/publication/research/sizing-the-impact-investing-market-2024/

Gutterman, A. S. (2024). What is Impact Investing, *SSRNpaper*, August 20, 2024. http://dx.doi.org/DOI: 10.2139/ssrn.3823837

Hand, D., Dithrich, H., Sunderji, S., & Nova, N. (2020). *2020 Annual Impact Investor Survey*, June 11, 2020, GIIN. https://thegiin.org/publication/research/impinv-survey-2020/

Höchstädter, A. K., & Scheck, B. (2015). What's in a name: An analysis of impact investing understandings by academics and practitioners. *Journal of Business Ethics*, *132*(2), 449–475. DOI: 10.1007/s10551-014-2327-0

IICPSD. (2024). Impact Investing, UNDP's Istanbul International Center for Private Sector in Development. https://www.undp.org/policy-centre/istanbul/impact-investing-0#:~:text=Impact%20investing%20is%20defined%20as,or%20environmental%20impact%20alongside%20a

Investopedia (2025). Impact Investing: Definition, Types, and Examples, Investopedia, February 09, 2025._https://www.investopedia.com/terms/i/impact-investing.asp#:~:text=Impact%20investing%20involves%20making%20investments%20to%20help%20create,such%20as%20stocks%2C%20bonds%2C%20mutual%20funds%2C%20or%20microloans

IRIS. (2024). IRIS+/About, GIIN. https://iris.thegiin.org/about/

Jaya, O. S. (2024). Nexus between Impact Investing and Green Finance in Driving Sustainable Development. *Advances in Applied Accounting Research*, *2*(1), 26–38. DOI: 10.60079/aaar.v2i1.229

Kumar, S., Sharma, D., Rao, S., Lim, M. W., & Mangla, S. K. (2022). *Past, present, and future of sustainable finance: insights from big data analytics through machine learning of scholarly research, Annals of Operations Research.* Springer., DOI: 10.1007/s10479-021-04410-8

Martiny, A., Taglialatela, J., Testa, F., & Iraldo, F. (2024). Determinants of environmental social and governance (ESG) performance: A systematic literature review. *Journal of Cleaner Production*, *456*, 142213. DOI: 10.1016/j.jclepro.2024.142213

Meng, T., Newth, J., & Woods, C. R. (2022). Ethical Sensemaking in Impact Investing: Reasons and Motives in the Chinese Renewable Energy Sector. *Journal of Business Ethics*, *179*(3), 1091–1117. DOI: 10.1007/s10551-022-05160-8

Montabon, F., Sroufe, R., & Narasimhan, R. (2007). An examination of corporate reporting, environmental management practices and firm performance. *Journal of Operations Management*, *25*(5), 998–1014. https://doi.org/https://doi.org/10.1016/j.jom.2006.10.003. DOI: 10.1016/j.jom.2006.10.003

Moran, M., & Ward-Christie, L. (2022). Blended Social Impact Investment Transactions: Why Are They So Complex? *Journal of Business Ethics*, *179*(15), 1011–1031. DOI: 10.1007/s10551-022-05153-7

Popkova, E. G., & Sergi, B. S. (Eds.). (2023). *Current problems of the global environmental economy under the conditions of climate change and the perspectives of sustainable development.* Springer. DOI: 10.1007/978-3-031-19979-0

Ripple, W. J., Wolf, C., Newsome, T., Barnard, P., & Moomaw, W. R. (2020). World scientists' warning of a climate emergency. *Bioscience*, *70*(1), 8–12. DOI: 10.1093/biosci/biz152

Rizzello, A., & Kabli, A. (2020). Sustainable financial partnerships for the SDGs: The case of social impact bonds. *Sustainability (Basel)*, *12*(13), 5362. DOI: 10.3390/su12135362

Roncalli, T. (2023). *Handbook of Sustainable Finance*, Creative Commons Attribution 4.0 International License. https://creativecommons.org/licenses/by/4.0

Roundy, P. T., Holzhauer, H., & Dai, Y. (2017). Finance or philanthropy? Exploring the motivations and criteria of impact investors. *Social Responsibility Journal*, *13*(3), 491–512. DOI: 10.1108/SRJ-08-2016-0135

Schilirò, D. (2019). Sustainability, Innovation, and Efficiency: A Key Relationship. In Ziolo, M., & Sergi, B. S. (Eds.), *Financing Sustainable Development* (pp. 83–102). Palgrave Macmillan. DOI: 10.1007/978-3-030-16522-2_4

Schilirò, D. (2020). Towards digital globalization and the covid-19 challenge. *International Journal of Business Management and Economic Research*, *11*(2), 1710–1716.

Schilirò, D. (2020a). Sustainable public finance system. In Ziolo, M. (Ed.), *Finance and Sustainable Development. Designing Sustainable Financial Systems* (pp. 163–177). Routledge., DOI: 10.4324/9781003011132

Schilirò, D. (2024). Sustainable finance and sustainable public finance system, *MPRA paper* No. 120216.

Taccuso, F. (2023). Finanza sostenibile: cos'è, come funziona, ESG e come investire, *Consulenza vincente*, 20 luglio 2023._https://www.consulenzavincente.it/finanza-sostenibile/

Zairis, G., Liargovas, P., & Apostolopoulos, N. (2024). Sustainable Finance and ESG Importance: A Systematic Literature Review and Research Agenda, *Sustainability*, *16*(7), 2878, 1-13. https://doi.org/DOI: 10.3390/su16072878

Ziolo, M., Bąk, I., Cheba, K., Spoz, A., & Niedzielski, P. (2021). Sustainable financial systems toward sustainability in finance. Institutional and managerial approach. *Procedia Computer Science*, *192*, 4237–4248. DOI: 10.1016/j.procs.2021.09.200

ADDITIONAL READING

Joshipura, M., Mathur, S., & Kedia, N. (2024). Sustainable investing and financing for sustainable development: A hybrid review. *Sustainable Development (Bradford)*, *32*(6), 4469–4485. Advance online publication. DOI: 10.1002/sd.2912

Roy, J. K., & Vasa, L. (2025, March 01). Financial technology and environmental, social and governance in sustainable finance: A bibliometric and thematic content analysis. *Discover Sustainability*, *6*(148), 1–22. DOI: 10.1007/s43621-025-00934-2

Seema, T., Singh, H., Wadhwa, S., & Tandon, D. (2021). Scaling Impact Investment for Sustainable Development Goals: An Empirical Analysis, *Australasian Accounting. Business and Finance Journal, 15*(5), 4–21. DOI: 10.14453/aabfj.v15i5.2

Sreenu, N. (2024). The impact of Fintech and green bonds on the Indian renewable energy production, *Renewable Energy*, 237, Part C, 121807, 1-10. https://doi.org/ DOI: 10.1016/j.renene.2024.121807

Vega, A. G., Torre Olmo, B., & de la Cuesta-González, M. (2025). A multistakeholder approach to impact investing: Focus on institutional investors and key dimensions. *Research in International Business and Finance, 75*(102766), 1–28. DOI: 10.1016/j.ribaf.2025.102766

KEY TERMS AND DEFINITIONS

Sustainable finance: is essentially integrating environmental, social, and governance (ESG) considerations into financial decisions.

Sustainability: is about using resources responsibly so that they are available for future generations. The most widely recognized definition comes from United Nations Commission (Brundtland, 1987): Sustainable development is development that meets the needs of the present without compromising the ability of future generations to meet their own needs.

ESG criteria: are a set of standards that socially conscious investors use to screen potential investments. They evaluate an organization's performance in three domains: Environmental, Social, and Governance.

Sustainable Development: is a concept addressing the need for economic growth while simultaneously protecting the environment and ensuring social equity.

Impact investing: is about intentionally generating positive social or environmental impact alongside financial returns.

Greenwashing: describes the practice of making misleading or unsubstantiated claims about the environmental benefits of a product, service, or organization.

Chapter 11
Contribution of Local E-Business to the Sustainable Development of Smart Territories:
The Mediation of Green Accounting in Logistics Complexes of Ethiopia

Shashi Kant
https://orcid.org/0000-0003-4722-5736
Bule Hora University, Ethiopia

Tamire Ashuro
Bule Hora University, Ethiopia

ABSTRACT

In order to augment sustainable progression in smart territories, this investigation depicts the association ships among green accounting as well as local e-business practices. The investigation employs exploratory factor analysis to uncover substantial constituents as well as their interactions in light of the growing implication of sustainability in communal procedures. The outcomes manifest that green accounting plays a critical mediating function in the interaction among local e-business activities as well as sustainable development. Establishments may improve their operational efficiency as well as sustainability outcomes by incorporating ecologically friendly accounting methods into their e-business initiatives. In order to maximize the influence of these activities, the investigation underscores the need of cultivating a sustainable

DOI: 10.4018/979-8-3693-8362-9.ch011

culture inside firms as well as the necessity of stakeholder participation. While the practical recommendations urge firms to establish quantifiable sustainability.

INTRODUCTION

The importance of local e-businesses in promoting economic progression as well as maintaining environmental sustainability has been brought to light in recent years by the worldwide emphasis on sustainable development (Kitukutha et al., 2023). The Brundtlas well as Commission's 1987 report served as the foundation for the idea of sustainable development, which emphasizes how important it is for economic activity to satisfy current needs without endangering future generations. This idea has acquired popularity in a number of settings, particularly in developing nations like Ethiopia, where there are both possibilities as well as problems due to the interaction of technology, business, as well as sustainability (Ishengoma & Shao, 2024). According to empirical investigation, e-business may greatly augment sustainable practices by increasing productivity as well as cutting waste. Investigation has manifest that digital platforms reduce carbon footprints by streamlining logistics as well as enabling improved resource management. Even if there have been notable developments, there are still real-world obstacles (Luhtala et al., 2024). The capacity of several local e-businesses in Ethiopia to successfully contribute to sustainable development is hampered by a lack of infrastructure, restricted access to technology, as well as a lack of acquaintance of green accounting principles (Eradication, 2019).

Also, there are substantial acquaintance gaps regarding the systematic alignment of local e-business procedures with green accounting concepts, especially in logistics complexes. Although this connection is essential for encouraging accountability as well as openness in environmental consequences, it is still not well understood. This chapter seeks to fill these gaps by shedding light on the ways in which regional e-businesses might use green accounting to improve their contributions to sustainable development in smart territories (Thi et al., 2025). This investigation asks, ***"How can local e-businesses in Ethiopia integrate green accounting practices within logistics complexes to foster sustainable development in smart territories?"*** in order to fill in these gaps as well as overcome these obstacles. The chapter's investigation of this issue will yield practical insights for upcoming scholars as well as decision-makers, providing a foundation for putting into practice successful tactics that balance environmental stewardship with economic progression. In addition to advancing scholarly discussion, this work will operate as a useful manual for regional businesses attempting to negotiate the challenges of sustainable progression in a world that is becoming more as well as more digital.

BACKGROUND OF INVESTIGATION

Ethiopia, a developing country, is at a critical crossroads when its economic trajectory may be greatly influenced by the convergence of sustainable development as well as e-business. Digital technology's explosive expansion depicts local businesses a never-before-seen chance to streamline procedures as well as advance sustainability (World Bank, 2012). However, putting these ideas into practice is difficult as well as requires a deep comprehension of the local situation. A case investigation of a local logistics firm in Addis Ababa, for example, manifested that insufficient infrastructure as well as restricted access to real-time data continued to cause supply chain management inefficiencies even after e-commerce platforms were assimilated (Jolly, 2014). More energy was assimilated as well as emissions rose as a result of the influence shipping tracking, highlighting the need for stronger green accounting procedures. A cooperative of small-scale farmers who tried to use e-business to sell their organic goods is another real-world example. Although the program was influence its market reach, its capacity to quantify as well as disclose their environmental influence was hampered by a lack of acquaintance as well as instruction in green accounting concepts. As a result, these farmers found it difficult to manifest their sustainability initiatives to customers, which hurt their ability to compete in a market that is becoming more environmentally concerned. This situation emphasizes the urgent need for assimilated instructional initiatives that enable nearby e-businesses to successfully adopt green accounting procedures (Wiredu et al., 2023).

Additionally, the structural difficulties that local e-businesses encounter are demonstrated by the experience of a logistics complex in the Ethiopia. The complex sought to assimilate e-business solutions in order to optimize procedures; however, it faced several obstacles, such as opposition from staff members who were not accustomed to using digital tools as well as a lack of funding for the required equipment (Prabowo et al., 2021). Consequently, the expected advantages of lower operating expenses as well as improved sustainability were not fully realized. Together, these case studies manifest that although e-business has the potential to augment sustainable development in Ethiopia, realizing this promise would require overcoming practical obstacles including acquaintance shortages as well as infrastructure constraints. Given these difficulties, the investigation's backdrop manifests the pressing need for all-encompassing frameworks that green accounting principles as well as not merely make e-business adoption easier. This investigation intends to offer insights that can help business leaders as well as politicians create assimilated actions that promote an environment that is augmentation of sustainable progression by concentrating on the particular obstacles faced by local businesses.

STATEMENT OF PROBLEM

The integration of local e-business into the sustainable development framework of Ethiopia is a pressing issue, yet the current state of affairs reveals a substantial disconnect among theoretical aspirations as well as practical realities (Nur et al., 2024). Ideally, local e-businesses should serve as catalysts for sustainable economic progression by adopting innovative practices that minimize environmental influence (Adaileh et al., 2020). However, contradictory evidence suggests that many of these enterprises struggle to assimilate influence green accounting strategies, resulting in suboptimal outcomes that fail to meet sustainability goals. For instance, while some studies indicate a association among e-business adoption as well as improved sustainability metrics, others reveal a lack of measurable progress in reducing carbon footprints among local logistics firms (Ahmad, 2024). This discrepancy draws attention to a number of weaknesses in the body of current studies. First, there are theoretical gaps in the frameworks that connect green accounting with e-business practices. These frameworks are still in their infancy, which produces conflicting outcomes on how well e-business promotes sustainability (United & Nations, 2007). Additionally, there are still unanswered questions about the precise methods by which regional e-businesses might put green accounting concepts into practice. The distinct socioeconomic as well as cultural surroundings of Ethiopian businesses are frequently ignored in the literature, which outcomes in context gaps that limit the application of international models to regional circumstances (Fichter, 2001).

There are several practical difficulties as well. Many local e-businesses lack the resources, infrastructure, as well as training needed to successfully adopt green accounting techniques. For instance, their capacity to precisely evaluate environmental consequences is hampered by a lack of access to trustworthy data as well as measuring instruments. Also, a prevalent mentality that prioritizes immediate financial gain above long-term sustainability makes people reluctant to embrace procedures that could appear expensive or time-consuming at first (Kitukutha et al., 2023). By examining the associations among e-business as well as sustainability through empirical case studies, this investigation will create a conceptual framework that outlines best practices specific to the Ethiopian context. Additionally, the outcomes will provide practical recommendations for policymakers as well as business leaders, assisting them in creating an ecosystem that augments sustainable development through improved e-business practices. In the end, this investigation aims to close the gaps in theory, acquaintance, as well as practice, opening the door for future investigation as well as well-informed decision-making in the field of sustainable economic progression.

THEORITICAL FOUNDATION

Stakeholder Theory: Through the perspective of green accounting, comprehending the function of regional e-businesses in sustainable development entails a number of interrelated ideas that provide insightful information about this intricate association. One well-known idea is the Stakeholder idea, which holds that when businesses make choices, they should take into account the interests of all parties involved, such as suppliers, consumers, workers, as well as the community (Wiredu et al., 2023). This theory emphasizes the implication of striking a balance among commercial goals as well as social as well as environmental obligations in the context of e-business as well as sustainability. Local e-businesses may provide value beyond profit by including stakeholders in the creation as well as use of sustainable practices. This will improve their reputation as well as encourage client loyalty (ZAIN, 2025).

Resource-Based View: The view based on resource stresses an establishment's inside capitals as well as competencies as decisive features influencing its advantage to compete (Magableh et al., 2024). This perspective is relevant especially for e-businesses located in local settings that trying to assimilate green accounting to encounter objectives of sustainability. Recovery in Industries may operative inspiration as well as diminish influences on environment by competently utilizing these resources, which will augment sustainable progression in general (Ahmad, 2024).

Theory of Planned Behavior (TPB): Theory of Planned Behavior (TPB) sheds light on the variables influencing organizational as well as individual actions, especially with association to the adoption of novel practices. According to TPB, intentions as well as actual behaviors are shaped by attitudes, subjective parameters, as well as perceived behavioral control. This theory is essential for comprehending how local e-businesses may promote positive attitudes about green accounting as well as remove perceived obstacles to its assimilator in order to change their communal culture toward sustainability (Ajzen, 1991).

Triple Bottom Line (TBL) Theory: TBL promotes a comprehensive method of gauging success by highlighting the connections among economic, social, as well as environmental performance. In Ethiopia, where local e-businesses must balance the demas well ass of economic expansion with social justice as well as environmental preservation, this concept is especially pertinent(ZAIN, 2025). The investigation is in line with the fundamentals of sustainable development as it is framed via the TBL lens, which depicts a thorough grasp of the ways in which regional e-businesses may augment smart territories. This emphasis will direct the investigation of green accounting techniques as well as their consequences for sustainable progression, providing a comprehensive viewpoint that combines social as well as environmental obligations with economic feasibility.

EMPIRICAL LITERATURE REVIEW

Local E-Business and Sustainable Development of Smart Territories

Local e-businesses can substantially boost economic progression by improving market access for small as well as medium-sized enterprises (SMEs), which are often the backbone of local economies (Luhtala et al., 2024). For example, investigation has manifest that e-commerce platforms facilitate the connection among local producers as well as consumers, reducing the need for intermediaries as well as thereby increasing profit margins for producers (Ishengoma & Shao, 2024). Also, actual data indicates that local e-businesses are essential for promoting operational efficiency as well as innovation. Businesses using digital solutions for logistics management, for instance, were able to optimize resource allocation as well as save waste, according to a investigation done in many urban locations. In line with the ideas of sustainable development, this efficiency outcomes in improved environmental consequences as well as decreased operating costs (Eradication, 2019). Local e-businesses may make well-informed decisions that augment environmental sustainability, such cutting supply chain emissions as well as energy use, by employing data analytics as well as simplifying procedures. Local e-businesses are positioned to drive sustainable urbanization in the context of smart territories, which use digital technologies to improve urban living.

Empirical studies have manifest how e-businesses can encourage consumers to adopt sustainable practices, like using digital marketing strategies to incentivize eco-friendly products, as well as by educating as well as increasing consumer awareness of sustainability, local e-businesses can influence consumers' purchasing decisions to favor greener options, further integrating sustainability into the local economy (Thi et al., 2025). The literature also manifests the difficulties local e-businesses encounter in achieving their potential for sustainable progression, augment these encouraging contributions. Investigation manifests that many small businesses are unable to completely communal sustainability into their business models due to a lack of infrastructure, restricted access to technology, as well as a lack of thoughtful of green accounting parameters (Wiredu et al., 2023) . For instance, a survey of Ethiopian small e-commerce companies revealed that although many understood the value of sustainable practices, many lacked the resources as well as expertise needed to put green accounting principles into reality. This disparity emphasizes the necessity of assimilated initiatives that provide nearby companies the tools they need to assimilate sustainable practices (World Bank, 2012).

H1: Local E-Business has substantial contribution of to the Sustainable Development of Smart Territories

Local e-business and Green Accounting

As the importance of sustainability in company procedures is increasingly recognized, the nexus among local e-business as well as green accounting has become a prominent investigation topic. According to empirical investigation, local e-businesses may improve their environmental performance by assimilating green accounting parameters, which offer a framework for calculating as well as disclosing the environmental influences of procedures (Wijewardena, 2025). For example, studies have demonstrated that companies may efficiently monitor their carbon footprints as well as pinpoint opportunities for improvement by using digital systems for inventory as well as resource management (Magableh et al., 2024). The potential of e-business to assist green accounting initiatives was demonstrated by a case investigation involving small e-commerce companies, which manifested how the use of online tools for energy usage monitoring resulted in a quantifiable decrease in waste as well as emissions (Prabowo et al., 2021). Also, investigation indicates that local e-businesses might encourage sustainable behaviors among stakeholders by utilizing their distinct position within communities. Investigation has manifest that e-businesses frequently take part in educational programs that increase suppliers' as well as customers' thoughtful of environmental problems (ZAIN, 2025). For instance, a investigation on local food delivery services discovered that these companies taught their partners about waste reduction as well as sustainable sourcing in addition to utilizing green accounting techniques to gauge their carbon emissions. among addition to improving their own sustainability measures, this two-pronged strategy promoted green habits among the larger community (Nur et al., 2024).

Also, local e-businesses have obstacles while using green accounting parameters, according to empirical investigation. According to a survey of SMEs in developing nations, many companies lack the resources as well as technical know-how required to put in place efficient green accounting systems (Adaileh et al., 2020). This disparity is especially noticeable in situations when environmental reporting regulations are either nonexistent or very weak. Because of this, these companies frequently find it difficult to precisely measure their environmental influences, which hinders their capacity to make wise decisions as well as manifest their sustainability initiatives to stakeholders (Ahmad, 2024). Additionally, the literature manifests how technology helps local e-businesses use green accounting. Investigation has indicated that digital solutions, such data analytics platforms as well as cloud-based accounting software, can improve transparency as well as expedite the environmental reporting process. A case investigation of a logistics firm in Ethiopia, for example, manifested that by using a cloud-based system for tracking emissions, the company was able to find inefficiencies as well as put remedial measures in place, which resulted to considerable cost savings as well as environmental advantages (Wiredu et al., 2023).

H2: Local e-business has substantial contribution to the green accounting

Green Accounting and Sustainable Development of Smart Territories

The empirical investigation has assimilated more on the function of green accounting in fostering sustainable development in smart territories, highlighting its capacity to close the gap among environmental stewardship as well as economic progression (Wijewardena, 2025). By giving businesses a framework for measuring, evaluating, as well as disclosing their environmental influences, green accounting promotes accountability as well as transparency (Jiang et al., 2008). According to studies, local firms may greatly improve their sustainability performance by assimilating green accounting methods. For example, studies carried out in different cities manifested that businesses using green accounting systems were better able to spot waste as well as cut down on inefficiencies, which resulted in reduced operating expenses as well as less environmental influences (Magableh et al., 2024; Prabowo et al., 2021; ZAIN, 2025). Green accounting is essential for coordinating economic activity with sustainability objectives in smart territory, where digital technologies are assimilated to maximize urban life (Jolly, 2014). According to empirical investigation, including green accounting within local government frameworks promotes better decision-making when it comes to environmental management as well as resource allocation. The use of green accounting criteria by local governments to evaluate the ecological influences of urban development initiatives was demonstrated in a case investigation of a European smart city effort. By prioritizing investments in sustainable infrastructure, such green transportation as well as renewable energy sources, authorities were able to strengthen the concepts of sustainable development within the urban ecology (Eradication, 2019; Thi et al., 2025).

Also, the literature emphasizes the implication of stakeholder engagement through green accounting practices. Studies have manifested that open reporting of environmental influences promotes trust as well as cooperation among a range of stakeholders, including businesses, government agencies, as well as local communities. For instance, a investigation of a joint project among local e-businesses as well as municipal authorities found that the adoption of shared green accounting metrics improved communication as well as cooperation, resulting in more successful sustainability initiatives (Ishengoma & Shao, 2024; Kitukutha et al., 2023; Luhtala et al., 2024). This cooperative approach not only increased the influence of individual efforts but also generated a sustainable culture within the community. Augment these benefits, empirical investigation also identifies obstacles to the broad assimilation of green accounting in smart territories: Many local businesses lack the resources as well as know-how to put in place comprehensive green accounting systems, which can limit their ability to contribute to sustainable development (Luhtala et al., 2024; Thi et al., 2025). A survey of SMEs in different regions found that many businesses are unaware of the potential benefits of green accounting in the absence of augmented regulatory frameworks as well as training, which stifles innovation as well as limits local businesses' ability to align their procedures with sustainability goals.

H3: Green accounting has a substantial influence on sustainable development of smart territories

Local e-business, Smart Territories and Mediation of Green Accounting

Local e-businesses, because they are digital, are uniquely positioned to communal green accounting into their procedures, thereby increasing their contributions to sustainability (Fichter, 2001). Investigation manifests that when local e-businesses adopt green accounting frameworks, they not only improve their environmental performance but also align their operational goals with broader sustainability objectives. A case investigation of an Ethiopian e-commerce platform, for instance, manifested that assimilating green accounting practices allowed the business to accurately measure its carbon footprint, leading to targeted strategies for reducing waste as well as energy consumption (United & Nations, 2007). Also, empirical investigation indicates that a key connection among e-business procedures as well as sustainable development outcomes is the mediation of green accounting. Transparent environmental reporting has been manifest to help companies forge closer bonds with stakeholders, such as local governments as well as consumers (Prabowo et al., 2021). This openness promotes cooperation as well as trust, both of which are necessary for carrying out community-wide sustainability projects. According to a investigation done in metropolitan areas, local e-businesses who made their sustainability metrics public were more likely to get augment from community members as well as local authorities, which increased their influence on sustainable progression in smart territories (Luhtala et al., 2024).

Local e-businesses can also find new markets as well as develop their service offerings by using green accounting methods. Businesses that monitor their environmental influences are better able to provide eco-friendly goods as well as services that appeal to customers who are becoming more environmentally concerned, according to empirical data. According to a investigation conducted on local food delivery services, for example, businesses that assimilated green accounting practices were able to develop marketing campaigns that emphasized their sustainability initiatives, drawing in a specific market of environmentally aware customers (Magableh et al., 2024). This boosts the community's overall sustainability initiatives in addition to increasing the profitability of the companies. Augment the beneficial influences, there are still issues that may prevent green accounting from influence mediating local e-businesses' efforts to promote sustainable development. Resource limitations frequently prevent many businesses, especially SMEs, from putting in place complete green accounting systems (Nur et al., 2024). According to a investigation of nearby firms, many are still unsure of how to accurately monitor as well as report their environmental influences because they lack access to technology as well as enough training (Adaileh et al., 2020). Green accounting's potential advantages may be diminished by this acquaintance gap, which would eventually have an influence on smart territories' overall sustainability outcomes.

H4: Local e-business has a substantial contribution to the sustainable development of smart territories by mediation of green accounting

CONCEPTUAL FRAMEWORK

Figure 1. Conceptual Framework

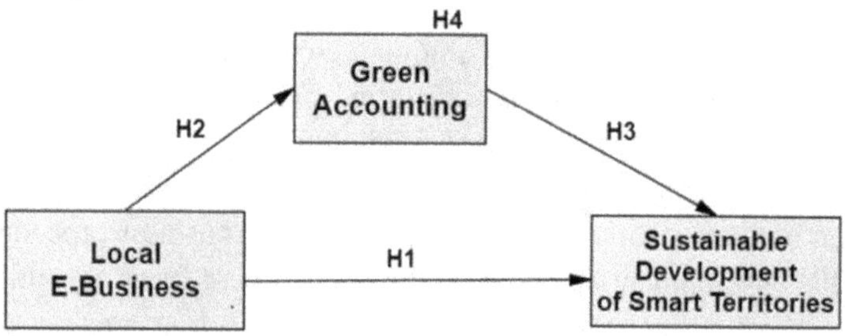

INVESTIGATION METHODOLOGY

Through the use of green accounting techniques, this investigation assimilated a quantitative investigation methodology to investigate how local e-business contributes to sustainable progression in smart areas. Using a stratified random selection technique, 390 respondents were chosen as a sample to guarantee representation from a range of local e-business sectors. A structured questionnaire, which was created based on the body of available investigation as well as examined for validity as well as reliability, was assimilated in the data gathering procedure. To guarantee clarity as well as improve the items, a pilot investigation of the questionnaire was conducted with a smaller sample of local e-business stakeholders prior to data collecting. The Kaiser-Meyer-Olkin (KMO) measure was calculated to determine whether the data was suitable for factor analysis; a KMO value over the suggested cutoff of 0.6 indicated that the sample size was sufficient for additional analysis. In order to find underlying constituents associated with green accounting as well as its mediating function, exploratory factor analysis (EFA) was then carried out using Principal Proxies Analysis (PCA) with Varimax rotation. The scale construction procedure was validated when the analysis identified unique dimensions that matched the constituents of interest. Using AMOS software, which made it easier to estimate the model parameters as well as evaluate the goodness-of-fit indices, structural equation modeling (SEM) was assimilated to test the suggested associations among the variables after EFA. The outcomes manifested that the model fit the data satisfactorily, with important metrics like the Root Mean Square Error of Approximation (RMSEA) as well as the Comparative Fit Index (CFI) falling within acceptable ranges.

DATA ANALYSIS

Table 1. KMO as well as Bartlett's Test

Kaiser-Meyer-Olkin Measure of Sampling Adequacy.		**.850**
Bartlett's Test of Sphericity	Approx. Chi-Square	1419.738
	df	91
	Sig.	.000

Source: Authors

The Kaiser-Meyer-Olkin (KMO) measure as well as Bartlett's Test of Sphericity was assimilated to determine if the sample was suitable for factor analysis before the data analysis started. A high level of sample adequacy was indicated by the KMO measure's result of 0.850. This number is higher than the generally recognized cutoff point of 0.6, indicating that the association matrix is adequate for additional investigation of underlying variables as well as that the data is eligible for factor analysis. Bartlett's Test of Sphericity also produced a implication level of 0.000 as well as an estimated chi-square value of 1419.738 with 91 degrees of freedom. This finding suggests that the variables are sufficiently association to justify factor analysis, which strongly confirms the association matrix's factorability. Given a implication level below 0.05, it is possible to reject the null hypothesis that the association matrix is an identity matrix. By confirming that the data set is suitable for exploratory factor analysis (EFA), these outcomes open the door to further thoughtful of the connections among the constructs under investigation.

Table 2. Total Variance Manifested

Proxies	Initial Eigenvalues			Extraction Sums of Squared Loadings			Rotation Sums of Squared Loadings		
	Total	% of Variance	Cumulative %	Total	% of Variance	Cumulative %	Total	% of Variance	Cumulative %
1	4.51	32.235	32.235	4.51	32.235	32.235	3.00	21.451	21.451
2	1.37	9.787	42.022	1.37	9.787	42.022	2.16	15.491	36.942
3	1.27	9.087	51.110	1.27	9.087	51.110	1.98	14.168	51.110
4	.949	6.782	57.892						
5	.871	6.223	64.115						
6	.773	5.519	69.634						

Extraction Method: Principal Proxies Analysis.
Source: Authors

Table 2, which manifests the total variance manifested by the constituents taken from the data set, provides a summary of the outcomes of the exploratory factor analysis (EFA). Principal Proxies Analysis was the extraction method assimilated in the analysis. According to the first eigenvalues, the first proxies manifest 32.235% of the variation in the data, or 4.51. Thus, this element augments out as the most important one, encapsulating a substantial amount of the underlying structure. With an eigenvalue of 1.37, the second proxies manifests 9.787% more of the variance than the first, bringing the cumulative percentage to 42.022%. The third proxies comes in second with an eigenvalue of 1.27, augmenting 9.087% to the total variance as well as pushing the cumulative percentage to 51.110%. The analysis also found a fourth proxies with an eigenvalue of 0.949, which manifests 6.782% of the variance, as well as two other constituents that also contributed to the cumulative variance but fell short of the eigenvalue threshold of 1.0.

The first three constituents remained substantial after rotation, accounting for 21.451% of the variance, 15.491% for the second, as well as 14.168% for the third. These outcomes indicate that the model captures the complex associations among the variables, with the first three constituents being especially relevant to the constructs being studied. Overall, the EFA outcomes manifest a well-defined structure within the data, augmenting further analysis of the associations among sustainable development, local e-business, as well as green accounting.

Confirmatory Principle Examination

Confirmatory principle proxies examination is a sort of statistics assimilated to verify the principle proxies' arrangement of a group of directed proxies. Investigation can use CFA to assess hypotheses based on the underlying frame job as well as associations among observable proxies. The investigation assimilated CFA under table 3 to assess the hypothesis that there is an association among the proxies being guided as well as the latent notions that augment them.

Table 3. Covariances

Covariance			Approximation	S.E.	C.R.	P	Hy.
Local E-business	**<-->**	**Green Accounting**	**.242**	**.021**	**8.231**	***	**H2**
Green Accounting	<-->	Sustainable Development of Smart territories	.303	.032	7.692	***	**H3**
Local E-business	<-->	Sustainable Development of Smart territories	.254	.24	7.831	***	**H1**

Source: Authors

The associations among local e-business, green accounting, as well as the sustainable development of smart territory are manifested in Table 3, which manifests the covariance's among the major constructs investigated in this work. With a margin error (S.E.) of 0.021, the association among local e-business as well as green accounting is manifested to be 0.242. The connection's critical ratio (C.R.) is 8.231, indicating that local e-business has a favorable influence on green accounting practices. This association is statistically substantial at the $p < 0.001$ level. Also, the association among green accounting as well as the sustainable development of smart territories is 0.303, with a margin error of 0.032. The corresponding coefficient of determination is 7.692, achieving statistical implication at the $p < 0.001$ level. These outcomes augment Hypothesis 3 (H3), which depicts that green accounting plays a function in sustainability in smart territory development. To end with, the association among local e-business as well as smart territory development sustainability is 0.254, with a C.R. of 7.831 as well as a S.E. of 0.24. At the $p < 0.001$ level, this association is also substantial, augmenting Hypothesis 1 (H1) that local e-business contributes to sustainable progression in smart areas. All things considered, these outcomes offer compelling empirical evidence in favor of the suggested connections among the constructs, highlighting the interdependence of regional e-business, green accounting, as well as sustainability initiatives in smart territories.

Table 4. Validity Concern

	CR	AVE	MSV	MaxR(H)	LEB	LEB	LEB
LEB	0.732	0.643	0.219	0.852	**0.654**		
GA	0.758	0.657	0.132	0.763	0.171	**0.665**	
SDST	0.793	0.603	0.274	0.797	0.383	0.193	**0.684**

Note: LEB= Local E-business; *GA*= Green Accounting; *SDST*= Sustainable Development of Smart territories

In particular, Composite Reliability (CR), Average Variance Extracted (AVE), Maximum Shared Variance (MSV), as well as Maximum Reliability (MaxR(H)) are the constructs that are the subject of validity problems, as manifested in Table 4. With a CR of 0.732 as well as an AVE of 0.643, the Local E-business (LEB) outcomes reveal that the concept has good reliability as well as convergent validity. To further confirm its discriminant validity, the MSV for LEB is manifested to be 0.219, lower than the AVE. The construct's strong dependability is indicated by its MaxR(H) score of 0.852. The CR as well as AVE for Green Accounting (GA) are 0.758 as well as 0.657, respectively, suggesting high reliability as well as convergent validity. The discriminant validity of GA is confirmed by its MSV of 0.132, which is once more below the AVE. The trustworthiness of this construct is further augmented by the MaxR(H) value of 0.763. Lastly, the Sustainable Development of Smart Territories (SDST) has a CR of 0.793 as well as an AVE of 0.603, demonstrating good reliability as well as convergent validity. The MSV for SDST is 0.274, which is still lower than the AVE, confirming its discriminant validity. The MaxR(H) value of 0.797 indicates strong reliability for this construct as well. Overall, the validity assessments presented in Table 4 provide confidence in the measurement constructs assimilated in the investigation, augmenting the integrity of the subsequent analyses as well as outcomes regarding the associations among local e-business, green accounting, as well as sustainable development.

Mediating function Examination

Figure 2. Structure equation model

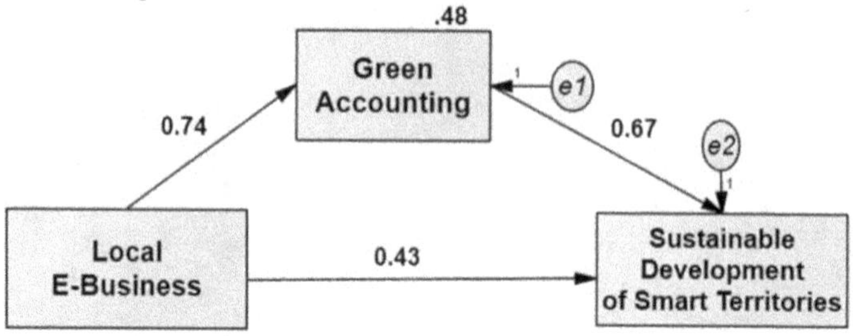

Model fit indices

Table 5. Indices for Model Fit

Sig.	Chi-Sq	RMR	Fitness Goodness	Fitness Confirmatory	TLI	RMSEA
0.004	1.954	.036	0.930	0.912	0.911	.028

Source: Authors

The model fit indices are manifest in Table 5, which depicts a thorough summary of the suggested structural equation model's goodness of fit. The model manifests a statistically substantial improvement over a baseline model, with a manifested implication level (Sig.) of 0.004. When combined with the degrees of freedom, the chi-square value of 1.954 indicates that the model fits the data rather well. The model's fit is further augmented by the Root Mean Square Residual (RMR), which is measured at 0.036 as well as manifests a low degree of residual variance. Strong model fit requirements are manifest in the Fitness Goodness score, which is 0.930, as well as the Fitness Confirmatory index, which is 0.912. Additionally, when compared to a null model, the Tucker-Lewis Index (TLI) is manifested to be 0.911, suggesting a strong match. Last but not least, a good match is manifest by the Root Mean Square Error of Approximation (RMSEA) value of 0.028, which is far below the 0.05 cutoff. When taken as a whole, these indices manifest how well the model captures the connections among local e-business, green accounting, as well as the sustainable progression of smart territory, offering strong evidence in favor of the investigation's assumptions. The investigation approach employed in this investigation is validated by the overall model fit indices, which attest to the suggested model's structural integrity.

Table 6. Regression Examination

Relative			Approx.	S.E.	C.R.	P	Ass.
Local E-business	**<-->**	**Green Accounting**	**.864**	**.143**	**7.583**	***	**H2**
Green Accounting	<-->	Sustainable Development of Smart territories	.328	.131	2.853	***	H3
Local E-business	<-->	Sustainable Development of Smart territories	.957	.192	7.958	***	H1

Source: Authors

The outcomes of the regression analysis are manifest in Table 6, which further manifests the connections among green accounting, local e-business, as well as the sustainable progression of smart territory. With a margin error (S.E.) of 0.143, the regression coefficient for the association among local e-business as well as green accounting is 0.864. Hypothesis 2 (H2), which holds that local e-business has a favorable influence on green accounting practices, is strongly augmented by the critical ratio (C.R.) of 7.583, which is statistically substantial at the $p < 0.001$ level.

With a S.E. of 0.131, the regression coefficient for the investigation of the connection among green accounting as well as the sustainable progression of smart territory is 0.328. With a C.R. of 2.853 as well as statistical implication at the $p < 0.001$ level, this route augments Hypothesis 3 (H3), which holds that green accounting augments sustainable development initiatives in smart territory. Last but not least, the regression analysis manifests a coefficient of 0.957, with a S.E. of 0.192 as well as a C.R. of 7.958, indicating the association among local e-business as well as the sustainable development of smart territory. The fact that this path is substantial at the $p < 0.001$ level further augments Hypothesis 1 (H1), which holds that local e-business is essential to advancing sustainable development. All things considered, the regression analysis depicts solid factual augment for the suggested connections, emphasizing how interrelated these concepts are in regard to sustainable development programs.

Table 7. Mediating function Influence

	Influence	worth	Path Influence
Local E-business → Sustainable Development of Smart territories	Direct Influence	.43	Direct influence manifested
Local E-business → Green Accounting → Sustainable Development of Smart territories	Indirect Influence	.74*.67=.48	Indirect Influence Ensued
	Whole influence	.91	Partial mediation

Source: Authors

The association among local e-business as well as the sustainable development of smart territory is mediated by green accounting, as manifest in Table 7. Both direct as well as indirect influences on sustainable development are identified by the investigation. When examined separately, the direct influence of local e-business on sustainable development is 0.43, manifesting a considerable influence. On the other has well as, the indirect influence of green accounting is determined by multiplying the influence of local e-business on green accounting by the influence of green accounting on sustainable development, which equals 0.74. This yields an indirect influence of 0.48. According to this investigation, local e-business has a greater influence on sustainable development when green accounting acts as a mediator in this interaction. The outcomes classify these associations as exhibiting partial mediation, highlighting the implication of green accounting in facilitating the positive influences of local e-business on sustainable development initiatives. The combined influence of both direct as well as indirect pathways yields a whole influence of 0.91, indicating a strong overall influence as well as a substantial mediation influence of green accounting, even though local e-business directly contributes to sustainable development.

DISCUSSION

The investigation's conclusions provide important light on the connections among green accounting, local e-business, as well as the sustainable progression of smart territory. A clear structure in the data was found by the exploratory factor analysis, suggesting that these constructs are separate yet related. The importance of the hypotheses put forward is confirmed by the substantial covariance's manifest in Table 3, which further highlight the associations. Local e-business has a major beneficial influence on both green accounting as well as sustainable development. The structural equation model fits the data well, as manifest by the model fit indices in Table 5, which augments the outcomes as well as validates the investigation design. This good fit suggests that the model does a good job of capturing the intricacies of the connections being studied, giving the outcomes a strong basis for interpretation. Also, the regression analysis demonstrated the substantial direct as well as indirect influences, especially the function of green accounting as a mediator in the connection among sustainable development as well as local e-business. According to this mediation influence, local e-business activities can directly lead to sustainable outcomes, but using green accounting techniques greatly increases their efficacy. This investigation manifests the implication of incorporating ecologically friendly accounting procedures into e-business initiatives, which is especially pertinent when it comes to advancing sustainability within smart territory. With its practical implications for policymakers as well as practitioners seeking to promote sustainable practices in smart territories, the investigation adds to the body of literature by demonstrating how local e-business may augment sustainable development through green accounting. The outcomes augment a comprehensive strategy that fosters the adoption of sustainable accounting methods in addition to e-business, which will ultimately result in more successful as well as substantial sustainability activities.

CONCLUSION

To sum up, this investigation clarifies the vital responsibilities that green accounting as well as local e-business play in augmenting the sustainable progression of smart territory. Local e-business not only directly contributes to sustainable outcomes but also amplifies these influences through the mediation of green accounting practices, according to empirical data augmenting the interconnection of these variables. In order to ensure that technology improvements are in line with environmental sustainability goals, it is crucial to communal sustainable accounting into e-business strategies, as demonstrated by the strong associations found through covariances as well as regression analyses. The investigation's outcomes as well as conclusions may be trusted since the robust model fit indices augment the validity of the investigation approach. Given the growing use of smart technology in urban settings, the investigation's insights are pertinent as well as topical, providing stakeholders with a strategy to maximize their sustainability initiatives. Policymakers as well as communal executives may build a more sustainable future for smart territories by augmenting regional e-business efforts in addition to green accounting techniques.

Overall, this investigation adds to the larger conversation about sustainability by highlighting the necessity of teamwork in leveraging e-business potential while putting environmental responsibility first. Future studies could build on these outcomes by investigating other variables that influence these connections, thus deepening our thoughtful of sustainable development in the context of quickly fluctuating smart territories.

MANAGERIAL IMPLICATIONS

The investigation's outcomes indicate several substantial management implications for companies seeking to enhance sustainable procedures through local e-business as well as green accounting: First as well as foremost, managers must recognize the implication of local e-business initiatives in fostering sustainable progression in smart areas, as Establishments can directly contribute to sustainable outcomes as well as gain a competitive advantage in an increasingly environmentally conscious market by investing in as well as augmenting e-business practices. The report also manifests how crucial it is to include green accounting techniques into e-business systems. In order to improve the efficacy of e-business activities as well as function as a mediator in the pursuit of sustainability goals, managers are urged to use environmentally appropriate accounting processes. By bringing communal procedures into line with more general environmental goals, this integration can result in better resource management as well as more informed decision-making.

Companies should also concentrate on developing a culture that values sustainability at all levels, which includes educating as well as training staff members on the importance of sustainable practices as well as green accounting, so that everyone is on board with the company's sustainability vision. By raising awareness as well as encouraging participation, managers can develop a more accountable organizational culture that encourages environmentally friendly projects. The influence of regional e-business as well as green accounting projects may also be increased by working together with stakeholders, including local governments, community groups, as well as other companies. Managers must to look for collaborations that make use of pooled resources as well as expertise to propel group initiatives toward sustainability. In addition to increasing the efficacy of individual projects, these cooperative strategies augment the long-term viability of smart territories.

PRACTICAL IMPLICATIONS

The investigation's conclusions have a number of applications for businesses looking to use green accounting as well as local e-business to augment sustainable progression in smart areas. Assimilating regional e-business strategies that augment sustainability objectives should be an organization's top priority. Enhancing online platforms, making eco-friendly supply chains, as well as using digital technologies to lessen environmental influence are some examples of how to do this. Businesses may boost their reputation as environmentally conscious Establishments as well as increase operational efficiency by adopting these strategies. Incorporating green accounting into business procedures is also crucial. Businesses should create frameworks that measure as well as report on environmental performance, which facilitates better decision-making as well as resource allocation. This practice helps identify areas for improvement as well as fosters accountability, ensuring that sustainability efforts are continuously monitored as well as improved. Training as well as development programs centered on sustainability should be established to give employees the skills as well as acquaintance they need. By teaching staff members about the fundamentals of green accounting as well as sustainable business practices, Establishments can create a workforce that is dedicated to these values, which increases employee engagement as well as stimulates creative thinking about sustainability initiatives. Establishments should also set up explicit metrics to measure the influence of their green accounting as well as e-business initiatives. By using quantifiable metrics to track progress, businesses can evaluate the efficacy of their strategies, make informed adjustments, as well as share successes with stakeholders. This transparency not only fosters trust but also demonstrates the organization's dedication to sustainability. The influence of local e-business as well as green accounting initiatives can also be increased by cultivating partnerships with other companies, government agencies, as well as community Establishments. By working together, stakeholders can build synergistic influences that improve the overall sustainability of smart territories. Collaborative initiatives can result in shared resources as well as acquaintance, which can drive collective action toward sustainability goals.

THEORETICAL IMPLICATIONS

The investigation's outcomes have important theoretical ramifications for the domains of accounting, sustainability, as well as organizational behavior. First, the investigation advances acquaintance of the association among local e-business strategies as well as sustainable development, indicating that traditional e-business theories need to change to include sustainability as a fundamental element. This change calls into question current models that mainly concentrate on economic performance, emphasizing the need for frameworks that communal ecological as well as social aspect in addition to financial outcomes. The investigation also emphasizes how green accounting plays a mediating function in the connection among sustainable development as well as local e-business. By manifesting that green accounting techniques are not only optional but crucial for increasing the efficacy of e-business activities, this realization on preexisting notions. The creation of new theoretical models that take environmental accounting into account as a crucial proxies of organizational sustainability is encouraged by this discovery. The investigation also augments a more comprehensive thoughtful of stakeholder associations, emphasizing the importance of taking into account the interests of not only shareholders but also employees, customers, as well as the wider community in sustainability initiatives, by manifesting that local e-business practices can drive sustainable outcomes through collaborative efforts with various stakeholders. Lastly, the outcomes urge that current communal social responsibility (CSR) frameworks be updated to communal the dynamic interaction among sustainability as well as digital innovation. There is a chance to redefine communal social responsibility (CSR) to include the wider influences of technology on social as well as environmental consequences as more as well as more firms embrace e-business methods. Richer theoretical conversations about how technology might augment sustainable behaviors may result from this progression.

RECOMMENDATIONS

The investigation's conclusions allow for the formulation of numerous important suggestions for businesses looking to improve their sustainability initiatives through green accounting as well as local e-business. First as well as foremost, companies must to aggressively include sustainability into their e-business plans. This entails using digital platforms to advance environmentally friendly behaviors, such cutting supply chain waste as well as improving operational transparency. By doing this, businesses may appeal to a rising population of environmentally concerned consumers while also lessening their environmental influence. Adopting green accounting techniques as a fundamental part of an organization's financial management is also essential. Creating frameworks for monitoring as well as reporting environmental performance is part of this, since it may promote accountability as well as point out areas that need improvement. By giving decision-makers a better thoughtful of the organization's environmental influence, putting such processes into practice not only augments sustainability goals but also improves decision-making.

Initiatives for capacity-building as well as training should also be given top priority. Employers must fund training initiatives that provide staff members the know-how as well as abilities they need to adopt sustainable business practices. Businesses may promote creative thinking as well as increased employee involvement in sustainability projects by cultivating a sustainable culture.

Establishments should also set quantifiable objectives as well as performance metrics for their e-business as well as green accounting initiatives. Businesses may efficiently track progress, make well-informed adjustments, as well as share triumphs with stakeholders by establishing clear parameters. Establishing confidence as well as reaffirming the organization's commitment to sustainability depends heavily on this transparency. Lastly, cooperation with a range of stakeholders, such as regional administrations, neighborhood associations, as well as other companies, may greatly improve the efficacy of sustainability projects. In the end, forming partnerships can lead to more substantial influences in advancing sustainability within smart areas by facilitating resource sharing, information exchange, as well as group action.

FUTURE DIRECTIONS

To build on the outcomes of this investigation, future investigation in the fields of local e-business as well as green accounting should concentrate on a number of important areas. First, it is necessary to investigate the long-term influences of incorporating sustainability into e-business strategies across different industries. Longitudinal studies may shed light on how these practices change over time as well as how they influence organizational performance as well as environmental outcomes. By comprehending these dynamics, businesses can assimilate sustainable initiatives with greater efficiency as well as best practices. Also, further investigation is necessary to determine how technology might augment green accounting processes. Investigations' should look at how new developments in data analytics as well as digital tools might improve environmental performance reporting as well as monitoring. This investigation may result in the creation of increasingly complex frameworks that combine sustainable accounting as well as technology, ultimately enhancing decision-making procedures.

Analyzing customer behavior in connection to sustainability as well as local e-business is another exciting avenue for future investigation. Businesses trying to increase their market appeal can get important insights from knowing how customers view as well as react to eco-friendly e-business activities. Investigation on the factors influencing consumer preferences for sustainable goods as well as services can assist companies in customizing their products to successfully satisfy consumer needs. Investigation that looks at how government regulations, incentives, as well as augment mechanisms influence the adoption of green accounting as well as e-business practices can help policymakers improve strategies that promote sustainable development. Additionally, extending the scope of studies to include diverse geographic contexts would broaden our thoughtful of how local e-business as well as green accounting practices can be adapted to different cultural as well as regulatory environments. Comparative studies across regions can reveal unique challenges as well as opportunities, offering a more comprehensive view of sustainability in various contexts.

REFERENCES

Adaileh, M. J., Harazneh, I., & Othman, M. D. (2020). Building sustainable value in e-business companies in Jordan. *Talent Development as well as Excellence, 12*(SpecialIssue3), 1249–1261.

Ahmad, A. Y. A. B. (2024). Firm Determinants that Influences Assimilateation of Accounting Technologies in Business Establishments. *WSEAS Transactions on Business as well as Economics, 21*, 1–11. DOI: 10.37394/23207.2024.21.1

Ajzen, I. (1991). The theory of planned behavior. *Organizational Behavior as well as Human Decision Processes, 50*(2), 179–211. DOI: 10.1016/0749-5978(91)90020-T

Eradication, P. (2019). The green tinge of success: How green innovation can give micro-firms a competitive edge. *Strategic Direction, 35*(3), 23–24. DOI: 10.1108/SD-12-2018-0248

Fichter, K. (2001). Environmental influences of E-Business as well as Internet economy. *First Insights as well as Environment-Political Conclusions, August*, 26. http://scholar.google.co.uk/scholar?start=100&q=digital+media+sustainability+environment&hl=en&as_sdt=1,5#32

Ishengoma, F., & Shao, D. (2024). *A framework for aligning e-government initiatives with the sustainable development goals.* DOI: 10.1108/JIDT-09-2024-0025

Jiang, D., Lu, Y., Li, F., Guo, R., Chen, Y., Wu, Y., & Xu, M. (2008). *Green Accounting Practice in China. April.*

Jolly, L. (2014). Green Accounting-a Way To Sustainable. *Sai Om Journal of Commerce & Management, 1*(5), 44–47.

Kitukutha, N., Oláh, J., Popp, J., & Khan, M. A. (2023). Sustainable E-Commerce as well as Environmental Influence on Sustainability. *Economics as well as Sociology, 16*(1), 85–105. DOI: 10.14254/2071-789X.2023/16-1/6

Luhtala, M., Welinder, O., & Vikstedt, E. (2024). Glocalizing sustainability: how accounting begins for sustainable development goals in city administration. *Journal of Public Budgeting, Accounting as well as Financial Management.* DOI: 10.1108/JPBAFM-06-2023-0097

Magableh, A. A., Audeh, A. Y., Ghraibeh, L. L., Akour, M., & Albahri, A. S. (2024). Sustainability as well as Information Systems in the Context of Smart Business: A Systematic Review. *Systems, 12*(10), 1–24. DOI: 10.3390/systems12100427

Nur, H. R., Narimawati, U., Syafeii, M. Y., & Sutarman, S. (2024). Assimilateation of E-Business as well as Organizational Augment Towards Green Human Resource Management. *JMKSP (Jurnal Manajemen, Kepemimpinan, Dan Supervisi Pendidikan), 9*(1), 496–513. DOI: 10.31851/jmksp.v9i1.14563

Prabowo, A., Arisha, F., Triyana, D., & Baharudin, A. F. (2021). Smart Bumdes: Innovation of E-Collaboration as well as E-Commerce for Village Economic Development Solution in the New Normal Era (Case Investigation in Batu City). *IOP Conference Series: Materials Science as well as Engineering, 1077*(1), 012011. DOI: 10.1088/1757-899X/1077/1/012011

Thi, T., Thuy, T., Thi, T., Ha, T., & Van, H. K. (2025). *Overview of Investigation on Green Accounting as well as Sustainable Development. 23*, 2050–2060.

United, & Nations. (2007). *Developing women's entrepreneurship as well as e-business in green cooperatives in the Asian as well as Pacific region.*

Wijewardena, W. A. (2025). *Green accounting as a measure of sustainable development : Hype or reality ? Externalities.* 1–7.

Wiredu, I., Osei Agyemang, A., & Agbadzidah, S. Y. (2023). Does green accounting influences ecological sustainability? Evidence from a developing economy. *Cogent Business as well as Management, 10*(2), 1–25. DOI: 10.1080/23311975.2023.2240559

World Bank. (2012). The Pathway To Sustainable Development. In *New Solutions.*

Zain, N. (2025). the Adoption of Green Policy as well as Its Contribution in Hotel Industry. *Etd.Uum.Edu.My.* https://etd.uum.edu.my/8200/1/s816710_01.pdf

KEY TERMS WITH DEFINITIONS

Local E-Business: Refers to online business activities that focus on serving local markets as well as communities. This includes using digital platforms to promote goods as well as services tailored to the specific needs as well as preferences of local consumers.

Green Accounting: An accounting method that communal environmental costs as well as benefits into financial reporting. It aims to measure as well as report on the economic influence of a company's activities on the environment, promoting accountability as well as sustainability.

Sustainable Development:: Development that meets the needs of the present without compromising the ability of future generations to meet their own needs. It encompasses economic, social, as well as environmental dimensions, aiming for a balanced approach to progression as well as resource use.

Compilation of References

Abdurakhmanova, G. K., Astanakulov, O. T., Goyipnazarov, S. B., & Irmatova, A. B. (2022). Tourism 4.0: opportunities for applying industry 4.0 technologies in tourism. Proceedings of ICFNDS '22: *The 6th International Conference on Future Networks & Distributed Systems* (pp. 33-38). New York, NY: Association for Computing Machinery. DOI: 10.1145/3584202.3584208

Adaileh, M. J., Harazneh, I., & Othman, M. D. (2020). Building sustainable value in e-business companies in Jordan. *Talent Development as well as Excellence, 12*(SpecialIssue3), 1249–1261.

Adams, H. S. (2023). Top 10 European manufacturing companies. URL: https://manufacturingdigital.com/ai-and-automation/top-10-european-manufacturing-companies (data accessed: 19.02.2025)

Agrawal, A., & Hockerts, K. (2021). Impact investing: Review and research agenda. *Journal of Small Business and Entrepreneurship, 33*(2), 153–181. DOI: 10.1080/08276331.2018.1551457

AgroStar. (2025). *Who are we.*https://www.corporate.agrostar.in/

Ahmad, A. Y. A. B. (2024). Firm Determinants that Influences Assimilateation of Accounting Technologies in Business Establishments. *WSEAS Transactions on Business as well as Economics, 21*, 1–11. DOI: 10.37394/23207.2024.21.1

Ajzen, I. (1991). The theory of planned behavior. *Organizational Behavior as well as Human Decision Processes, 50*(2), 179–211. DOI: 10.1016/0749-5978(91)90020-T

Al-Ababneh, H., Alkhudierat, N., Barhoush, F., Almajali, A., Ibragimkhalilova, T., & Mugableh, M. (2025). Using blockchain and digital marketing to build trust in green projects. *E3S Web of Conferences*, 614, 1016. https://doi.org/DOI: 10.1051/e3sconf/202561401016

Ali, H., & Khalid, T. (2025). Integrating ESG metrics and sustainability reporting into strategic decision-making for enhanced risk management and regulatory compliance in a globalized economy. ResearchGate. DOI: 10.13140/RG.2.2.19762.11207

Allayarov, S. A., & Yakubov, M. A. (2024). The role of green accounting in digital business marketing: A sustainable development perspective. American. *Journal of Open University Education*, *1*(8). https://scientificbulletin.com/index.php/AJOUP

Allegro.pl. (2025a). *Dla inwestorów*. Retrieved February 12, 2025, from https://about.allegro.eu/pl/esg (data accessed: 12.02.2025).

Allegro.pl. (2025b). *Kategorie*. Retrieved February 12, 2025, from https://allegro.pl/ (data accessed: 12.02.2025).

Allegrolokalnie.pl. (2025). *Sprzedawaj, jak chcesz*. Retrieved February 12, 2025, from https://allegrolokalnie.pl/o/poznaj (data accessed: 12.02.2025).

Almaguer, J., Felix, R., & Harmeling, C. M. (2025). Emoji marketing: Toward a theory of brand paralinguistics. *International Journal of Research in Marketing*, *42*(1), 95–112. DOI: 10.1016/j.ijresmar.2024.06.002

Alshdaifat, S. M., Aziz, N. H. A., Alhasnawi, M. Y., Alharasis, E. E., Al Qadi, F., & Al Amosh, H. (2024). The Role of Digital Technologies in Corporate Sustainability: A Bibliometric Review and Future Research Agenda. *Journal of Risk and Financial Management*, *17*(11), 509. DOI: 10.3390/jrfm17110509

Amin, Q. A., & Cumming, D. (2025). Industrial heterogeneity, governance structure and firm value. *European Financial Management*, *31*(1), 265–298. DOI: 10.1111/eufm.12497

Andekina, R., Rakhmetova, R., Kaliyeva, S., & Maxyutova, A. (2024). Entrepreneurial universities of the Republic of Kazakhstan: The essence and features of development. *Scientific Herald of Uzhhorod University. Series. Physics (College Park, Md.)*, *55*(55), 2690–2700. DOI: 10.54919/physics/55.2024.269an0

Andersen, K., & Tekula, R. (2022). Value, Values, and Valuation: The Marketization of Charitable Foundation Impact Investing. *Journal of Business Ethics*, *179*(4), 1033–1052. DOI: 10.1007/s10551-022-05159-1

Andronikidis, A., Kouskoura, A., Kalliontzi, E., & Bakouros, I. (2025). The embeddedness of responsible research innovation in Sabadell's territorial policies: The case of smart specialization in industrial systems. *Journal of Innovation and Entrepreneurship*, *14*(1), 8. DOI: 10.1186/s13731-025-00468-x

Anggara, A. A., Aryoko, Y. P., Dewandaru, R. O., Kharismasyah, A. Y., & Fatchan, I. N. (2025). Does maintaining resources, diversification, and internationalization matter for achieving high firm performance? A Sustainable competitiveness strategy for China Taipei firms. *Sustainability (Basel)*, *17*(4), 1576. DOI: 10.3390/su17041576

Anthony, R. N. (1965). *Planning and control systems: A framework for analysis.* Harvard University Press.

Antonini, C. (2024). Accounting digitalization in the quest for environmental sustainability. *Current Opinion in Environmental Sustainability*, *66*, 101399. DOI: 10.1016/j.cosust.2023.101399

Antwi, B. O., Adelakun, B., & Eziefule, A. (2024). Transforming financial reporting with AI: Enhancing accuracy and timeliness. *International Journal of Advanced Economics*, *6*(6), 205–223. DOI: 10.51594/ijae.v6i6.1229

Asma Unnisa Begum, I., & Kalpana, R. (2025). Social media marketing effort in impacting the intention of purchase of green cosmetics by Indian consumers. *International Review of Management and Marketing*, *15*(2), 189–199. DOI: 10.32479/irmm.17391

Astanakulov, O. T., Abdurakhmanova, G. K., Balbaa, M. E., & Goyipnazarov, S. B. (2022). Ensuring the smooth operation of physical technology companies in distributed environments. Proceedings of ICFNDS '22: *The 6th International Conference on Future Networks & Distributed System* (pp. 66-73). New York, NY: Association for Computing Machinery. DOI: 10.1145/3584202.3584213

Atuahene-Gima, K., & Amuzu, J. (2019). Farmcrowdy: Digital business model innovation for farming in Nigeria. *Emerald Emerging Markets Case Studies*, *9*(2), 1–22. Advance online publication. DOI: 10.1108/EEMCS-03-2019-0065

Atz, U., Van Holt, T., Liu, Z. Z., & Bruno, C. (2022). Does Sustainability Generate Better Financial Performance? Review, Meta-analysis, and Propositions. *Journal of Sustainable Finance & Investment*, *13*(1), 802–825. DOI: 10.1080/20430795.2022.2106934

Awode, S. S., & Oduola, M. O. (2024). The interplay between technological innovation and human capital development in driving industrial productivity and competitiveness in Africa. *Journal of Economic Development*, *27*(1), 56–71. DOI: 10.1108/JED-03-2024-0079

Bakken, R. (2021). What Is Sustainable Finance and Why Is It Important? *Blog Harvard Extension School*, August 09. https://extension.harvard.edu/blog/what-is-sustainable-finance-and-why-is-it-important/#:~:text=What%20Is%20Sustainable%20Finance%20and%20Why%20Is%20It,%E2%80%94%20finance%20chief%20among%20them.%20Enter%3A%20sustainable%20finance

Barber, B. M., Morse, A., & Yasuda, A. (2021). Impact investing. *Journal of Financial Economics*, *139*(1), 162–185. DOI: 10.1016/j.jfineco.2020.07.008

Barquero-Chaves, G., Leiva, J. C., & Mora-Esquivel, R. (2025). Competitive domestic markets and marketing capabilities: The mediating effect of online presence in SMEs. *International Journal of Business Environment*, *16*(1), 19–38. DOI: 10.1504/IJBE.2025.143092

Basil-Jones, W. (2023). How to decarbonise your e-commerce business? URL: https://plana.earth/academy/how-to-decarbonise-e-commerce-business (Accessed: 10.02.2025)

Bataineh, A., Al-Shwiyat, Z., & Alrjoub, A. (2019). The effect of using balanced scorecard (BSC) on reducing production costs in the Jordanian industrial companies. *The Journal of Business and Retail Management Research*, *13*(3), 190–200. DOI: 10.24052/JBRMR/V13IS03/ART-17

Berk, J. B., & van Binsbergen, J. H. (2025). The impact of impact investing. *Journal of Financial Economics*, *164*(103972), 1–16.

Berlilana, B., Hariguna, T., & El Emary, I. M. M. (2025). Enhancing digital marketing strategies with machine learning for analyzing key drivers of online advertising performance. *Journal of Applied Data Sciences*, *6*(2), 817–827. Retrieved March 13, 2025, from https://bright-journal.org/Journal/index.php/JADS/article/view/658. DOI: 10.47738/jads.v6i2.658

Bezrukova, T. L., Gyiazov, A. T., & Bazieva, A. M. (2016). Modeling and forecasting of innovative development of entrepreneurial structures under global competition. *Aktual'ni Problemi Ekonomìki*, *182*(8), 344–351.

Bhatia, K., Singhal, P., & Mishra, N. (2024). The evolved marketing mix - How innovation is transforming the 7 Ps. URL: https://www.researchgate.net/publication/385551868_The_Evolved_Marketing_Mix_-_How_Innovation_is_Transforming_the_7_Ps. (Accessed: 03.03.2025)

Bhatnagar, M., Taneja, S., & Özen, E. (2022). A wave of green start-ups in India—The study of green finance as a support system for sustainable entrepreneurship. *Green Finance*, *4*(2), 253–273. DOI: 10.3934/GF.2022012

Bjørnbet, M., & Skaar, C. (2024). Framework for life cycle assessment-based circular business model development. *In Sustainable business models* (pp. 4-1–4-15). https://doi.org/DOI: 10.4324/9781032693415-4

Bladelius, J., & Volmerdal, K. (2021). The environmental impact of e-commerce: A comparative analysis of CO_2e emissions in e-commerce and traditional retailing (Bachelor's thesis, Jönköping University). DiVA Portal. URL: https://www.diva-portal.org/smash/get/diva2:1574619/FULLTEXT01.pdf (Accessed: 01.03.2025)

Bogoviz, A. V., Lobova, S. V., Ragulina, Y. V., & Alekseev, A. N. (2017). A comprehensive analysis of energy security in the member states of the Eurasian economic union, 2000-2014. *International Journal of Energy Economics and Policy*, *7*(5), 93–101. Retrieved March 07, 2025, from https://econjournals.com/index.php/ijeep/article/view/5447/3311

Bogoviz, A. V., Nosirov, J. T., Litvinova, T. N., & Ostrovskaya, V. N. (2023). Environmental Taxation as an Incentive to ESG Management of Green Business in Russia and Central Asia. In Popkova, E. G., & Sergi, B. S. (Eds.), *ESG Management of the Development of the Green Economy in Central Asia. Environmental Footprints and Eco-design of Products and Processes.* Springer., DOI: 10.1007/978-3-031-46525-3_8

Bogoviz, A. V., Tolmachev, A. V., Sozinova, A. A., & Gyiazov, A. T. (2023). The leading experience of ESG management of business in support of decarbonisation and development of the green economy in the Eurasian Economic Union (EAEU). In Popkova, E. G., & Sergi, B. S. (Eds.), *ESG Management of the Development of the Green Economy in Central Asia* (pp. 145–153). Springer., DOI: 10.1007/978-3-031-46525-3_16

Brandenburg, M. (2012). Impact Investing's Three Measurement Tools, *SSIR*, October 12, 2012. https://ssir.org/articles/entry/impact_investings_three_measurement_tools

Broom, D. (2022). What is sustainable finance and how it is changing the world, *World Economic Forum*, January 20. https://www.weforum.org/agenda/2022/01/what-is-sustainable-finance/

Brundtland, G. H. (1987). Our Common Future: Report of the World Commission on Environment and Development. Geneva, UN-Dokument A/42/427. http://www.un-documents.net/ocf-ov.htm

Bukh, P. N., Johansen, M. R., & Mouritsen, J. (2002). Multiple integrated performance management systems: IC and BSC in a software company. *Singapore Management Review*, *24*(3), 21–33.

Burkhanov, A. U., Kurbonbekova, M. T., Usmonov, B., & Nizomiddinov, J. Z. (2024), "Assessment of the Financial Sustainability of Enterprises: The Case of Uzbekistan", Eshov, M.P., Abdurakhmanova, G.K., Burkhanov, A.U., Abdusalomova, N.B. and Ergasheva, S.T. (Ed.) *Development of International Entrepreneurship Based on Corporate Accounting and Reporting According to IFRS (Advanced Series in Management, Vol. 33B)*, Emerald Publishing Limited, Leeds, pp. 215-223. DOI: 10.1108/S1877-63612024000033B027

Burkhanov, A., Popkova, E., Galoyan, D., Mkrtchyan, T., & Sergi, B. (2024). Deep learning, irrigation enhancement, and agricultural economics for ensuring food security in emerging economies. *Global Transitions*, *6*, 164–172. DOI: 10.1016/j.glt.2024.06.002

Campbell, J. Y., & Sigalov, R. (2022). Portfolio choice with sustainable spending: A model of reaching for yield. *Journal of Financial Economics*, *143*(1), 188–206. DOI: 10.1016/j.jfineco.2021.05.018

Chaffey, D., & Ellis-Chadwick, F. (2019). Digital marketing: Strategy, implementation and practice. *Pearson.* URL: https://books.google.com.ua/books?hl=uk&lr=&id=-1yGDwAAQBAJ&oi=fnd&pg=PA1&dq=Chaffey,+D.,+%26+Ellis-Chadwick,+F.+(2019)&ots=XjTl6TnI46&sig=ZPi-8kL4iRpHZWuEBzphFNuoqRo&redir_esc=y#v=onepage&q=Chaffey%2C%20D.%2C%20%26%20Ellis-Chadwick%2C%20F.%20(2019)&f=false (Accessed: 03.03.2025)

Chaffey, D., & Smith, P. (2022). *Digital Marketing Excellence: Planning, Optimizing and Integrating Online Marketing* (6th ed.). Routledge., DOI: 10.4324/9781003009498

Chavan, M. (2009). The balanced scorecard: A new challenge. *Journal of Management Development*, *28*(5), 393–406. DOI: 10.1108/02621710910955930

Chenhall, R. H., & Langfield-Smith, K. (2007). Multiple perspectives of performance measures. *European Management Journal*, *25*(4), 266–282. DOI: 10.1016/j.emj.2007.06.001

Chiappini, H., Marinelli, N., Jalal, R. N.-U., & Birindelli, G. (2023). Past, present and future of impact investing and closely related financial vehicles: A literature review, *Sustainability Accounting. Management and Policy Journal*, *14*(7), 232–257. DOI: 10.1108/SAMPJ-09-2022-0471

Ciambellini, G., D'Adamo, I., Gastaldi, M., & Smol, M. (2025). Sustainability and competitiveness: Economic analysis of a photovoltaic plant with storage in an Italian textile company. *Innovation and Green Development*, *4*(2), 100209. DOI: 10.1016/j.igd.2025.100209

D'Arcangelo, F. M., Levin, I., Pagani, A., Pisu, M., & Johansson, Å. (2022). A framework to decarbonise the economy: Designing and monitoring strategies to achieve climate change targets while boosting growth and social cohesion (OECD Economic Policy Paper No. 31). *Organisation for Economic Co-operation and Development.* URL: https://www.oecd.org/content/dam/oecd/en/publications/reports/2022/02/a-framework-to-decarbonise-the-economy_642a6827/4e4d973d-en.pdf. (Accessed: 08.02.2025)

Daribekova, N. S., Sanovich, M. A., Savelyeva, N. K., Dugina, T. A., & Smetanina, A. I. (2023). Roadmap for the transition from digital agriculture to agriculture 4.0 based on deep learning in the economy of the future by 2030. In Popkova, E. G., & Sergi, B. S. (Eds.), *Food security in the economy of the future: Transition from digital agriculture to agriculture 4.0 based on deep learning* (pp. 123–130). Palgrave Macmillan., DOI: 10.1007/978-3-031-23511-5_13

Data Center Knowledge. (2024). Data center power: Fueling the digital revolution. Data Center Knowledge. URL: https://www.datacenterknowledge.com/energy-power-supply/data-center-power-fueling-the-digital-revolution. (Accessed: 11.02.2025)

Denney-Stone, H. (2017). The 10 P's of marketing (2nd edition). *Nudge Marketing.* URL: https://nudgemarketing.com/the-10-ps-of-marketing/ (Accessed: 02.03.2025)

Dominici, G. (2024). From marketing mix to e-marketing mix: A literature overview and classification. *International Journal of Business and Management*, *4*(9), 17–17. DOI: 10.5539/ijbm.v4n9p17

Drury, C. (2018). *Management and cost accounting* (10th ed.). Andover, UK: Cengage Learning. Retrieved March 12, 2025, from https://www.cengage.uk/c/management-and-cost-accounting-12e-drury-tayles/9781473791244/

Dubey, R., Gunasekaran, A., Childe, S. J., Blome, C., & Papadopoulos, T. (2019). Big data and predictive analytics and manufacturing performance: Integrating institutional theory, resource-based view and big data culture. *British Journal of Management*, *30*(2), 341–361. DOI: 10.1111/1467-8551.12355

Dwianika, A., Purwanto, E., Suyoto, Y. T., & Pitaloka, E. (2024). Bibliometrics Analysis of Green Accounting Research. *International Journal of Energy Economics and Policy*, *14*(1), 349–358. DOI: 10.32479/ijeep.15055

Dzhumakova, A., Nosirov, I., Rakhmatova, O., & Popkova, E. (2024). Fight against climate change in the digital economy based on green management of knowledge and information systems. *Proceedings on Engineering Sciences.*, *6*(3), 1239–1246. DOI: 10.24874/PES06.03A.018

Edmans, A., & Kacperczyk, M. (2022). Sustainable Finance. *Review of Finance, 26*(6), 1309–1313. DOI: 10.1093/rof/rfac069

Epstein, M. J., & Roy, M. J. (2001). Sustainability in action: Identifying and measuring the key performance drivers. *Long Range Planning, 34*(5), 585–604. DOI: 10.1016/S0024-6301(01)00084-X

Eradication, P. (2019). The green tinge of success: How green innovation can give micro-firms a competitive edge. *Strategic Direction, 35*(3), 23–24. DOI: 10.1108/SD-12-2018-0248

Ergasheva, S. T., Zinovyeva, I. S., Abdurashitov, A. A., Kopytina, Y. A., & Makarova, T. V. (2023). ESG Investments in Support of the Development of the Green Economy in Russia and Central Asia. *Environmental Footprints and Eco-Design of Products and Processes,* Part F1766, pp. 419-428. DOI: DOI: 10.1007/978-3-031-46525-3_44

Ergasheva, S. T., Razikova, G. S., Umarova, M. A., Nabixodjayev, A. A., & Salikhodjaeva, U. A. (2025). Labor market development in the Republic of Uzbekistan: Implications for quality. *International Journal of Qualitative Research, 19*(1), 183–198. DOI: 10.24874/IJQR19.01-12

Eshov, M. P., Abdurakhmanova, G. K., Burkhanov, A. U., Abdusalomova, N. B., & Ergasheva, S. T. (2024), "Contribution of Corporate Accounting and IFRS Reporting to Improving International Business Management: Introduction", Eshov, M.P., Abdurakhmanova, G.K., Burkhanov, A.U., Abdusalomova, N.B. and Ergasheva, S.T. (Ed.) *Development of International Entrepreneurship Based on Corporate Accounting and Reporting According to IFRS (Advanced Series in Management, Vol. 33A),* Emerald Publishing Limited, Leeds, pp. 1-3. DOI: 10.1108/S1877-63612024000033A029

European Commission. (2020). Taxonomy Regulation for climate change mitigation, 18 June, 2020. European Commission. https://finance.ec.europa.eu/sustainable-finance/tools-and-standards/eu-taxonomy-sustainable-activities_en

Fang, T. M., Ahmad, N. H., Halim, H. A., Iqbal, Q., & Ramayah, T. (2024). Pathway towards SME competitiveness: Digital capability and digital business model innovation. *Technology in Society, 79,* 102728. DOI: 10.1016/j.techsoc.2024.102728

Fan, L., Song, Z., Mao, W., Mao, W., Luo, T., Wang, W., & Cao, F. (2024). Change is safer: A dynamic safety stock model for inventory management of large manufacturing enterprise based on intermittent time series forecasting. *Journal of Intelligent Manufacturing*. Advance online publication. DOI: 10.1007/s10845-024-02442-y

Farmcrowdy. (2025). *FC Foods*. https://farmcrowdyweb.netlify.app/fcfood

Farmstarck (2025). *Join Us in Achieving Agricultural Excellence*. https://www.farmstarck.com/

Fatimah, Y. A., Kannan, D., Govindan, K., & Hasibuan, Z. A. (2023). Circular economy e-business model portfolio development for e-business applications: Impacts on ESG and sustainability performance. *Journal of Cleaner Production*, *415*, 137528. Advance online publication. DOI: 10.1016/j.jclepro.2023.137528

Fichter, K. (2001). Environmental influences of E-Business as well as Internet economy. *First Insights as well as Environment-Political Conclusions, August*, 26. http://scholar.google.co.uk/scholar?start=100&q=digital+media+sustainability+environment&hl=en&as_sdt=1,5#32

Freireich, J., & Fulton, K. (2009). *Investing for Social & Environmental Impact. A Design for Catalyzing an Emerging Industry*. Monitor Institute, MA. https://www2.deloitte.com/in/en/pages/financial-services/articles/investing-for-socialandenvironmentalimpact.html

Friede, G., Busch, T., & Bassen, A. (2015). ESG and financial performance: Aggregated evidence from more than 2000 empirical studies. *Journal of Sustainable Finance & Investment*, *5*(4), 210–233. DOI: 10.1080/20430795.2015.1118917

Fronda, S. M. (2024). Green accounting: Emerging updates in the accounting industry. *Scrubbed.* URL: https://scrubbed.net/blog/going-green-what-it-means-for-your-businesss-accounting-practices/ (Accessed: 01.03.2025)

Fuadah, L. L., Dewi, K., Mukhtaruddin, M., Kalsum, U., & Arisman, A. (2022). The Relationship between Sustainability Reporting, E-Commerce, Firm Performance and Tax Avoidance with Organizational Culture as Moderating Variable in Small and Medium Enterprises in Palembang. *Sustainability (Basel)*, *14*(7), 3738. DOI: 10.3390/su14073738

Galoyan, D., Mkrtchyan, T., Hrosul, V., Buhrimenko, R., Smirnova, P., & Balamut, H. (2023)... *Formation of Adaptation Strategy for Business Entities in the Context of Digital Transformation of the Economy.*, *21*, 2023. refpress.org/ref-vol21-a64/

Gantino, R., Ruswanti, E., & Widodo, A. M. (2023). Green accounting and intellectual capital effect on firm value moderated by business strategy. *Jurnal Akuntansi*, *27*(1), 38–61. DOI: 10.24912/ja.v27i1.1118

Gao, Y., & Hoepner, A. G. F. (2024). Virtues of impact financing: Do financial institutions benefit from considering the environmental impact on financing decisions? *Journal of Environmental Management*, *359*(120259), 1–14. DOI: 10.1016/j.jenvman.2024.120259 PMID: 38350274

Garrigós-Simón, F., Sanz-Blas, S., Narangajavana, Y., & Buzova, D. (2021). The Nexus between Big Data and Sustainability: An Analysis of Current Trends and Developments. *Sustainability (Basel), 13*(12), 6632. DOI: 10.3390/su13126632

Gaurav, A., Gupta, B. B., Bansal, S., & Psannis, K. E. (2025). Bankruptcy forecasting in enterprises and its security using hybrid deep learning models. *Cyber Security and Applications, 3*, 100070. DOI: 10.1016/j.csa.2024.100070

GIIN. (2024). *Sizing the Impact Investing Market 2024*, Global Impact Investing Network. https://thegiin.org/publication/research/sizing-the-impact-investing-market-2024/

Gimbert, X., Bisbe, J., & Mendoza, X. (2010). The role of performance measurement systems in strategy formulation processes. *Long Range Planning, 43*(4), 477–497. Retrieved March 12, 2025, from https://merit.url.edu/en/publications/the-role-of-performance-measurement-systems-in-strategy-formulati-4. DOI: 10.1016/j.lrp.2010.01.001

Global Green Growth Institute (GGGI). (2023). Green growth index 2023: Measuring performance in achieving SDG targets. *GGGI Technical Report No. 32*. Seoul, Republic of Korea: GGGI. Retrieved March 07, 2025, from https://gggi.org/report/green-growth-index-2023/

Godrej Agrovet Limited. (2025a). *Annual Reports*. https://www.godrejagrovet.com/investors/annual-reports

Godrej Agrovet Limited. (2025b). *Sustainability*. https://www.godrejagrovet.com/sustainability

Gogoleva, T. N., & Bakhturina, Yu. I. Environmental accounting in the system of accounting types // International accounting. 2016. No. 12 (402). URL: https://cyberleninka.ru/article/n/ekologicheskiy-uchet-v-sisteme-vidov-ucheta-1 (Accessed: 06.02.2025).

Goi, C. L. (2024). A review of marketing mix: 4Ps or more? *International Journal of Marketing Studies, 1*(1), 2. DOI: 10.5539/ijms.v1n1p2

Goldmann, S., & Knörzer, M. (2023). Technology advancement propels work productivity: Empirical efficiency potential determination in marketing and sales. *MDE. Managerial and Decision Economics, 44*(4), 1962–1977. DOI: 10.1002/mde.3793

Gonzalez, C. C., & Peña-Vinces, J. (2023). A framework for a green accounting system-exploratory study in a developing country context, Colombia. *Environment, Development and Sustainability, 25*(9), 9517–9541. DOI: 10.1007/s10668-022-02445-w

Gou, X., & Wang, S. (2025). How does the anti-trust policy stimulate firms' product market competitiveness? Evidence from the implementation of the Anti-trust Law. *Finance Research Letters*, *77*, 107062. DOI: 10.1016/j.frl.2025.107062

Government of India. (2024). Agriculture *Sector has registered an average annual Growth Rate of 4.18 per cent over the last five years: Economic survey.*https://pib.gov.in/PressReleasePage.aspx?PRID=2034943

Guo, J., Huang, Z., & Zhou, B. (2025). How does industrial policy affect corporate M&A Activities? *Finance Research Letters*, *75*, 106909. DOI: 10.1016/j.frl.2025.106909

Gutterman, A. S. (2024). What is Impact Investing, *SSRNpaper*, August 20, 2024. http://dx.doi.org/DOI: 10.2139/ssrn.3823837

Gyiazov, A. T., Gamulinskaya, N. V., Markeev, S. A., & Popkova, Z. V. (2023). Case experience of conducting climate-responsible entrepreneurship in the digital economy markets in Russia. In Popkova, E. G. (Ed.), *Smart green innovations in industry 4.0* (pp. 97–109). Springer., DOI: 10.1007/978-3-031-45830-9_11

Hand, D., Dithrich, H., Sunderji, S., & Nova, N. (2020). *2020 Annual Impact Investor Survey*, June 11, 2020, GIIN. https://thegiin.org/publication/research/impinv-survey-2020/

Hausfather, Z. (2017). Analysis: Why scientists think 100% of global warming is due to humans. Carbon Brief. URL: https://www.carbonbrief.org/analysis-why-scientists-think-100-of-global-warming-is-due-to-humans/ (Accessed: 10.02.2025)

Heriqbaldi, U., Esquivias, M. A., Lau, W., & Cesilia, A. F. (2025). Export promotion programs and firm performance: Linking knowledge, commitment, and market strategy to enhance competitiveness. *Journal of Open Innovation*, *11*(1), 100479. DOI: 10.1016/j.joitmc.2025.100479

Höchstädter, A. K., & Scheck, B. (2015). What's in a name: An analysis of impact investing understandings by academics and practitioners. *Journal ofBusiness Ethics*, *132*(2), 449–475. DOI: 10.1007/s10551-014-2327-0

Hrosul, V., Kruhlova, O., Mkrtchyan, T., Zubkov, S., & Timchenko, O. (2021). Enterprise integration and formation of cluster structures in the field of food sector. *Agricultural and Resource Economics*, *7*(2), 119–140. DOI: 10.51599/are.2021.07.02.07

Huang, Z., Li, H., Song, M., & Ma, L. (2025). Intersecting sustainability and governance: The impact of industrial land price distortion on carbon emission efficiency in China. *Applied Geography (Sevenoaks, England)*, *176*, 103510. DOI: 10.1016/j.apgeog.2025.103510

Iacob, A., Ciobanu, I., & Coman, E. L. (2023). Application Of Environmental Accounting Methods In Business. *Social-Economic Debates*, *12*(1), 1–8.

Ibrahim, A. A., Ahmad, S. Z., & Abu Bakar, A. R. (2025). Impact of competitive intelligence on firm sustainable competitiveness and performance: Strategic design collaboration's mediating role. *Management Research Review*, *48*(2), 231–257. DOI: 10.1108/MRR-04-2024-0280

IICPSD. (2024). Impact Investing, UNDP's Istanbul International Center for Private Sector in Development. https://www.undp.org/policy-centre/istanbul/impact-investing-0#:~:text=Impact%20investing%20is%20defined%20as,or%20environmental%20impact%20alongside%20a

Imran, M., Khan, I., Nassani, A. A., Binsaeed, R. H., Khan, H. R., Abro, M. M. Q., Zaman, K., & Haffar, M. (2023). A green perspective: Investigating the optical effects of e-commerce, renewable energy demand, and services trade on carbon emissions. *Optik (Stuttgart)*, *283*, 170918. Advance online publication. DOI: 10.1016/j.ijleo.2023.170918

Inshakova, A. O., Sozinova, A. A., & Litvinova, T. N. (2021). Corporate fight against the COVID-19 risks based on technologies of industry 4.0 as a new direction of social responsibility. *Risks*, *9*(12), 212. DOI: 10.3390/risks9120212

International Energy Agency. (2025). Climate pledges explorer: Data and statistics. International Energy Agency. URL: https://www.iea.org/data-and-statistics. (Accessed: 08.02.2025)

Investopedia (2025). Impact Investing: Definition, Types, and Examples, Investopedia, February 09, 2025. https://www.investopedia.com/terms/i/impact-investing.asp#:~:text=Impact%20investing%20involves%20making%20investments%20to%20help%20create,such%20as%20stocks%2C%20bonds%2C%20mutual%20funds%2C%20or%20microloans

Iqbal, M., Kalim, R., & Arshed, N. (2024). Evaluating industrial competitiveness strategy in achieving environmental sustainability. *Competitiveness Review*, *34*(2), 353–369. DOI: 10.1108/CR-12-2022-0191

IRIS. (2024). IRIS+/About, GIIN. https://iris.thegiin.org/about/

Ishengoma, F., & Shao, D. (2024). *A framework for aligning e-government initiatives with the sustainable development goals*. DOI: 10.1108/JIDT-09-2024-0025

Ittner, C. D., & Larcker, D. F. (2003). Coming up short on nonfinancial performance measurement. *Harvard Business Review*, *81*(11), 88–95. PMID: 14619154

Jabłoński, M. (2018). Value migration to the sustainable business models of digital economy companies on the capital market. *Sustainability (Basel), 10*(9), 3113. DOI: 10.3390/su10093113

Jakob, M., & Mehling, M. (2025). Addressing competitiveness concerns of EU exporters with industrial policy: The role of innovation support. *World Trade Review*, 1–20. Advance online publication. DOI: 10.1017/S1474745624000405

Jaya, O. S. (2024). Nexus between Impact Investing and Green Finance in Driving Sustainable Development. *Advances in Applied Accounting Research*, *2*(1), 26–38. DOI: 10.60079/aaar.v2i1.229

Jiang, D., Lu, Y., Li, F., Guo, R., Chen, Y., Wu, Y., & Xu, M. (2008). *Green Accounting Practice in China. April.*

JinRu, L., Qamruzzaman, M., Hangyu, W., & Kler, R.JinRu. (2022). Do environmental quality, financial inclusion, and good governance ensure the FDI sustainably in Belt and Road countries? Evidence from an application of CS-ARDL and NARDL. *Frontiers in Environmental Science*, *10*, 936216. DOI: 10.3389/fenvs.2022.936216

Jolly, L. (2014). Green Accounting-a Way To Sustainable. *Sai Om Journal of Commerce & Management*, *1*(5), 44–47.

Jula, N. M., Staicu, G. I., Moraru, L. C., & Bodislav, D. A. (2024). Toward a sustainable development of e-commerce in EU: The role of education, internet infrastructure, income, and economic freedom on e-commerce growth. *Sustainability (Basel)*, *16*(9), 3809. DOI: 10.3390/su16093809

Kalieva, S. A. (2012). Integration capacity of Kazakhstan and Russia. *Ekonomika regiona* [Economy of Regions], *4*, 227-233. DOI: 10.17059/2012-4-27

Kaplan, R. S. (1990). *Measures for manufacturing excellence*. Harvard Business School Press.

Kaplan, R. S., & Anderson, S. R. (2022). The impact of strategic cost management on financial performance: The role of balanced scorecard. *Harvard Business Review*, *100*(3), 72–83.

Kaplan, R. S., & Norton, D. P. (1992). The balanced scorecard: Measures that drive performance. *Harvard Business Review*, *70*(1), 71–79. PMID: 10119714

Kaplan, R. S., & Norton, D. P. (1996). *The balanced scorecard: Translating Strategy into Action*. Harvard Business School Press.

Kaplan, R. S., & Norton, D. P. (2001). *The strategy-focused organization: How balanced scorecard companies thrive in the new business environment.* Harvard Business School Press. DOI: 10.1108/sl.2001.26129cab.002

Kare, M. Š., Gavurová, B., & Porada Rochoń, M. (2024). Digitalization and carbon footprint: Building a path to sustainable economic growth. *Technological Forecasting and Social Change, 199*(1), 123045. Advance online publication. DOI: 10.1016/j.techfore.2023.123045

Kazambayeva, A. M., Begeyeva, M. K., Nursapina, K. U., & Rakhmetova, R. (2023). Systematic approach to sustainable development in agricultural and food systems – Example of Republic of Sakha (Yakutia) and the Arctic Zone. [Problems of Sustainable Development]. *Problemy Ekorozwoju, 18*(1), 226–234. DOI: 10.35784/pe.2023.1.24

Kelchevskaya, N. R., & Zhaparov, R. N. (2024) Integration of digital technologies into the strategy of company's sustainable development // Bulletin of South Ural State University, Series "Economics and management", 2024, No. 3. URL: https://cyberleninka.ru/article/n/integratsiya-tsifrovyh-tehnologiy-v-strategiyu-ustoychivogo-razvitiya-promyshlennogo-predpriyatiya (Accessed: 06.02.2025).

Khan, S., & Gupta, S. (2024). The interplay of sustainability, corporate green accounting and firm financial performance: A meta-analytical investigation. Sustainability Accounting. *Management and Policy Journal, 15*(5), 1038–1066. DOI: 10.1108/SAMPJ-01-2022-0016

Kim, K., Park, K., Jeon, H. W., & Kremer, G. E. (2024). Design complexity based flexible order dispatching for additive manufacturing production. *International Journal of Production Economics, 274*, 109307. DOI: 10.1016/j.ijpe.2024.109307

Kirillova, E., Otcheskiy, I., Ivanova, S., Verkhovod, A., Stepanova, D., Karlibaeva, R., & Sekerin, V. (2023). Developing methods for assessing the introduction of smart technologies into the socio-economic sphere within the framework of open innovation. *International Journal of Sustainable Development and Planning, 18*(3), 693–702. DOI: 10.18280/ijsdp.180305

Knowledge for All. (2025). *Economic competitiveness: Country ranking.* Retrieved March 13, 2025, from https://www.knowledge4all.com/ranking?Id=59&Color=A1A881

Kobilov, A. U., Bozorov, J. R., Rajabov, Sh. B., Abdulakhatov, M. M., & Sapaev, I. B. (2023). Development of the digital economy in the Republic of Uzbekistan. *E3S Web of Conferences, 402*, 08038. DOI: 10.1051/e3sconf/202340208038

Kumar, A., Shankar, A., Shaik, A. S., Jain, G., & Malibari, A. (2025). Risking it all in the metaverse ecosystem: Forecasting resistance towards the enterprise metaverse. *Information Technology & People, 38*(1), 198–218. DOI: 10.1108/ITP-04-2023-0374

Kumar, S., Sharma, D., Rao, S., Lim, M. W., & Mangla, S. K. (2022). *Past, present, and future of sustainable finance: insights from big data analytics through machine learning of scholarly research, Annals of Operations Research.* Springer., DOI: 10.1007/s10479-021-04410-8

Kurowska-Pysz, J., Czart, P., & Kot, S. (2024). Familiness as a determinant of competitiveness of family businesses – The organisational effectiveness-based approach. *Journal of Competitiveness, 16*(2), 182–209.

Kwilinski, A., Lyulyov, O., & Pimonenko, T. (2023). The Impact of Digital Business on Energy Efficiency in EU Countries. *Information (Basel), 14*(9), 480. DOI: 10.3390/info14090480

Laatsit, M., & Johansson, G. (2025). Fostering industrial symbiosis in process industries: An innovation policy perspective. *Environmental Technology & Innovation, 37*, 104027. DOI: 10.1016/j.eti.2025.104027

Lannelongue, L., Grealey, J., & Inouye, M. (2021). Green algorithms: Quantifying the carbon footprint of computation. *Advancement of Science, 8*(12), 2100707. DOI: 10.1002/advs.202100707 PMID: 34194954

Lestari, D. I., Adi, P. P., Kustinah, S., Jayanti, D., Mulyandini, V. C., Purwanti, M., & Kurniawan, A. (2023). Green accounting, environmental accounting, and carbon accounting: Is it the same? *Kurdish Studies, 11*(2), 2359–2366. kurdishstudies.net/menu-script/index.php/KS/article/view/801

Lin, J., & Qamruzzaman, M. (2023). The impact of environmental disclosure and the quality of financial disclosure and IT adoption on firm performance: Does corporate governance ensure sustainability? *Frontiers in Environmental Science, 11*, 1002357. DOI: 10.3389/fenvs.2023.1002357

Litvinova, T. N., Kulikova, E. S., Kuznetsov, V. P., & Taranov, P. M. (2017). Marketing as a determinant of the agricultural machinery market development. In Popkova, E. (Ed.), *Overcoming uncertainty of institutional environment as a tool of global crisis management* (pp. 465–471). Springer., DOI: 10.1007/978-3-319-60696-5_59

Liu, Y., Du, H., Wu, Y., & Mo, T. (2025). FPGA accelerated deep learning for industrial and engineering applications: Optimal design under resource constraints. *Electronics (Basel), 14*(4), 703. DOI: 10.3390/electronics14040703

Li, W., Liu, X., & Zhou, L. (2025). The role of digital finance in enhancing export competitiveness: Insights from China's listed companies. *Finance Research Letters*, *71*, 106376. DOI: 10.1016/j.frl.2024.106376

Li, X., Jiang, X., & Yang, C. (2025). Dynamic evolution of the manufacturing international competitiveness of China and the U.S. against the U.S. Manufacturing Reshoring Policy. *China Journal of Econometrics*, *5*(1), 129–147.

Li, Z., Chen, J., Li, Z., & Zhang, Y. (2024). Strengthen or weaken? How industrial internet platform affects the core competitiveness of manufacturing companies. *Operations Management Research : Advancing Practice Through Research*, *17*(1), 220–232. DOI: 10.1007/s12063-023-00426-4

Luhtala, M., Welinder, O., & Vikstedt, E. (2024). Glocalizing sustainability: how accounting begins for sustainable development goals in city administration. *Journal of Public Budgeting, Accounting as well as Financial Management*. DOI: 10.1108/JPBAFM-06-2023-0097

Maama, H., & Appiah, K. O. (2019). Green accounting practices: Lesson from an emerging economy. *Qualitative Research in Financial Markets*, *11*(4), 456–478. DOI: 10.1108/QRFM-02-2017-0013

Magableh, A. A., Audeh, A. Y., Ghraibeh, L. L., Akour, M., & Albahri, A. S. (2024). Sustainability as well as Information Systems in the Context of Smart Business: A Systematic Review. *Systems*, *12*(10), 1–24. DOI: 10.3390/systems12100427

Malina, M. A., & Selto, F. H. (2001). Communicating and controlling strategy: An empirical study of the effectiveness of the balanced scorecard. *Journal of Management Accounting Research*, *13*(1), 47–90. DOI: 10.2308/jmar.2001.13.1.47

Mariotti, S. (2024). "Open strategic autonomy" as an industrial policy compass for the EU competitiveness and growth: The good, the bad, or the ugly? *Economia e Politica Industriale*, *52*(1), 1–26. DOI: 10.1007/s40812-024-00327-y

Marr, B., & Schiuma, G. (2003). Business performance measurement – Past, present and future. *Management Decision*, *41*(8), 680–687. DOI: 10.1108/00251740310496198

Martiny, A., Taglialatela, J., Testa, F., & Iraldo, F. (2024). Determinants of environmental social and governance (ESG) performance: A systematic literature review. *Journal of Cleaner Production*, *456*, 142213. DOI: 10.1016/j.jclepro.2024.142213

Matos, S., & Hall, J. (2007). Integrating sustainable development in the supply chain: The case of life cycle assessment in oil and gas and agricultural biotechnology. *Journal of Operations Management*, *25*(6), 1083–1102. DOI: 10.1016/j.jom.2007.01.013

Meng, T., Newth, J., & Woods, C. R. (2022). Ethical Sensemaking in Impact Investing: Reasons and Motives in the Chinese Renewable Energy Sector. *Journal of Business Ethics, 179*(3), 1091–1117. DOI: 10.1007/s10551-022-05160-8

Mkrtchyan, T. M., Karbekova, A. B., Zakharov, D. S., & Pakhomova, O. K. (2024). AI and machine learning in inclusive development to personalize user experience and increase digital literacy. In Popkova, E. G. (Ed.), *Digital inclusiveness: Bridging the divide in the digital economy* (pp. 25–35). World Scientific Publishing., DOI: 10.1142/9789811270826_0003

Mkrtchyan, T. M., Tovmasyan, G. R., & Dallakyan, S. A. (2023). Sustainable Development of the Tourism Sector of the Republic of Armenia in the Context of an Innovative Economy. In Popkova, E. G. (Ed.), *Smart Green Innovations in Industry 4.0. Springer Climate*. Springer., DOI: 10.1007/978-3-031-45830-9_43

Montabon, F., Sroufe, R., & Narasimhan, R. (2007). An examination of corporate reporting, environmental management practices and firm performance. *Journal of Operations Management, 25*(5), 998–1014. https://doi.org/https://doi.org/10.1016/j.jom.2006.10.003. DOI: 10.1016/j.jom.2006.10.003

Moran, M., & Ward-Christie, L. (2022). Blended Social Impact Investment Transactions: Why Are They So Complex? *Journal of Business Ethics, 179*(15), 1011–1031. DOI: 10.1007/s10551-022-05153-7

Neely, A., Adams, C., & Kennerley, M. (2002). *The performance prism: The scorecard for measuring and managing business success.* Harlow, UK: Financial Times Prentice Hall.

Neely, A., Gregory, M., & Platts, K. (1995). Performance measurement system design: A literature review and research agenda. *International Journal of Operations & Production Management, 15*(4), 80–116. DOI: 10.1108/01443579510083622

Neill, S., & Dang, L. (2025). The integration of entrepreneurial marketing processes and controls. *Journal of Research in Marketing and Entrepreneurship*. DOI: 10.1108/JRME-06-2024-0138

Ngwakwe, C., & Ambe, C. (2016). Business sustainability performance measurement: Eco-ratio analysis. Risk Governance and Control. *Financial Markets & Institutions, 6*(4), 516–520. Advance online publication. DOI: 10.22495/rgcv6i4siart10

Nico, A. (2023). Green accounting and firm value. *Accounting and Finance Review, 7*(4), 12–18. DOI: 10.35609/afr.2023.7.4(2)

Niven, P. R. (2002). *Balanced scorecard step-by-step: Maximizing performance and maintaining results*. John Wiley & Sons.

Nosirov, J. T., Kukaeva, L. I., Hussein, B. A. A., & Ustenko, V. S. (2023). Disclosure of the Export Potential of High-Tech Enterprises in the Context of Industry 4.0 Through Quality Management. *Proceedings on EngineeringSciences*, *5*(S2), 295–310. DOI: 10.24874/PES.SI.02.009

Nur, H. R., Narimawati, U., Syafeii, M. Y., & Sutarman, S. (2024). Assimilateation of E-Business as well as Organizational Augment Towards Green Human Resource Management. *JMKSP (Jurnal Manajemen, Kepemimpinan, Dan Supervisi Pendidikan), 9*(1), 496–513. DOI: 10.31851/jmksp.v9i1.14563

Nurjannah, N., Yunus, M. H., Nurimansjah, R. A., & Erwina, E. (2024). Total quality management and productivity performance of SMEs: The moderating effect of marketing strategy. *Quality - Access to Success*, *25*(199), 272–278. DOI: 10.47750/QAS/25.199.30

Oláh, J., Popp, J., Khan, M. A., & Kitukutha, N. (2023). Sustainable e-commerce and environmental impact on sustainability. *Economics & Sociology (Ternopil)*, *16*(1), 85–105. DOI: 10.14254/2071-789X.2023/16-1/6

Omanov, S., Usmonov, B., & Tashbaev, B. (2024), "Improving the Analysis of Profitability Indicators of Joint-Stock Company", Eshov, M.P., Abdurakhmanova, G.K., Burkhanov, A.U., Abdusalomova, N.B. and Ergasheva, S.T. (Ed.) *Development of International Entrepreneurship Based on Corporate Accounting and Reporting According to IFRS (Advanced Series in Management, Vol. 33A)*, Emerald Publishing Limited, Leeds, pp. 213-219. DOI: 10.1108/S1877-63612024000033A025

Onwude, D. (2023). *What is the role of digitalisation for a sustainable agri-food system?*https://energy-base.org/news/what-is-the-role-of-digitalisation-for-a-sustainable-agri-food-system/

Opoku, R. K. (2025). Resilience capabilities and performance dimensions of manufacturing supply chains in a developing economy. *Business Process Management Journal.* Advance online publication. DOI: 10.1108/BPMJ-07-2024-0577

Oyewo, B., Tawiah, V., & Alta'any, M. (2025). Determinants and impact of strategy-driven manufacturing accounting techniques on organisational competitiveness: A structural equation modelling approach. *Journal of Accounting and Organizational Change*, *21*(1), 114–142. DOI: 10.1108/JAOC-10-2022-0165

Parthasarathy, V., & Kumar, V. (2012). Cloud computing for business sustainability. *Asia-Pacific Journal of Management Research and Innovation*, *8*(4), 461–474. DOI: 10.1177/2319510X13481905

Patiño, E., & Maya, J. (2025). A toolbox of analog form-finding techniques: Experiments for the generation of bioinspired forms in industrial design. *International Journal of Designed Objects*, *19*(1), 41–89. DOI: 10.18848/2325-1379/CGP/v19i01/41-891

Petcu, M. A., Sobolevschi-David, M.-I., & Curea, S. C. (2024). Integrating Digital Technologies in Sustainability Accounting and Reporting: Perceptions of Professional Cloud Computing Users. *Electronics (Basel)*, *13*(14), 2684. DOI: 10.3390/electronics13142684

Petrenko, Y. S., Burkhanov, A. U., Bukalerova, L. A., & Ustenko, V. S. (2024). Counter-Cyclical Approach to Change Management in Banks for the Sustainable Development of the Financial System. *Global Journal of Flexible Systems Management*, *25*(S1, Suppl 1), 31–47. DOI: 10.1007/s40171-023-00362-z

Piechucka, J., Sauri-Romero, L., & Smulders, B. (2024). Competition and industrial policies: Complementary action for EU competitiveness. *Journal of Competition Law & Economics*, *20*(4), 384–408. DOI: 10.1093/joclec/nhae015

Pinheiro, C. (2025). Relatedness and economic complexity as tools for industrial policy: Insights and limitations. *Structural Change and Economic Dynamics*, *72*, 1–10. DOI: 10.1016/j.strueco.2024.09.019

Popkova, E. G., Kaurova, O. V., & Maloletko, A. N. (2024). Introduction. Popkova, E.G., Kaurova, O.V., Maloletko, A.N. (Ed.) Sustainable Cooperation for the Creation of Green Supply Chains Based on Environmental Technologies and Responsible Innovations (Sustainable Civil Infrastructures, Part F3650), *Springer Nature Switzerland*. pp. V-VIII. DOI: DOI: 10.1007/978-3-031-70962-3

Popkova, E. G., Litvinova, T. N., & Zemskova, O. M. (2024), "Smart Automation of Corporate Accounting and Reporting in International Business According to IFRS: Global Premises and Prospects for Russia", Eshov, M.P., Abdurakhmanova, G.K., Burkhanov, A.U., Abdusalomova, N.B. and Ergasheva, S.T. (Ed.) *Development of International Entrepreneurship Based on Corporate Accounting and Reporting According to IFRS* (Advanced Series in Management, Vol. 33A), Emerald Publishing Limited, Leeds, pp. 91-98. https://doi.org/DOI: 10.1108/S1877-63612024000033A011

Popkova, E. G. (Ed.). (2024). *Smart Technologies and Innovations in E-Business*. IGI Global., DOI: 10.4018/978-1-6684-7840-0

Popkova, E. G., & Ergasheva, S. T. (2024). Favorable business climate for transition to international financial reporting standards: criteria and pathways for achievement. In Eshov, M. P., Abdurakhmanova, G. K., Burkhanov, A. U., Abdusalomova, N. B., & Ergasheva, S. T. (Eds.), *Development of international entrepreneurship based on corporate accounting and reporting according to IFRS* (pp. 7–13). Emerald Publishing Limited., DOI: 10.1108/S1877-63612024000033A001

Popkova, E. G., & Sergi, B. S. (Eds.). (2023). *Current problems of the global environmental economy under the conditions of climate change and the perspectives of sustainable development*. Springer. DOI: 10.1007/978-3-031-19979-0

Popkova, E. G., Ustenko, V. S., Petrenko, Y. S., & Bratukhina, E. A. (2024). ENVIRONMENTAL FRIENDLINESS OF PRODUCTS AS A MEASURE OF QUALITY: MANAGEMENT FROM THE POSITION OF SUSTAINABLE DEVELOPMENT. *International Journal of Qualitative Research, 18*(4), 1159–1170. DOI: 10.24874/IJQR18.04-15

Prabowo, A., Arisha, F., Triyana, D., & Baharudin, A. F. (2021). Smart Bumdes: Innovation of E-Collaboration as well as E-Commerce for Village Economic Development Solution in the New Normal Era (Case Investigation in Batu City). *IOP Conference Series: Materials Science as well as Engineering, 1077*(1), 012011. DOI: 10.1088/1757-899X/1077/1/012011

President of the Republic of Uzbekistan. (2024). *Decree of the President of the Republic of Uzbekistan No. DP-37 "On the state program for the implementation of the Strategy 'Uzbekistan – 2030' in the 'Year of support for youth and business'"* (February 21, 2024). Tashkent, Uzbekistan. Retrieved March 10, 2025, from https://lex.uz/uz/docs/6811938

President of the Republic of Uzbekistan. (2025a). *Decree "On approval of the Strategy 'Digital Uzbekistan-2030' and measures for its effective implementation"* (October 5, 2020 No. DP-6079 as amended on November 14, 2024). Tashkent, Uzbekistan. Retrieved March 13, 2025, from https://online.zakon.kz/Document/?doc_id=39012756

President of the Republic of Uzbekistan. (2025b). *Decree "On additional measures for further development of competitive environment and reduction of state participation the economy"* (July 6, 2020 No. DP-6019, in the edition of the Decrees of the President of the Republic of Uzbekistan from March 17, 2022 No. DP-89, July 6, 2023 No. DP-108). Tashkent, Uzbekistan. Retrieved March 13, 2025, from https://base.spinform.ru/show_doc.fwx?rgn=138760

Przhedetskiy, Yu. V., Przhedetskaya, N. V., Borzenko, K. V., & Bondarenko, V. A. (2019). Blockchain technologies in healthcare institutions: Focus on security and effective cooperation with the government. *International Journal of Economics and Business Administration*, *7*(Special Issue 2, SI2), 92–99. DOI: 10.35808/ijeba/373

Przhedetsky, Y. V., Przhedetskaya, N. V., Przhedetskaya, V. Y., Bondarenko, V. A., & Borzenko, K. V. (2018). The role of social-ethical marketing and information and communication technologies in response to challenges of oncology. *European Research Studies*, *21*(Special Issue 1, SI1), 377–386. DOI: 10.35808/ersj/1188

Ragin-Skorecka, K., Grobelna, K., & Nowak, F. (2024). Identifying e-commerce processes is key to sustainable automation using AI. *European Research Studies*, *27*(Special Issue A, S2), 621–633. DOI: 10.35808/ersj/3740

Ratang, W. (2025). Entrepreneurship, market orientation and marketing performance in culinary business: Mediating effects of innovation and competitive advantage. *Journal of Information Systems Engineering & Management*, *10*(5s), 234–243. DOI: 10.52783/jisem.v10i5s.608

Ripple, W. J., Wolf, C., Newsome, T., Barnard, P., & Moomaw, W. R. (2020). World scientists' warning of a climate emergency. *Bioscience*, *70*(1), 8–12. DOI: 10.1093/biosci/biz152

Ritchie, H., Rosado, P., & Roser, M. (2025). CO_2 and greenhouse gas emissions. Our World in Data. URL: https://ourworldindata.org/co2-and-greenhouse-gas-emissions. (Accessed: 09.02.2025)

Rizzello, A., & Kabli, A. (2020). Sustainable financial partnerships for the SDGs: The case of social impact bonds. *Sustainability (Basel)*, *12*(13), 5362. DOI: 10.3390/su12135362

Rödl & Partner. (2024). *Current ESG and product compliance – New regulatory requirements due to the EU Green Deal*. Retrieved February 12, 2025, from https://www.roedl.com/insights/esg-news/2024-3/esg-product-compliance-new-regulatory-requirements-due-to-eu-green-deal- (data accessed: 12.02.2025).

Rogachev, A. F., Ostrovskaya, V. N., Natsubidze, A. S., Litvinova, T. N., & Yakovleva, E. A. (2018). Tools for sustainability management of socio-ecological systems in the globalizing world. In Popkova, E. (Ed.), *The impact of information on modern humans* (pp. 241–247). Springer., DOI: 10.1007/978-3-319-75383-6_31

Roncalli, T. (2023). *Handbook of Sustainable Finance*, Creative Commons Attribution 4.0 International License. https://creativecommons.org/licenses/by/4.0

Rosário, A. T., & Dias, J. C. (2023). The New Digital Economy and Sustainability: Challenges and Opportunities. *Sustainability (Basel)*, *15*(14), 10902. DOI: 10.3390/su151410902

Rounaghi, M. M. (2019). Economic analysis of using green accounting and environmental accounting to identify environmental costs and sustainability indicators. *International Journal of Ethics and Systems*, *35*(4), 504–512. DOI: 10.1108/IJOES-03-2019-0056

Roundy, P. T., Holzhauer, H., & Dai, Y. (2017). Finance or philanthropy? Exploring the motivations and criteria of impact investors. *Social Responsibility Journal*, *13*(3), 491–512. DOI: 10.1108/SRJ-08-2016-0135

Rozite, V. (2023). Data centres and data transmission networks. International Energy Agency. URL: https://www.iea.org/energy-system/buildings/data-centres-and-data-transmission-networks. (Accessed: 10.02.2025)

Sahraen, A. N. (2020). Risk mitigation using integration enterprise risk management and balanced scorecard model: A case study in a consulting services company in Indonesia. *Spektrum Industri*, *18*(1), 73–85. DOI: 10.12928/si.v19i1.17830

Sai, F., Zhu, G., Qin, Z., & Zheng, L. (2025). Linking technological relatedness to firm innovation: The moderating roles of environmental dynamism, competitiveness and enterprise life cycle. *Baltic Journal of Management*, *20*(1), 52–71. DOI: 10.1108/BJM-08-2024-0435

Salahodjaev, R., Djalilov, B., Kobiljonov, I., Otajonov, S., & Kasimova, N. (2023). Industrialization and CO_2 emissions: Accounting for the role of renewable energy in OIC member states. *International Journal of Energy Economics and Policy*, *13*(5), 37–43. DOI: 10.32479/ijeep.12544

Sandoval-Caraveo, M. D. C., Surdez-Pérez, E. G., & Lamoyi-Bocanegra, C. L. (2024). Internal and external competitiveness of small industrial companies in COVID-19. *Aibi. Revista de Investigacion Administracion e Ingenierias*, *12*(1), 11–17. DOI: 10.15649/2346030X.3434

Schilirò, D. (2024). Sustainable finance and sustainable public finance system, *MPRA paper* No. 120216.

Schilirò, D. (2019). Sustainability, Innovation, and Efficiency: A Key Relationship. In Ziolo, M., & Sergi, B. S. (Eds.), *Financing Sustainable Development* (pp. 83–102). Palgrave Macmillan. DOI: 10.1007/978-3-030-16522-2_4

Schilirò, D. (2020). Towards digital globalization and the covid-19 challenge. *International Journal of Business Management and Economic Research*, *11*(2), 1710–1716.

Schilirò, D. (2020a). Sustainable public finance system. In Ziolo, M. (Ed.), *Finance and Sustainable Development. Designing Sustainable Financial Systems* (pp. 163–177). Routledge., DOI: 10.4324/9781003011132

Schneider Electric, S. E. (2025). Financial and Sustainable Development Report 2023 Universal Registration Document. URL: chrome- https://www.se.com/ww/en/assets/564/document/462018/2023-universal-registration-document.pdf (data accessed: 19.02.2025)

Seddaoui, R., Abdullah, S. S., Ahmad, S., & Gorundutse, A. H. (2025). Influence of marketing innovation and advanced technologies on firm performance: The case of Algeria. *Journal of Advanced Research in Applied Sciences and Engineering Technology*, *48*(2), 183–196. DOI: 10.37934/araset.48.2.183196

Sheth, J. (2024). AI-powered sustainability in e-commerce: How smart technologies are reducing carbon footprints. *LinkedIn*. URL: https://www.linkedin.com/pulse/ai-powered-sustainability-e-commerce-how-smart-carbon-nyeff/. (Accessed: 12.02.2025)

Shin, W. S., Dahlgaard, J. J., Dahlgaard-Park, S. M., & Kim, M. G. (2018). A quality scorecard for the era of Industry 4.0. *Total Quality Management & Business Excellence*, *29*(9-10), 959–976. DOI: 10.1080/14783363.2018.1486536

Singh, D., & Cohen, V. (2025). Socio-economic dimensions and human centricity in Industry 5.0: A study on manufacturing sectors in central and Eastern European economies. *Journal of Economic Studies (Glasgow, Scotland)*, *52*(2), 254–275. DOI: 10.1108/JES-02-2024-0067

Soraya, B., Nurrochmah, A., & Hwihanus. (2024). Business transformation towards sustainability: The role of green accounting in sustainability management. *Journal of Environmental Economics and Sustainability*, 1(3). URL: https://www.researchgate.net/publication/381573968_Business_Transformation_Towards_Sustainability_The_Role_of_Green_Accounting_in_Sustainability_Management. (Accessed: 08.02.2025)

Soraya, B., Nurrochmah, A., & Hwihanus, H. (2024). Business Transformation Towards Sustainability: The Role of Green Accounting in Sustainability Management. *Journal of Environmental Economics and Sustainability*, *1*(3), 1–8. DOI: 10.47134/jees.v1i3.342

Statista (2024a) Leading e-commerce companies worldwide as of December 2024, by market cap. URL: https://www.statista.com/statistics/245340/leading-large-cap-e-commerce-companies-market-cap/ Accessed: 06.02.2025

Statista (2024b). Market capitalization of the largest internet companies worldwide as of October 2024. URL: https://www.statista.com/statistics/277483/market-value-of-the-largest-internet-companies-worldwide/ Accessed: 06.02.2025

Statista. (2025). *Income statement of Allegro in Poland from 2020 to 2023 (in million zloty).* Retrieved February 12, 2025, from https://www.statista.com/statistics/1219445/poland-income-statement-of-allegro/ (data accessed: 12.02.2025).

Stocker, T. F., Qin, D., Plattner, G.-K., Alexander, L. V., Allen, S. K., Bindoff, N. L., Bréon, F.-M., Church, J. A., Cubasch, U., ... (2013). Technical Summary. In: Climate Change 2013: The Physical Science Basis. Contribution of Working Group I to the Fifth Assessment Report of the Intergovernmental Panel on Climate Change [Stocker, T.F., D. Qin, G.-K. Plattner, M. Tignor, S.K. Allen, J. Boschung, A. Nauels, Y. Xia, V. Bex and P.M. Midgley (eds.)]. Cambridge University Press, Cambridge, United Kingdom and New York, NY, USA. URL: URL: https://www.climatechange2013.org/images/report/WG1AR5_TS_FINAL.pdf. (Accessed: 09.02.2025)

Sun, D., Dong, J., Gu, X., & Chen, Z. (2025). Scenario simulation and regulation policy optimization of industrial enterprise production water considering scale heterogeneity: A case study in the chemical industry. *Computers & Industrial Engineering*, *202*, 110961. DOI: 10.1016/j.cie.2025.110961

Sundarasen, S., Rajagopalan, U., & Alsmady, A. A. (2024). Environmental Accounting and Sustainability: A Meta-Synthesis. *Sustainability (Basel)*, *16*(21), 9341. DOI: 10.3390/su16219341

Su, X., & Zhao, Y. (2025). Asymmetric time-frequency risk spillovers between the Fourth Industrial Revolution assets and commodity futures: Is economic policy uncertainty a driving factor? *Global Finance Journal*, *64*, 101076. DOI: 10.1016/j.gfj.2025.101076

Sydow, J., Schreyögg, G., & Koch, J. (2020). On the theory of organizational path dependence: Clarifications, replies to objections, and extensions. *Academy of Management Review*, *45*(4), 717–734. DOI: 10.5465/amr.2020.0163

Taccuso, F. (2023). Finanza sostenibile: cos'è, come funziona, ESG e come investire, *Consulenza vincente*, 20 luglio 2023. https://www.consulenzavincente.it/finanza-sostenibile/

Taneja, G., & Bala, A. (2024). Adapting to digital: A review of the e-marketing mix and its evolution beyond the 4Ps. *Zenodo*. https://doi.org/DOI: 10.5281/zenodo.14560872

Tao, X., & Cai, W. (2025). The impact of digital finance on export competitiveness: Evidence from Chinese manufacturing enterprises. *Finance Research Letters, 73*, 106629. DOI: 10.1016/j.frl.2024.106629

Tashbaev, B., Usmonov, B., & Omanov, S. (2024), "Analysis of Public Debt Policy and Its Effectiveness in Uzbekistan", Eshov, M.P., Abdurakhmanova, G.K., Burkhanov, A.U., Abdusalomova, N.B. and Ergasheva, S.T. (Ed.) *Development of International Entrepreneurship Based on Corporate Accounting and Reporting According to IFRS (Advanced Series in Management, Vol. 33B)*, Emerald Publishing Limited, Leeds, pp. 191-195. DOI: 10.1108/S1877-63612024000033B024

The Otto Group. (2025a). *About us*. Retrieved February 12, 2025, from https://www .ottogroup.com/en/nachhaltigkeit/ (data accessed: 12.02.2025).

The Otto Group. (2025b). *Annual reports*. Retrieved February 12, 2025, from https:// www.ottogroup.com/en/medien/downloads/?categoryDocs=geschaeftsberichte (data accessed: 12.02.2025).

The Otto Group. (2025c). *Sustainability*. Retrieved February 12, 2025, from https:// www.ottogroup.com/en/nachhaltigkeit/ (data accessed: 12.02.2025).

Thi, T., Thuy, T., Thi, T., Ha, T., & Van, H. K. (2025). *Overview of Investigation on Green Accounting as well as Sustainable Development. 23*, 2050–2060.

ThyssenKrupp AG. (2025). Environment, Social, Governance (ESG). URL: https:// www.thyssenkrupp.com/en/investors/esg-information-for-capital-markets (data accessed: 19.02.2025)

Tizroo, A., Esmaeili, A., Khaksar, E., Šaparauskas, J., & Mozaffari, M. M. (2017). Proposing an agile strategy for a steel industry supply chain through the integration of balance scorecard and Interpretive Structural Modeling. *Journal of Business Economics and Management, 18*(2), 288–308. DOI: 10.3846/16111699.2017.1279683

Tolmachev, A. V., Lifanov, P. A., Ketko, N. V., & Smetanina, A. I. (2023). The model of organisation of green entrepreneurship and the climate-responsible management of production factors in the digital economy markets. In Popkova, E. G. (Ed.), *Smart green innovations in industry 4.0 for climate change risk management* (pp. 145–153). Springer., DOI: 10.1007/978-3-031-28457-1_15

Trading View, Inc. (2025). Overview Godrej Agrovet LTD.https://www.tradingview .com/symbols/NSE-GODREJAGRO/

Treiblmaier, H., & Sillaber, C. (2021). The impact of blockchain on e-commerce: A framework for salient research topics. *Electronic Commerce Research and Applications, 48*, 101054. DOI: 10.1016/j.elerap.2021.101054

Tursunov, B. O., Uktamov, K. F., & Tukhtamuratova, A. (2022). Ways to ensure food security in the development of a digital economy. Proceedings of ICFNDS '22: *The 6th International Conference on Future Networks & Distributed Systems* (pp. 548-555). New York, NY: Association for Computing Machinery. DOI: 10.1145/3584202.3584284

UNDP & MBRF. (2023). *Global Knowledge Index 2023.* Retrieved March 07, 2025, from https://knowledge4all.com/admin/2023/Methodology/GKI2023_Methodology_EN.pdf

UNDP & MBRF. (2024). Global Knowledge Index 2024. Retrieved March 13, 2025, from https://www.undp.org/arab-states/publications/global-knowledge-index-2024

United Nations. (2015). Sustainable development goals. United Nations. URL: https://sdgs.un.org/goals (Accessed: 01.03.2025)

United Nations. (2015a). The Paris Agreement. United Nations Framework Convention on Climate Change. URL: https://unfccc.int/sites/default/files/english_paris_agreement.pdf. (Accessed: 10.02.2025)

United Nations. (2015b). Transforming our world: The 2030 agenda for sustainable development. United Nations. URL: https://sdgs.un.org/2030agenda. (Accessed: 11.02.2025)

United, & Nations. (2007). *Developing women's entrepreneurship as well as e-business in green cooperatives in the Asian as well as Pacific region.*

Usman, A. B., Babaji, A. U., & Muhammad, R. (2022). Performance of Cooperatives among Farmers in Gombe State, Nigeria. *Nigerian Journal of Agriculture and Agricultural Technology*, *2*, 2. DOI: 10.59331/njaat.v2i2.351

Usmonov, B. (2024), "Evaluation of Efficiency of Capital Management in Joint-Stock Companies in the Chemical Sector: The Case of Uzbekistan", Eshov, M.P., Abdurakhmanova, G.K., Burkhanov, A.U., Abdusalomova, N.B. and Ergasheva, S.T. (Ed.) *Development of International Entrepreneurship Based on Corporate Accounting and Reporting According to IFRS (Advanced Series in Management, Vol. 33B),* Emerald Publishing Limited, Leeds, pp. 67-74. DOI: 10.1108/S1877-63612024000033B009

van der Valk, H., Schmelzer, R., Rose, D., & Dinter, B. (2024). Towards a Process Model for Digital Twin Implementation: The Implementation Canvas. *Procedia CIRP*, *122*, 903–908. DOI: 10.1016/j.procir.2024.01.123

Vanchukhina, L. I., Leybert, T. B., Ergasheva, S. T., Khalikova, E. A., & Khanafieva, I. R. (2022). Integration of the higher education systems of Russia and the Republic of Uzbekistan in training for the digital economy. In E. G. Popkova & B. S. Sergi (Eds.), *Digital education in Russia and Central Asia* (*Education in the Asia-Pacific Region: Issues, Concerns and Prospects,* Vol. 65). Springer. https://doi.org/DOI: 10.1007/978-981-16-9069-3_1

Van, H. T. T. (2012). Environmental accounting – A new challenge for the accounting system. *Public Finance Quarterly*, *57*, 437–452. https://api.semanticscholar.org/CorpusID:15291846

Wall Street Mojo. (2024). What is green accounting? Wall Street Mojo. URL: https://www.wallstreetmojo.com/green-accounting/. (Accessed: 10.02.2025)

Wang, L., Chen, L., Jin, S., & Li, C. (2025). Forecasting the green behaviour level of Chinese enterprises: A conjoined application of the autoregressive integrated moving average (ARIMA) model and multi-scenario simulation. *Technology in Society*, *81*, 102825. DOI: 10.1016/j.techsoc.2025.102825

Wang, Z., Gao, L., & Wang, W. (2025). The impact of supply chain digitization and logistics efficiency on the competitiveness of industrial enterprises. *International Review of Economics & Finance*, *97*, 103759. DOI: 10.1016/j.iref.2024.103759

Wigand, R. (1997). Electronic Commerce: Definition, Theory, and Context. *The Information Society*, *13*(1), 1–16. DOI: 10.1080/019722497129241

Wijewardena, W. A. (2025). *Green accounting as a measure of sustainable development : Hype or reality ? Externalities*. 1–7.

WIPO. (2024). *Global Innovation Index 2024: Unlocking the promise of social entrepreneurship* (17th ed.). Geneva, Switzerland: WIPO. Retrieved March 10, 2025, from https://www.wipo.int/web-publications/global-innovation-index-2024/assets/67729/2000%20Global%20Innovation%20Index%202024_WEB3lite.pdf

WIPO. (2024). *Global Innovation Index 2024: Unlocking the promise of social entrepreneurship* (17th ed.). Geneva, Switzerland: WIPO. Retrieved March 13, 2025, from https://www.wipo.int/web-publications/global-innovation-index-2024/assets/67729/2000%20Global%20Innovation%20Index%202024_WEB3lite.pdf

Wiredu, I., Osei Agyemang, A., & Agbadzidah, S. Y. (2023). Does green accounting influences ecological sustainability? Evidence from a developing economy. *Cogent Business & Management*, *10*(2), 2240559. Advance online publication. DOI: 10.1080/23311975.2023.2240559

Wismansyah, A. R., Kadir, A. R., Baja, S., & Amar, M. Y. (2024). Dynamic capabilities and competitiveness: Relationship among industrial policy, structural transformation, and economic growth in Indonesian regional industries. *Journal of Infrastructure. Policy and Development*, *8*(5), 3773. DOI: 10.24294/jipd.v8i5.3773

World Bank Group. (2025a). Agriculture, forestry, and fishing, value added (constant 2015 US$) – India, Nigeria. https://data.worldbank.org/indicator/NV.AGR.TOTL.KD?locations=IN-NG&view=chart

World Bank Group. (2025b). *Cereal yield (kg per hectare) – India, Nigeria.*https://data.worldbank.org/indicator/AG.YLD.CREL.KG?locations=IN-NG&view=chart

World Bank Group. (2025c). *School enrollment, secondary (% gross). – India, Nigeria.*https://data.worldbank.org/indicator/SE.SEC.ENRR?locations=IN-NG&view=chart

World Bank. (2012). The Pathway To Sustainable Development. In *New Solutions*.

World Bank. (2025). *Ease of doing business score (0 = lowest performance to 100 = best performance).* Retrieved March 13, 2025, from https://data.worldbank.org/indicator/IC.BUS.DFRN.XQ?view=chart

World Bank. (2025). *Industry (including construction), value added (% of GDP).* Retrieved March 10, 2025, fromhttps://data.worldbank.org/indicator/NV.IND.TOTL.ZS?view=chart

Xie, H., Chang, S., Wang, Y., & Afzal, A. (2022). The impact of e-commerce on environmental sustainability targets in selected European countries. *Ekonomska Istrazivanja*, *36*(1), 230–242. DOI: 10.1080/1331677X.2022.2117718

Xu, D., Fei, X., Chen, Q., Hong, X., & Shen, G. (2025). Interplay of industrial transformation, diversified governance, and talent gathering on the ruralization of China. *Journal of Urban Planning and Development*, *151*(1), 04024055. DOI: 10.1061/JUPDDM.UPENG-5240

Xu, J., She, S., & Liu, W. (2022). Role of digitalization in environment, social and governance, and sustainability: Review-based study for implications. *Frontiers in Psychology*, *13*, 961057. DOI: 10.3389/fpsyg.2022.961057 PMID: 36533022

Yang, C., Yan, J., & Wang, G. (2024). Time series trends forecasting for manufacturing enterprises in the digital age. *Journal of Organizational and End User Computing*, *36*(1), 1–22. DOI: 10.4018/JOEUC.345242

Yudelson, J. (1999). Adapting McCarthy's Four P's for the Twenty-First Century. *Journal of Marketing Education*, *21*(1), 60–67. DOI: 10.1177/0273475399211008

Yuldashev, T. K., Qodirov, N. N., Eshov, M. P., & Abdurakhmanova, G. K. (2024). Optimal control problems for the Whitham type nonlinear differential equations with impulse effects. In: Azimov, D. (Ed.), *Proceedings of the IUTAM Symposium on Optimal Guidance and Control for Autonomous Systems 2023* (pp. 205-217). Cham, Switzerland: Springer. DOI: 10.1007/978-3-031-39303-7_25

Zain, N. (2025). the Adoption of Green Policy as well as Its Contribution in Hotel Industry. *Etd.Uum.Edu.My*. https://etd.uum.edu.my/8200/1/s816710_01.pdf

Zairis, G., Liargovas, P., & Apostolopoulos, N. (2024). Sustainable Finance and ESG Importance: A Systematic Literature Review and Research Agenda, *Sustainability, 16*(7), 2878, 1-13. https://doi.org/DOI: 10.3390/su16072878

Zarubin, S. G., & Deev, K. A. (2017). Process model of digital manufacturing. *Russian Engineering Research, 37*(8), 714–719. DOI: 10.3103/S1068798X17080214

Zhang, L., Xu, M., Chen, H., Li, Y., & Chen, S. (2022). Globalization, green economy, and environmental challenges: State of the art review for practical implications. *Frontiers in Environmental Science, 10*, 870271. DOI: 10.3389/fenvs.2022.870271

Zhang, Y., Wang, J., Sun, J., Sun, R., & Qin, D. (2025). Power load forecasting system of iron and steel enterprises based on deep kernel–multiple kernel joint learning. *Processes (Basel, Switzerland), 13*(2), 584. DOI: 10.3390/pr13020584

Zhang, Y., Wu, D., Luo, G., Lv, H., Yang, P., Zhou, J., & Liu, L. (2025). The impact of BEV manufacturing on China's economy and environment: An input–output perspective. *Journal of Cleaner Production, 490*, 144773. DOI: 10.1016/j.jclepro.2025.144773

Zhao, J., Hu, P., & Cui, L. (2025). Economic and non-economic impact of digital transformation on ehnterprise competitiveness: Evidence from Chinese-listed companies. *Technology Analysis and Strategic Management*, 1–17. Advance online publication. DOI: 10.1080/09537325.2025.2467927

Zheng, X., Huang, J., & Yuan, Z. (2025). Move to innovation: Place-based industrial relocation policy and firm innovation in China. *International Journal of Emerging Markets, 20*(1), 157–186. DOI: 10.1108/IJOEM-08-2022-1299

Zhu, H., Bao, W., & Qin, M. (2024). Impact analysis of digital trade on carbon emissions from the perspectives of supply and demand. *Scientific Reports, 14*(1), 14540. DOI: 10.1038/s41598-024-65658-1 PMID: 38914673

Ziolo, M., Bąk, I., Cheba, K., Spoz, A., & Niedzielski, P. (2021). Sustainable financial systems toward sustainability in finance. Institutional and managerial approach. *Procedia Computer Science, 192*, 4237–4248. DOI: 10.1016/j.procs.2021.09.200

Zrnić, A., Pekanov Starčević, D., & Mijoč, I. (2020). Evaluating environmental accounting and reporting: The case of Croatian listed manufacturing companies. *Pravni Vjesnik*, 36(1), 47-63. URL: https://www.academia.edu/52291685/Evaluating_Environmental_Accounting_and_Reporting_The_Case_of_Croatian_Listed_Manufacturing_Companies. (Accessed: 11.02.2025)

About the Contributors

Shakhlo T. Ergasheva graduated from Tashkent Institute of National Economy (speciality "Organisation of machine processing of economic information") in 1991. She started work activities in 1986 as a laboratory assistant at the Chair "Higher Mathematics" at Tashkent Institute of Engineers in Irrigation and Agricultural Mechanisation. In 1993-2002, she worked as the Head of the Chair of "Higher Mathematics" at Tashkent Institute of Engineers in Irrigation and Agricultural Mechanisation, in 2002-2004 – assistant of the Chair of "Financial Accounting and Finance" at Tashkent Institute of Engineers in Irrigation and Agricultural Mechanisation, in 2004-2005 – associate professor of the Chair of "Financial Accounting and Audit" at Tashkent Institute of Irrigation and Melioration, in 2005-2012 – Head of the Chair "Financial accounting and audit" at Tashkent Institute of Irrigation and Melioration, in 2012-2017 – associate professor of the Chair of "Financial Accounting" at Tashkent State University of Economics, since February 2017 – until now – professor of the Chair of "Financial Accounting" at Tashkent State University of Economics. She holds a PhD in Economics – awarded by the dissertation committee D 067.06.01 at Tashkent State University of Economics on 07.05.2004, approved by the Higher Attestation Committee of the Republic of Uzbekistan on 25.11.2004. The academic rank of associate professor of the Chair "Financial Accounting and Audit" was awarded by the decree of the Higher Attestation Committee of the Republic of Uzbekistan 03 No. 005467 dated 26.04.2007. The academic rank of professor of the Chair of "Financial Accounting" was awarded by the decree of the Higher Attestation Committee of the Republic of Uzbekistan o5 No. 002911 dated 28.02.2018. She has more than 200 publications, including a monograph, patent, regulatory and economic documents of companies of agricultural economy and water management, two study guides, nine teaching aids and guidances, articles in peer-reviewed journals, scientific and methodological works in collections and conference proceedings of various levels. Shakhlo T. Ergasheva performs research works supported by grants from the Republic of Uzbekistan. Shakhlo T. Ergasheva was a finalist (for scientific and pedagogical achievements) in the Republican competition "Best Pedagogue of the Year" (Tashkent, 2015-2016). Member of the Democratic Party of Uzbekistan "Milliy tiklanish". Letter of gratitude from the Head of the Women's Committee of the Republic of Uzbekistan for the contribution to the training of professional personnel and support of the creative initiative of youth in 2010. Gratitude from the university for successful work and high indicators in labour (2012), active participation in research work and results (2013) and for the 1st place of the Chair of "Financial Accounting" in the ranking of educational and scientific activity for 2015. Represented at the Honours Board of the university (2012-2019). She was awarded the university's honorary diploma for scientific achievements in the sphere of fundamental and applied studies (2011).

***

Fazilat K. Abdullaeva is an assistant teacher at the department of "Financial analysis", Tashkent State University of Economics (Tashkent, Uzbekistan). She published with the co-authorship "Practical training and independent study the organization" on financial analysis subject. In addition, she published more than 10 articles and theses in economic journals. Currently, her research is being conducted on the topic of "Improving the analysis of the financial stability of business entities".

Tamire Ashuro is a Lecturer in the Department of Logistics and Management of supply chain, Bule Hora University, Ethiopia.

Inna P. Bandurina is a senior lecturer at the Department of Management and Marketing of the Kuban State Agrarian University named after I.T. Trubilin. He is the author of seven textbooks for students in the fields of Management and Animal Science, as well as two monographs. She has published over 100 scientific articles, of which 27 are indexed in the Scopus database, which underlines the high level of her scientific activity. The Hirsch index for all publications on elibrary.ru 25, and in the Scopus database – 4, which confirms a significant scientific contribution. His research interests include the ecological and economic development of the regional economy, irrigated agriculture, the economic efficiency of managing the resource base of the agro-industrial complex at the regional level, product quality management, monitoring the state of land reclamation complexes in the region, evaluating the effectiveness of investment projects in land reclamation, as well as advanced technologies in agriculture and animal husbandry.

Mavluda Sh. Akhmedova is a Candidate of Economic Sciences, Associate Professor, Department of Management, Institute of International School of Finance Technology and Science. She is the author of three textbooks on "Industrial Statistics," a textbook on "Economic statistics" (in authorship), and articles and abstracts at more than 200 international and local conferences. She published three articles in Scopus. During 2006–2024, she worked as a teacher at the Department of Statistics at the Tashkent State University of Economics. During the 2022–2024 academic year, she served as deputy dean for spiritual and educational affairs. She is a member of the editorial board of the scientific, practical, and popular journal "Marketing."

Aktam U. Burkhanov is the Doctor of Economic Sciences, Professor, Alfraganus University and Tashkent State University of Economics. He is the author of more than 35 publications in Scopus (h-index: 11). Moreover, Aktam U. Burkhanov is the author (co-author) of more than 300 scientific and educational works. He has published eight textbooks, four monographs, five tutorials, and 14 academic and methodological manuals. He is a member of the editorial board of the international journals "Uluslararası İşletme, Ekonomi ve Yönetim Perspektifleri Dergisi," and "Journal of Turkish Studies." He is also the editor of special issues of two books.

Ikram R. Davletov completed his undergraduate studies in "Accounting and Auditing" at Tashkent State Agrarian University in 2003, followed by a master's degree in "Accounting Accounting" in 2006. On May 25, 2018, he successfully defended his Candidate Dissertation titled "Improving Accounting and Auditing of Intellectual Property Objects in the Agricultural Sector" and earned the degree of Candidate of Economic Sciences. With a strong academic background and extensive research experience, Davletov has contributed significantly to the field of accounting. Since September 5, 2022, he has been serving as an associate professor in the Department of Accounting at Tashkent State University of Economics, where he is actively engaged in teaching, research, and mentoring students to advance their academic and professional aspirations.

Vadim H. Grigoryan holds a PhD in Economics, Associate Professor. Since 2018, he has been the Head of the Chair of Marketing of the Armenian State University of Economics (ASUE) and the Head of the Bachelor's "Marketing" and Master's Marketing Communications" programs. Before that, he was the deputy dean of the Faculty of Marketing and Business Organization of the same university for about 6 years. He was involved in the ASUE "Amberd" Research Center as a member of the "Educational Process and Technology Research" project group.

Currently, he is a member of the ASUE Scientific Council, the Expert Council of the ASUE "Amberd" Research Center, and the Editorial Board of the "Messenger of ASUE" scientific journal.

Shashi Kant is an Assistant Professor, College of Business and Economics, Department of Management, Bule Hora University, Ethiopia.

Yulduz P. Khalikulova is an assistant teacher at the department of "Financial analysis", Tashkent State University of Economics (Tashkent, Uzbekistan). She is the author of more than 10 publications in Google scholar. Simultaneously, she is doing research on topic "Improving rent accounting in accordance with international financial standards" and published 4 papers accordingly.

Arzybek O. Kozhoshev is a Member of the Collegium (Minister) for Energy and Infrastructure of the Eurasian Economic Commission; Honored Economist of the Kyrgyz Republic, Doctor of Economic Sciences, Professor; Honorary Professor at the Research Institute of the Kyrgyz Economic University, Kyrgyz State Academy of Physical Culture and Sport, the Academy of Public Administration under the President of the Kyrgyz Republic, Kyrgyz National University, and Bishkek State University. He has over 150 scientific publications in Kyrgyz and international journals, including seven monographs and textbooks, as well as three higher education textbooks. He has been awarded the Medal of the Ministry of Energy of the Russian Federation (2024), the Order of "Dostyk" II Class of the Republic of Kazakhstan (2022), and the Badge of the Eurasian Economic Commission (2019, 2024). He is also an honored coach of the Kyrgyz Republic, a Master of Sports of the USSR in Greco-Roman (classical) wrestling, and the President of the Greco-Roman Wrestling Federation of the Kyrgyz Republic.

Kholisa K. Kuldasheva is an assistant teacher at the Department of Financial analysis, Tashkent state university of economics (Tashkent, Uzbekistan). She is the author of more than 2 publications in Google scholar. At the same time, she is doing research on topic "Enhancing the management accounting and internal control effectiveness evaluation system in the production process based on international practice" and according to this topis 3 high impact ranked papers published.

Nazgul T. Kutusheva is a lecturer at Osh State University of the Kyrgyz Republic, and by profession, she is an economist-mathematician. She has been working at the university for many years and has currently published around 15 scientific papers in journals indexed in the RINC and Scopus databases. Having successfully completed her postgraduate studies, she conducts research on the issues of state regulation of external migration in Kyrgyzstan, actively participating in scientific conferences and seminars on this topic.

Tatiana N. Litvinova is the Doctor of Economic Sciences, Professor, Department of Management and Logistics in Agro-industrial Complex, Volgograd State Agricultural University. Tatiana N. Litvinova is the head of the main professional educational program of higher education in the direction of training "Management," orientation "Business management in risk conditions." She actively participates in conferences and publishes research materials in international scientific publications, including those indexed by Scopus and WOS (more than 30 publications). Tatiana N. Litvinova is the author of more than 120 publications in Russian and English. Her research interests include agricultural machinery market, entrepreneurship infrastructure, entrepreneurial activity in the agricultural machinery market, economic growth, sustainable development, and strategic planning.

Tuygunoy Mamadjanova is a Candidate of Economic Sciences, Head of Department of Economics, Termiz University of Economics (Surkhandarya, Uzbekistan). She is also the editor of eight books and many special issues of international peer-reviewed scientific journals. She is a member of the editorial board of the Bulletin of Scientific Research of TISU. She is the author of more than 30 publications in Google Scholar (h-index: 5) and more than five research papers in Scopus. She is also the editor of more than ten teaching aids and many syllabuses. She is a selfless teacher who loves her profession. With her courtesy and attention, she is respected among the team and students.

Maksatbek O. Orozov is an engineer, programmer, and mathematician. He is the vice-director for Academic and Research Affairs at the Higher School of International Educational Programs of Osh State University and is an Associate Professor in the "Integration of Turkic-speaking States" department. Also, he is a highly-qualified lecturer in the Software Engineering program. He has completed a Master Program in Information Systems and Technologies and postgraduate studies in Differential Equations and Dynamic Systems of the Osh State University (Osh,Kyrgyzstan). He has authored 11 scientific publications, including 4 indexed in Scopus and Web of Science, and holds 2 scientific patents. He is also a certified expert for the Ministry of Education and Science of the Kyrgyz Republic in the accreditation of educational Institutions in the Kyrgyzstan. For his contributions to research and education, he has received multiple awards, including honorary diplomas from Osh State University and Kyrgyz-Uzbek University, along with certificates from international conferences.

Elena G. Popkova is a Doctor of Economics, is a Director of the Laboratory of Scientometrics and International Rankings at Armenian State University of Economics (Yerevan, Armenia) and Research Professor at the Department of Finance and Banking at the Institute of Economics, Business and Management of Osh State University (Osh, Kyrgyzstan). She is the author of more than 300 publications in Scopus (h-index: 40). She is also editor of more than 50 books and a large number of special issues of international peer-reviewed scientific journals. She is a member of the editorial board of the International Journal of Economic Policy in Emerging Economies and the International Journal for Quality Research. She is the Recipient of Highly Commended Paper Award for the journal On the Horizon for 2020 (Emerald). Elena G. Popkova is Honoured worker of science and high technologies of the Russian Federation and Honoured professor of Osh State University (Osh, Kyrgyzstan). She is among Scopus top 2% of most-cited scholars of the world in 2019-2024.

Ilham M. Saipidinov is a Candidate of Economic Sciences, Associate Professor, and Head of the Department of the Higher School of International Educational Programs at Osh State University in Osh, Kyrgyz Republic. Ilham is the author of more than 60 articles in journals indexed in the RINC and Scopus databases. He has extensive experience in international educational projects where he has served as an expert. In 2025, he was awarded a diploma of the winner in the nomination 'Foresight Technologies for Economic Growth in Central Asia' as part of the international grant competition 'Emerging Markets: Central Asian Studies' of the 2024 Eurasian Scientific Publications Competition.

Jaloliddin U. Suyunov graduated from the Faculty of Finance of the Samarkand Institute of Economics and Service in 2015. In the following two years, he obtained master's degree from the Tashkent State University of Economics in the subject of accounting. After that, he successfully defended his doctoral thesis on "Diversification of service in food trade entrepreneurs and ways to increase efficiency" on May 8, 2024, at Samarkand Institute of Economics and Service. Currently, he is working as a senior teacher of the department of accounting in Tashkent State University of Economics. He is contributing to the learning environment with a positive and professional manner to help other peers to reach their full potential.

Nargul A. Sydykova is a lecturer at the Higher School of International Educational Programs at Osh State University. From 2012 to 2015, I worked as a lecturer at the Kyrgyz-Chinese Humanitarian Institute. In 2018, I worked as a laboratory assistant at the Faculty of International Relations at Osh State University. In 2019, I worked at Jusup Balasagyn National University as a lecturer at the

Faculty of Natural Sciences in Osh. I studied Applied Informatics and Mathematics at the Faculty of Mathematics and Information Technology at Osh State University in 2012. In 2020, I completed my master's degree in the specialty of Pedagogical and Information Technologies at the MIT faculty of Osh State University. From 2012 to 2015, I worked as a teacher at the Kyrgyz-Chinese Humanitarian Institute. In 2018, I worked as a laboratory assistant at the Faculty of International Relations at Osh State University.

Golib D. Tashmanov earned his bachelor's degree in "Accounting and Audit" from the Tashkent Institute in 2004. Between 2014 and 2016, he pursued and successfully completed a master's degree in "Business Administration" at Binary University of Management and Entrepreneurship in Malaysia. Currently, Golib serves as an associate professor in the Department of Accounting at Tashkent State University of Economics. With a wealth of academic and professional experience, he is actively engaged in fostering a dynamic and supportive learning environment. His dedication to teaching is evident in his efforts to guide and inspire peers and students, helping them achieve their full potential. His positive and professional approach has made him a valued contributor to the academic community and the field of accounting education.

Begaim T. Toichieva worked as an economist-engineer at Alai Agricultural Machinery from 1981 to 1987, and then from 1988 to May 1998, I worked there as a financial accountant. I also worked as an economist-engineer at Osh State University. After that, I was a cashier and accepted payments from students for contract-based education. In 1999, I was appointed deputy chief accountant. In 2011, I was appointed chief accountant of Osh State University. Since 2021, I have been working as a financial accountant for research to this day. I am a lecturer and the author of more than 20 articles in journals indexed in the RINC database.

Alexey V.Tolmachev is a Doctor of Economics, Professor of Kuban State Agrarian University named after I.T Trubilin (KubSAU), Krasnodar, Russia. He is the author of more than 40 publications in the data bases of Scopus (h-index: 4) and Web of Science, more than 270 publications in RSCI (h-index: 40). He was the first in our country to propose the current price mechanism for regulating the grain market with the participation of the state. Alexey V. Tolmachev is Honored Worker of the Higher School of Russia and Honored Worker of the Agro-Industrial Committee of Russian, Member of the Dissertation Council of KubSAU in the field of agricultural Economics, heads the University's postgraduate program in Economics, 12 PhD theses were defended under his supervision. He is the head of the Department of Management and Marketing at KubSAU.

Anna A. Tubalets is a Candidate of Economic Sciences, is an Associate Professor at the Department of Management and Marketing, Faculty of Economics, Kuban State Agrarian University named after I.T. Trubilin (Krasnodar, Russia). She is the author of 3 publications in Scopus (h-index: 2), over 80 publications in RSCI (h-index: 20), 5 textbooks, and 5 monographs. She has been awarded an honorary certificate by the administration of Krasnodar for her significant contribution to the training of qualified personnel for the agro-industrial complex of Russia and the Krasnodar region, as well as for many years of dedicated work.

Ibrokhimjon U. Tursunaliev completed his undergraduate studies in 2021 at Westminster International University in Tashkent, earning a degree in Economics with Finance. Building upon this foundation, he pursued a Master's degree in Accounting at Tashkent State University of Economics, where he studied from 2021 to 2023. Currently, Ibrokhimjon is serving as an assistant teacher in the Department of Accounting at Tashkent State University of Economics. In this role, he brings a positive and professional approach to the academic environment, dedicating himself to fostering a supportive learning atmosphere. His efforts aim to guide and inspire his peers and students to achieve their full potential, contributing significantly to the advancement of the department and the institution. He is committed to the field of education and accounting, demonstrating a passion for teaching and professional growth, making him a valued member of the academic community.

Bobir O. Tursunov is a Doctor of Economic Sciences, Head of Department "Economic and financial security," Tashkent State University of Economics (Tashkent, Uzbekistan) and Research Professor at the International School of Finance and Technology (Tashkent, Uzbekistan). He is the author of more than 20 publications in Scopus (h-index: 10), his ranking is No. 4 in Tashkent State University of Economics and No. 69 in Uzbekistan. He is also editor of more than ten books and a monograph. He is a member of the Central Asian Journal of Economics and Management (Uzbekistan), Marketing Journal (Uzbekistan), Global Journal of Business and Management (India), and Journal of Current Marketing Approaches and Research (Turkey).

Bunyod Usmonov is a Candidate of Economic Sciences, Associate Professor, Department of Financial Analysis, Tashkent State University of Economics. He is the author of more than 12 publications in Scopus (h-index: 5) and the author of more than 30 publications in Google Scholar (h-index: 8). Moreover, he is the author of 3 monographs, a textbook on "Financial Management" and the author of articles more than 50 international and local conferences. He is also editor of more than two large special issues of international and national peer-reviewed scientific journals, namely, “International Advance Journal of Engineering Research – IAJER” and the local journal “Scientific Journal of Actuarial Finance and Accounting.”

Rustam U. Xolpulotov is an Assistant in the Department of Accounting at Tashkent State University of Economics. He is an active participant in academic conferences. The author regularly publishes research in international scientific journals. Currently, he has authored eight publications in Russian and Uzbek, contributing significantly to the academic discourse in his field. Rustam’s research expertise spans a wide range of topics, including financial assets, financial liabilities, equity instruments, and debt instruments. He is well-versed in specialized areas such as bonds, private equity, preferred shares, and various financial derivatives, including options, forwards, futures, and swaps. With a strong commitment to advancing knowledge in finance and accounting, Rustam continues to engage in scholarly activities, demonstrating a passion for research and education that supports the academic and professional growth of his peers and students.

Sirengul T. Zholdubaeva, was born on November 21, 1985, in the village of Myrza-Ake, Uzgen district, Osh region. In 1992, I was enrolled in the first grade of secondary school No. 29 named after V.V. Tereshkova. In 2003, I graduated from the K. Rayymbekov Gymnasium. In 2003, I enrolled in Osh State University, from which I graduated in 2008 with a degree in Geography Education. After graduating from university, in the 2008-2009 academic year, I worked at the school named after J. Moidunov. In 2017, I became a methodologist at the Kyrgyz-European Faculty of Osh State University. Since 2019, I have been teaching at this university. Currently, I have published about 10 scientific works in journals indexed in the RINC database.

Tolgonay S. Zhusueva is a lecturer at the Higher School of International Educational Programs at Osh State University. From 2008 to 2014, she worked as a teacher-methodologist at Jalal-Abad University of Economics and Entreprise. From 2014 to 2018, she worked as an accountant-cashier at the Southern Branch of OJSC “EcoIslamicBank”. In 2012, she received a “Gratitude” award from the city administration of Jalal-Abad for her contribution to youth education. She also participated in the conference “International Opportunities: Bilateral and Multilateral Cooperation Programs / TUBITAK-2009, Elazig, Turkey.” She studied at the University of Economics and Entreprise in Jalal-Abad from 2003 to 2009. From 2012 to 2014, she pursued a master's degree in Management.

Index

A

C

D

E

F

G

I

L

M

O

P

S

U

Y

www.ingramcontent.com/pod-product-compliance
Lightning Source LLC
LaVergne TN
LVHW061538290926
849162LV00004B/835